GOLDEN

o o o

THE MIRACULOUS RISE OF
STEPH CURRY

MARCUS THOMPSON II

TOUCHSTONE

New York   London   Toronto   Sydney   New Delhi

Touchstone
An Imprint of Simon & Schuster, Inc.
1230 Avenue of the Americas
New York, NY 10020

First Touchstone hardcover edition April 2017

TOUCHSTONE and colophon are registered trademarks of Simon & Schuster, Inc.

For information about special discounts for bulk purchases,
please contact Simon & Schuster Special Sales at 1-866-506-1949
or business@simonandschuster.com.

The Simon & Schuster Speakers Bureau can bring authors to your live event.
For more information or to book an event contact the Simon & Schuster Speakers
Bureau at 1-866-248-3049 or visit our website at www.simonspeakers.com.

Manufactured in the United States of America

1   3   5   7   9   10   8   6   4   2

Library of Congress Cataloging-in-Publication Data
Names: Thompson, Marcus, II, 1977– author.
Title: Golden : the miraculous rise of Steph Curry / by Marcus Thompson II.
Description: New York : Touchstone, 2017.
Identifiers: LCCN 2016052824| ISBN 9781501147838
(hardcover) | ISBN 9781501147845 (pbk.)
Subjects: LCSH: Curry, Stephen, 1988– | Basketball
players—United States—Biography.
Classification: LCC GV884.C88.T46 2017 | DDC 796.323092 [B]—dc23
LC record available at https://lccn.loc.gov/2016052824

ISBN 978-1-5011-4783-8
ISBN 978-1-5011-4785-2 (ebook)

To my wife,
my greatest tangible proof that God loves me
and wants the best for me.
I am perennially at a loss for the words
to express what you mean to me.

Thank you, Dawn.

• • •

Daddy,

You are still, and forever, my favorite reader.
I wrote this missing you and your big nose.

CONTENTS

INTRODUCTION

The Bay Area is a vibrant basketball town, maybe even under-rated. Oakland's had a long history with hoop, producing Hall of Famers like Bill Russell, Jason Kidd, and Gary Payton, and other noteworthy NBA names like Paul Silas, Antonio Davis, Brian Shaw, J.R. Rider, and now Damian Lillard. This area's relationship with basketball is why the NBA is beloved in these parts. Even when the Warriors were bad, they still drew well, much better than several good teams draw now. Especially since the early 2000s, the Warriors have had a steady base of hardcore fans who have lived and died with the franchise. Mostly died.

Worse than being bad, worse than being onto something and blowing it on the biggest stage, the Warriors were irrelevant. Fans suffered in obscurity. Being tucked way out West in an East Coast–dominated sports media, California teams not named the Lakers have to do something spectacular to draw national attention. For the Warriors, that was usually something like Latrell Sprewell choking the coach. Or trading Chris Webber.

Unlike with the Chicago Cubs, who played day games on a nationally syndicated channel, few outside the Bay Area got to watch the Warriors enough to develop an affinity through sympathy and childhood memories. The Warriors' franchise, and its fans, was terrible *and* invisible. Every longtime Warriors fan has a story of coming across a non-Californian who didn't even know the city in which the Golden State Warriors played. No one cared enough to attach a curse to their decades-long plight, turn it into history worth following.

INTRODUCTION

The Warriors always felt so far from a championship that was never even the goal. Fans just wanted them to go to the playoffs and put a scare into a really good team. Get some respect. Though lofty, relevance was more realistic than a ring. It would have been parade worthy if the Warriors made it to the level of the Sonics or the Blazers or the Jazz—good enough to lose to the Michael Jordan–led Chicago Bulls in the Finals.

Stephen Curry changed all that.

Before James delivered Cleveland's first championship in fifty-four years, before the Cubs won the World Series for the first time in more than a hundred years, Golden State was the doomed franchise to break its title drought. It wasn't the national love story it was for those other teams, or for the Boston Red Sox when they finally broke through. Part of that was because the Bay Area had produced several champions in the meantime: the A's, the 49ers, and the San Francisco Giants. It's hard to throw some of that sympathy out this way.

And now, after just two magical years, the newness and freshness of the Warriors has already rubbed off in the national picture. There is already such a thing as Warriors fatigue. In a span of a few years, the Warriors went from a cute start-up, the trendy watch for those in the know, to champion, to despised favorite whose fall is celebrated. Meanwhile, in the Bay Area, people's heads are still spinning. Many fans are just getting settled in their championship skin, and already their beloved Warriors are national villains.

Nobody knew it at the time, but this all began on June 25, 2009. The future of the Warriors changed with the No. 7 pick. They got the cornerstone in the rebuilding of the franchise, the piece that would make them a power. It took three years to even see the possibility of the Warriors being a contender. Another two to build on it. And before it could be expected, they were blowing through the NBA like a sports car on an empty highway. And Curry was the epicenter. He delivered everything for which Warriors fans had been pining.

INTRODUCTION

He was a talent special enough to draw in respect from outside the Bay Area. Relevance from a national perspective had always been on the wish list of Warriors fans, and of most fans whose team is not in the regular *SportsCenter* rotation. Curry's highlights and feats made the sports shows, and forced experts and analysts to talk about the Warriors positively. Such was an acceptable consolation prize for a franchise so far from a championship.

Curry was good enough to compete with other credible stars. He was somebody they had to worry about, somebody who could land a couple of haymakers. The Warriors stars rarely stacked up with the game's elite. That is why they went sixteen years without an all-star. Their players were good enough to become fan favorites to desperate followers. But usually once they faced the league's best, they were exposed as in over their head. Those that were good enough to challenge the league's best didn't stay with the Warriors long. But Curry had even the elite worried. He was giving the business to the best teams, going blow for blow with the best players.

Curry brought wins. A playoff upset. Then fifty-one wins. Then sixty-seven wins. A championship. Then seventy-three wins. Another Finals appearance. He wasn't alone, by any means. But history will define this as Curry's era of Warriors basketball, just like it was Rick Barry's in the seventies, and Curry produced winning like these parts had never imagined.

It is fitting that it's a little guard who led the Warriors to big things. Dubs fans have always fallen in love with the small, productive guards. There is a reason they are so popular—they reflect the spirit of Warriors fans.

For decades, as the NBA bloomed into a popular and profitable league, the Warriors wallowed in the shadows. At their core, the Warriors have a self-made fan base, forged against the grain, in violation of the populace. It is a contingent of diehards that embraced their underdog status and savored the chance to dethrone giants.

That's what the productive small guard does in the NBA—welcomes an existence of being slighted and relishes the pursuit of respect. That same mindset is why the Bay Area has produced so many guards with giant-sized talent. That's why those who come here and carry that spirit become legend.

Curry embodies all of the little guys Warriors fans have adored over the years, but with a software upgrade.

He has the toughness of Tim Hardaway, the never-back-down mindset that inwardly hopes someone will try to challenge him. Curry is a gamer like Sleepy Floyd, but even better at taking over games and more often than not rising to the occasion. He has the energy of Keith "Mister" Jennings, infusing games with frenzy and excitement. He has the reliable touch of Earl Boykins, the quiet fury of Monta Ellis, the star power of Baron Davis.

No one saw this coming back in 2009. Not even Curry's own mother, who during the draft process asked Steve Kerr, then the general manager of the Phoenix Suns, if he thought Curry could make it in the league. Not even she saw a first-team all-NBA point guard and two-time MVP. Not even she saw her son putting a woeful franchise on his back and lifting it to heights it had never imagined, let alone seen.

But with the No. 7 pick, the Warriors selected a preadolescent-looking kid out of Davidson College. And he turned out to be golden.

Baby Faced Assassin

o o o

"I never seen anything like this in my life. I was a certified serial killer. But this dude has it all. Gawd, maaaan. This dude right here is unreal."

—Allen Iverson

CHAPTER 1

It would be a safe bet that the Spurs had Stephen Curry in mind when they signed Jonathon Simmons, a prototype of an NBA player from the late 1990s, early 2000s. Simmons is six-foot-six, 195 pounds. He's a super-athlete who explodes off the floor. He's got a wiry strength, which combined with his height and wingspan makes him a versatile defender. He couldn't shoot well and his ball-handling needed work coming out of the University of Houston. But he made it to the big leagues because of his potential to disrupt offenses. He was a first-team selection for the NBA Development League's 2015 all-defensive squad.

In the past, San Antonio had used point guard Cory Joseph off the bench to pester Curry, who usually had his way with Spurs all-star point guard Tony Parker. Joseph was small and quick, the perfect attributes for staying on Curry's hip. Curry thrives in space and Joseph was great at taking it away. And playing for a loaded Spurs squad, Joseph could focus on his primary job: pressuring the ball-handler. He did it well enough to earn a free agent contract from the Toronto Raptors in the 2015 off-season.

When the Warriors hosted the Spurs on January 25, 2016, the first showdown between two teams that had already separated themselves from the rest of the NBA, it was Simmons's first opportunity to shadow Curry.

What better way to make his mark? Curry had the Warriors off to a 40–4 start. And the Spurs, at 38–6, were right on the Warriors' tail. No two teams had ever faced off before with such a high combined winning percentage. And it was the first meeting between the West's top contenders. Everybody was watching. Shutting down Curry was the kind of performance that could catapult Simmons's career.

And for the first thirty-one minutes of the game, neither Parker, his backup Patty Mills, nor Kawhi Leonard, the reigning Defensive Player of the Year, had much luck slowing Curry.

Following a pair of free throws the previous possession, putting the Warriors up by 14, Curry broke LaMarcus Aldridge down with a crossover and dropped in a floater. The next time down, he quickly pulled up from twenty-eight feet while the defense was relaxed. And then with Leonard stalking him, Curry curled off a screen and dropped in another three. His ten straight points helped push the Warriors' lead to 20.

Curry galloped down court smiling. That's how he gets when he's feeling it. His playfulness geysers up and produces an awkward celebration. That's when he's having fun.

The lead was still 20 points when Simmons finally got his chance, with just under five minutes left in the third quarter. The eager defender jumped on Curry as soon as the Warriors guard received the next inbounds pass. It was as if this was what Simmons had been waiting for, and his eagerness was obvious as he smothered Curry down the sidelines.

Curry crossed over from right to left, then whipped it around his back to his right hand. The move didn't lose Simmons. "I hate when people pick me up full-court," Curry said. "It's disrespectful." He took two more dribbles, and Simmons was still crowding him, pestering him, as he crossed half-court. This was about the time Curry probably should have backed it out and reset. He could have lured Simmons out toward half-court and passed the ball to a teammate, to take advantage of the space. Or Curry could've signaled for a screen to get Simmons off him.

Instead, Curry took one more dribble and powered through

the chest bumping of Simmons, then pulled up for a floater as the whistle blew. Off the glass. Plus the foul.

Once he saw the shot go in, Curry let off a right hook in the air and screamed "LET'S GO!" several times, so vociferously that spit flew out of his mouth. The happy-go-lucky player who was just smiling and skipping minutes ago had disappeared. Surfaced was the stubborn, angry player with a drive to obliterate.

Simmons was officially a victim of the Baby Faced Assassin. He had brought out another side of Curry, fashioned from years of dealing with players doing exactly what Simmons was doing— treating Curry like he was a weakling.

Off the court, there is a legion of people who vouch for Curry's authenticity as a stand-up guy. His next-door-neighbor humility shines as he looks people in the eye and converses with them as if they are the star. He remembers details no one would ever expect a superstar to remember, asks questions like one who is genuinely interested. He has an uncanny ability to make people walk away from a Curry interaction feeling like they have a new friend who is really good at basketball.

"Don't get fooled by that smile," LeBron James said.

On the court he can be a completely different guy. His kindness tends to morph into aggressiveness. The gentleness that marks his personality off the court is replaced by vengeance. It's his survival mechanism.

The reason Curry despises being defended full-court is because he sees it as an indictment. It makes him feel like prey. To pressure a player the entire court is to deem him a non-threat. Against good players, smart defenders retreat on defense and get set up with the rest of the team, because that help will be needed. But to leave the pack to defend a player on an island is announcing help isn't needed. That's what bigger players do to smaller ones, what good players do to scrubs. The message Curry receives from that defensive posture is "all you have to do is put pressure on him and he'll fold."

Curry has been dealing with this all of his basketball life. He has always been relatively short on the court. He has always had an appearance that looks more innocent than intimidating. And because of it, Curry has always been under attack. He was perennially dismissed by his opponents. But constantly having players try to physically dominate him over the years has given Curry something of a complex on the court.

That's what Simmons had tapped into. That's the killer he'd awakened. Curry scored 37 points in twenty-eight minutes of action against the Spurs that night. He watched the entire fourth quarter from the bench as the Warriors beat the Spurs by 30, ending all suspense in the hyped matchup.

"As gifted and skilled as he is, I think one of his greatest attributes is his competitive fire," Steve Kerr said. "A lot of people don't know that because of his demeanor. But he's an incredible competitor."

Kerr played with Michael Jordan. Even got a black eye from an altercation with Jordan in practice. He knows how to spot maniacal competitors.

Jordan is revered for his killer instinct, the way he ripped the hearts out of his opponents. He was merciless, finding joy in their frustration as he repeatedly squashed his foes. The bigger the game, the larger the moment, the more Jordan was driven to own it. So many Hall of Famers don't have a championship—Charles Barkley, Patrick Ewing, John Stockton and Karl Malone, Gary Payton, Reggie Miller—because Jordan refused to let them win one.

And Jordan did it with a flair that embarrassed his victims. He looked so good doing it. They weren't just losing, they were antagonists in his performance. Making it worse, Jordan talked trash the whole time. He destroyed with his game and belittled with his tongue.

Kobe Bryant followed in Jordan's footsteps with his insane desire to dominate. He attacked relentlessly, until his opponent wilted under his barrage. Bryant even feuded with teammates who didn't share his approach to domination. He gave himself a nickname to personify his ultracompetitiveness: Black Mamba. Like Jordan, Bryant is praised for that element of his game.

Allen Iverson was a special athlete who made up for his lack of size by disregarding it. He, too, was as competitive as they come, honed on the streets of Hampton, Virginia. Iverson used his quickness and leaping ability to work his way inside the lane, where the giants dwelled, where he was not supposed to exist. His resilience was in embracing the physicality, scaling the trees. He was little in stature but proved big in heart and toughness. He became iconic for it.

Larry Bird said he hated when opposing teams would put white players on him. He saw it as a sign of disrespect. He believed he was good enough to be defended by the best. He took a white defender on him as a slap in the face. He saw it as his opponent saying "Larry Bird isn't much of a threat." So Bird would make it his mission to destroy the white guy defending him, mercilessly abusing him to force the other team to make a switch. They had better put their best athlete on Bird.

Curry has that same spirit, an edge groomed from life as a miniature in a sport of Goliaths. It's not unique that Curry is so competitive. Many little guys have been. But his antagonism is different because of how it plays out. His retaliation is exerted in a way that we've never seen. His competitiveness produces the same results. It's just so jarring because of his framework.

Curry doesn't prove he belongs by tapping into an unbecoming strength. He is stronger than he looks, but that's not how he evens the field.

Instead, Curry belittles strength. He mocks size. He negates physical stature. And his slingshot is the 3-pointer, the equalizer compensating for the size he lacks. With his impressive aim, he delivers shot after shot after shot. And the Baby Faced Assassin isn't satisfied with winning, but appeased only by overwhelming destruction. His goal is to dominate in such a way that his supremacy can't be questioned.

In that way, Curry is like the giants. His conquering spirit wreaked havoc on the NBA, and that spirit was developed in a constant fight to not be conquered. He can transform into a wolf in sheep's clothing.

The earliest stories of this alter ego in Curry date as far back as the early 2000s in Toronto. His mother, Sonya, had moved the whole family, including Steph, his younger brother, Seth, and sister, Sydel, up to Canada to spend the year with their father, Dell Curry, as he played his final NBA season with the Toronto Raptors.

Sonya couldn't find a Montessori school in Toronto, so she opted for one of the only Christian schools nearby, Queensway Christian College. A tiny school in the Etobicoke district of Toronto, about fourteen kilometers up the Gardiner Expressway from the Air Canada Centre. Oddly enough, a strip club and the Toronto headquarters for Hells Angels were across the street. The school was basically a few classrooms in the back of a church on the Queensway, plus an adjacent portable and decrepit gymnasium that housed all the physical education activities during the thick Toronto winters.

"Soft-spoken," James Lackey, the Queensway Christian College basketball coach, said of Steph during his time there. "Few words. Real quiet. Friendly. Personal."

Steph attended as an eighth grader. He played floor hockey, indoor soccer, and volleyball, and then basketball season rolled around.

There were no tryouts at Queensway. The school was so small, everyone who wanted to play was on the team. And usually the same athletes played all the sports.

Lackey started the first practice by rolling out the balls and telling the players to warm up. He really wanted to get a first look at the two NBA player sons, Stephen and Seth, to see what he was working with.

The eldest Curry stood out immediately. As is the case before every NBA game now, Steph's warm-up was a show. Crossovers, net-splashing jumpers, advanced footwork as he practiced certain shots.

"After about five minutes," Lackey said, "I went over to him and said, 'Can you teach me some of those things for my men's league tonight? I want to use some of those moves on the guys.' He was doing stuff at age twelve that I've never seen before."

These middle school warm-ups were small potatoes for Curry. He'd been in practice with his father, having shootouts with NBA players. He'd give Toronto point guard Mark Jackson all he could handle in shooting competitions. When Sonya allowed him and Seth to attend Raptors games, they'd spend most of the evening facing off on the Raptors practice court—which was across the concourse from a concession stand. Curry would constantly beat his younger brother, swishing jumpers in full-court games of one-on-one. When the fourth quarter began, or when they heard an uproar from the crowd, they'd scamper across the concourse to the tunnels overlooking the court, to see what amazingness Vince Carter had pulled off. After witnessing the replay, they'd run back to the practice court and finish going at it.

They had done the same in Charlotte, when their dad played for the Hornets. Steph and Seth groomed their game against each other in backyard one-on-ones. Steph spent quite a bit of time at NBA practices with his dad, in the Hornets locker rooms, and perfecting his shot on NBA courts. The boys didn't play AAU ball. The first six years of their schooling was at the Christian Montessori School of Lake Norman, where their mother is founder and principal.

When Curry hit the seventh grade, he transferred to Charlotte Christian. He played for the middle school team. That's when Shonn Brown, the high school coach, first saw him.

"He could shoot the ball, but he was really small," Brown said. "The way he handled the ball. The way he moved on the court.

The way he shot it. You could just tell he had been around basketball."

So what Lackey saw as amazing was merely a Tuesday for Curry.

As a small Christian college, Queensway's schedule consisted of playing other similar schools. It wasn't great basketball by any means, a bunch of short players tossing the ball around, learning the intangibles of teamwork and adversity more than honing their hoop skills. But with Curry on the team, Queensway was suddenly winning by 40 and 50 points each game.

Lackey, for the spirit of competition, started scheduling games against big high schools from the city. Curry torched them, too.

As legend has it, one of the big high schools had enough of Curry—who played shooting guard while his brother ran the point—and decided to get physical with him. Lackey got the sense that the opposing coach told them to bump Curry around.

Lackey tried everything he could to free up Curry, to get some scoring on this bigger, physical team. He put Curry at point guard. He ran him off screens. He used Curry as a decoy. He pulled out fancy plays they hadn't really practiced.

With about a minute left, Lackey was resigned to their perfect season being over. They were down 6 points, which at this level of hoops meant you were done. It typically takes four or five trips for a middle school team to score 6 points, as each trip requires time-consuming plays to get a good shot. He ran out of ideas.

Lackey called a timeout because he wanted to prepare his team for the inevitable loss, use it as a teaching moment about how to handle losing properly. He told them to finish out the game strong, to hold their heads up because they'd played hard against a team they had no business being on the court against.

Lackey, though, did have one move left. He just didn't know it until Curry spoke up.

Curry saying anything in the huddle was a surprise. He barely talked. Normally, he would just listen to the play, say OK, then go run the play. But something had been triggered in Curry.

"That's when Steph got serious," Lackey recalled. "He just said, 'We're not losing this game. Give me the ball.' That's exactly what he said. So I said give the ball to Steph. That's the play."

What happened over the next minute was a stunning takeover. Two quick 3-pointers by Curry rattled the opponent and changed the whole tenor of the game. The Queensway Saints won by 6.

The Baby Faced Assassin was born that day. The alter ego that would turn the kindest, cutest kid around into a vindictive, explosive predator on the court. The Baby Faced Assassin would eventually come out more often, grow stronger and more determined as his basketball career evolved.

Now it is a switch he can flip on and off. Curry is one of the most positive stars the NBA has ever seen. But once he flips that switch, he becomes as mean as it gets on the court. He is merciless in his pursuit of respect. He seeks validation through conquests. He is unconcerned about embarrassing his foe.

The Baby Faced Assassin usually surfaces when opponents are attempting to bully him. But anytime he's doubted, anytime he gets the sense he's being sized up, when he bumps against the limitations being placed on him, Curry goes into that zone. When his name is on the line, when he needs to extract respect, his alter ego comes out.

After Dell Curry retired from the NBA in 2002, the family moved back to Charlotte. Curry and Seth, and their cousin Willie Wade, who moved in with the Currys, would hunt for pick-up games in Charlotte. That usually led them to the YMCA in the city.

Inevitably, other players would look at the Curry brothers and think nothing of them. Or they would recognize they were the offspring of an NBA player and look to make an example of them. So many times, they'd leave the court having made believers of their doubters. On several occasions, Curry would enrage his opponent with his shot-making. They couldn't stop him, so they'd want to fight. But the Currys had an enforcer with them in the older Wade.

"My cousin, he was huge," Seth said. "He was rough. One of them real country-boy enforcers. They didn't want none with him. We used to run them out the gym. They would get so mad. Maybe it was because of our looks or whatever."

It was more of the same when Curry got to high school. He landed in another small, intimate setting at Charlotte Christian School. Before the goatee and the muscles, Curry was a giant toddler with his uniform draped off him. He looked more like a kid dressed up as a basketball player for Halloween than an actual player.

But, my, was he good. He dribbled with an impressive command. He could shoot with a range that contradicted his biceps. He passed with a level of instinct most high schoolers don't have. He was exceptional at changing direction, manipulating angles, and maximizing his short-area quickness, though his end-to-end speed trailed most point guards. Curry was an obvious prodigy. Obvious.

"He was as skilled as he is now," said Oklahoma City guard Anthony Morrow, who starred at Charlotte Latin School and has played against Curry since they were kids. "He was a late bloomer. But you could never leave him open. He never missed open shots. He had everything. He was always a guy you had to make sure you knew where he was."

The book on Curry was to swarm him. Morrow remembers his team's plan was to spring traps on Curry. They would fall back on defense, then, when he was bringing the ball up court, they'd suddenly blitz him with a double-team. They screamed and waved their arms wildly, hoping to rattle him into a turnover. They knew they had to do something because once Curry got into the half-court set, it was over. He would break down the defense or get freed by a screen and hit the 3.

When Curry finally made it to the state championship game his senior season, Greensboro Day used a strategy the NBA would eventually adopt. Johnny Thomas—a junior small forward who was six-foot-six and boasted the kind of athleticism Curry lacked—drew the assignment of defending Curry. Greensboro Day was more than one hundred miles northwest of Charlotte Christian. But the buzz beat Curry to the North Carolina Independent Schools Athletic Association 3A Championships. And the Bengals had a plan.

Thomas shadowed Curry everywhere, denying him the ball and using his size to frustrate the Charlotte Christian star. Curry had just 8 points as Greensboro Day pulled out the championship. Curry didn't have the strength then. But Thomas got to know the fight trapped inside Curry's underdeveloped body.

"He was tough," said Thomas, now a Harlem Globetrotter dubbed Hawk. "He didn't back down. He came at us all game. We handled him pretty well. He was just too small. I got the best of him that day."

This has been Curry's hoop existence, being too small in stature and that being used against him on the court. And his response has always been the same—make sure there is a price to pay. Attack in a way that makes underestimating him become untenable. He likes to make examples out of foes.

One Curry legend comes from the Pro-Am Tournament at Charlotte. At the time it was run by NBA point guard Jeff McInnis, a former Tar Heel who hailed from West Charlotte High.

The Pro-Am was some of the best basketball in Charlotte, which has an underrated hoop scene. Bismack Biyombo, Hassan Whiteside, P. J. Hairston, Ish Smith, Morrow, and the Curry brothers are all NBA players with Charlotte Pro-Am appearances under their belt. And those who grew up in that scene could probably tell you about one night at the Grady Cole Center in downtown Charlotte.

"I remember that," Curry said. "It was after my freshman year at Davidson."

Curry playing was an event. He was the well-known son of an NBA player. And he was still slight enough for other players to doubt the hype he received.

They went after Curry that game. It's not that they were talking trash. But it was obvious to everyone watching that the intensity thrown his way was heightened. The way they defended him. The way they tried to score on him. The way they fouled him. A whole team of players were trying to build their reputation on him.

Curry felt what was happening. After halftime, the Baby Faced Assassin came out. He made an example out of the players who were looking to make a name at his expense.

"He came back and had like 40 in the second half," said Morrow, who watched from the stands after his team had just played. "And it was 40 just like how it looks now. They were trying to pick him up full-court. I remember his dad went up to him afterwards like, 'You need to play like that from now on. Don't worry about missing, don't worry about what nobody says.' Everybody remembers that. If you know basketball and you come to the Pro-Am, you remember that game."

If there is a difficulty in having this switch to flip, it is knowing when to flip it. It has taken experience for Curry to master this, and it is still a work in progress. He takes pride in being a point guard. He wants to be known as one who plays the game the right way, unselfish and cerebral. But then there is a part of him that wants to nuke the enemy.

In that way, Curry is a dichotomy on the court, both of his personalities fighting over how to use his considerable talent. It's as if he gets pulled in two directions.

On one hand, his shooting ability and ball-handling can be used for good. The threat of his 3-pointer spaces the floor and opens up driving lanes. A simple pump fake or mere hesitancy prompts the defense to react. His ball-handling also allows him to penetrate without having to use speed, creating angles for him to pass by his defender and space for him to get his shot. All of those contribute to the purest ideas of basketball. Sharing the rock, making his teammates better, and every other cliché that makes coaches smile.

It's one of the reasons the Warriors' motion offense works so well. It is predicated on motion and passing. And the best thing going for it is that Curry buys in, using his gravitational pull to draw the defense toward him and open up the floor for his teammates. It is part of what attracted Kevin Durant, an offense that values diverse skills and feeds off players' unselfishness.

On the other hand, the Baby Faced Assassin in Curry wants to use those same skills for evil. They are tools for revenge, to announce his superiority. His range is payback for trying to put bigger players on him. His handles exact punishment for attempts to pressure him.

And the jaw-dropping way in which he wields them both is designed to strike fear. It can be ball-hogging. There is an arrogance to his game, taking shots that for anyone else would be ill-advised, and making them leaves defenses demoralized.

The trick for Curry has been growing the latter while maintaining the former. He is an all-time great because of his ability to be both. But first he had to get comfortable in his skin as the Baby Faced Assassin.

That persona grew in the 2008 NCAA tournament. As a sophomore, Curry took over in the second half of a first-round game against seventh-seeded Gonzaga. He scored 30 of his 40 points to lead No. 10 Davidson in the upset. He hit the game-winning 3 with a minute left and pointed to his parents in the crowd as he backpedaled on defense.

The next game, he exploded in the second half to take down No. 2 Georgetown. Curry wasn't being personally attacked. But the same doubt hovered over him as part of his underdog team. He was a small school guard going against a college basketball power. He was one of the top scorers in the country, who most believed had skewed stats against weaker competition. It was symbolic of the fight he's been in all of his basketball life.

So, fittingly, Curry put up 25 in the second half to erase a 17-point deficit and advance to the Sweet 16.

"Curry was known to be a good player, but I had no idea he was that good," said Barker Davis, who covered Georgetown and was the first to label Curry as the "baby-faced assassin" in print. "GU had a kid named Jessie Sapp who was an all–Big East level defender and he couldn't stay in the same area code as Curry. Then they doubled him with Sapp and six-foot-eight Patrick Ewing Jr., who is now a GU assistant and was a great athlete, and the two of them still couldn't contain this scrawny little runt from Davidson. It was just an awesome display."

Curry scored 33 more points, Davidson smacked No. 3 Wisconsin, and it was on to the Elite Eight. The Wildcats almost won that, too, over No. 1 Kansas. Curry struggled shooting all game but had the ball, down 2, with a chance to hit the game-winner. Double-teamed, he passed the ball and the game-winning 3 was missed, ending Davidson's chance at a Final Four bid. He didn't flip the switch, but instead made the smart play, and it cost the Wildcats.

But the nation now knew about the Baby Faced Assassin.

The next season, Curry and Thomas met again. Curry was a junior star at Davidson. Thomas, a year behind Curry, was a sophomore at North Carolina State.

Rehabbing from a knee injury, Thomas didn't get to defend Curry this time. He watched from the bench in street clothes. The game was a big enough deal to be played in the NBA stadium in downtown Charlotte, big enough for LeBron James to come to the arena and sit courtside hours before his Cavaliers played the then-Bobcats.

North Carolina State was coming off a rough season, finishing last in the ACC. But the Wolfpack were 4–0 to start the 2008–9 season. And they were a major conference team with a lesson to teach the mid-major star. They were going to rough him up, shut him down.

Thomas tried to warn his teammates. He'd seen Curry's body start to match his fight within. He knew Curry was going to be a handful. Roughing him up wasn't going to be enough. They would have to play smart and execute, be focused. They needed to be on point.

The game plan did not call for trapping Curry. Instead, they played him straight up. And Curry went through defender after defender.

The Wolfpack became part of Curry's growing legend that day, with James gesturing in disbelief on the sidelines. And Thomas, who would later transfer to Marshall, couldn't help but laugh and shake his head while on the bench.

"I remember he was at the free throw line and boooooy he was letting us have it," Thomas said. "He was laughing and talking to me. 'You better tell 'em, Johnny! You better tell 'em!' He put on a show. He was always a real humble guy. Real down to earth. Carried himself well. But he will let you have it on the court."

Curry dropped 44. He missed ten of his fourteen 3s but lit up North Carolina State with an array of mid-range runners and bank shots. The biggest shot of the night was a thirty-footer he hit with just over a minute left, a dagger he followed by staring at LeBron James and then pointing.

These kinds of moments are peppered throughout Curry's career. In high school, college, and the pros, there are stories about him shifting gears and destroying his foe. Of him responding to doubt with dominance and slights with something sensational.

The entire 2015–16 NBA season, in a sense, was one big response. Because even though Curry won the 2014–15 MVP, and went on to win the championship, the slights didn't stop. They came even more relentlessly, at his team and at him.

And they fueled Curry. He's always had something to prove. That he should have been recruited by high-level Division I. That he deserved to be drafted No. 7 overall. That he wasn't too small and weak to play point guard in the NBA. That his ankle injuries wouldn't be his undoing. That he could lead a team to the playoffs. That he was an elite NBA player.

One of the most driven players around was given new motivation. Even though he'd passed every test, accomplished what no one thought he could, Curry found himself in the same spot: having to prove himself. He was once again in pursuit of validation.

The first shot fired came from the NBA players' union. In April of 2015, at the height of the national debate about who should win MVP—Curry or Houston Rockets guard James Harden—the NBPA announced it would be having its own awards show. In protest of the media selecting the annual awards, the union came up with the Players' Choice Awards.

A month later it was announced by the NBA, which has used media voting since 1981, that Curry had won the league MVP. The players' union over the summer picked Harden as their MVP.

Curry's teammates expected that to happen. The scuttlebutt all season during the Warriors' run, especially behind the scenes in the inner circle of past and present NBA players, was that the Warriors were flukey jump shooters, and Curry was being propped up by a loaded roster and a free-flowing system. The Warriors players heard the talk, and they knew what was coming, so they refused to participate and did not vote for that award.

Curry won the Players' Choice "Hardest to Guard" award and "Clutch Performer." But the most coveted prize among his peers, the one that establishes a player as one of the all-time greats, they didn't think Curry deserved it. And that was all Curry needed to hear.

The Baby Faced Assassin stopped making momentary appearances and hung out for the whole season. And the continued slights, veiled as some were, made sure the alter ego didn't disappear.

Curry took twelve 3-pointers in the 2015–16 opener. He took

fourteen while scoring 53 in the third game of the season, a road game in New Orleans. In Game No. 6, he took sixteen 3-pointers. This was the Curry who refused to lose in the eighth grade, the Curry who shot Davidson to the Elite Eight, the Curry who went ballistic in the second half of a pro-am game. Curry was going for the kill with his greatest weapon.

He had nine 40-point games over the first six years of his career. He had seven from the start of the season to Christmas 2015.

For years, Curry was bent on proving he could play point guard in the NBA. Enamored with his shooting, and turned off by his propensity for turnovers, analysts and critics labeled him a shooting guard playing out of position. Curry didn't like it. He'd always been more than a shooter, and he took to proving it on the court. He would flex his underrated passing skills and impressive vision, and make the extra effort to run the offense and get his teammates involved. He resisted scoring binges unless they were needed.

But this was a new gear. He shook off the unselfishness and sought to dominate. He blitzed the league with scoring explosions and deep shooting that made him the NBA's must-watch player. It was largely because Curry let his alter ego be his guide.

And the fuel kept coming. In January 2016, ESPN ranked their top 100 players of all time. They ranked Curry as the No. 4 guard on their list, ahead of Detroit Pistons great Isiah Thomas. Magic Johnson, selected as the best point guard ever, immediately denounced the idea of Curry being better than Thomas. Grant Hill and Dennis Rodman echoed Magic's sentiments.

More fuel.

Then Cleveland really irritated Curry on January 18. The Warriors were making their first appearance in Quicken Loans Arena since they clinched the championship. Curry was asked about his feelings returning to the scene of his greatest basketball moment. His reply: "Hopefully, it still smells a little bit like champagne."

That set off a firestorm in The Land. Several Cavaliers players and coaches and fans took offense at Curry's comments. Being cast as the villain, arrogant and disrespectful, prompted Curry to be arrogant and disrespectful on the court.

He had 38 points in twenty-eight minutes. The Warriors won by 34.

Later in the season, Curry was stuck in a slump. Over three games, he averaged 16.7 points on 37.8 percent shooting—well below the rampage he'd been on all year. It came after he and the Warriors destroyed San Antonio, the only real competition remaining for them.

He then disappointed in his return to New York. Curry usually has something special for Madison Square Garden. That was where he unofficially announced his NBA stardom with 54 points in 2013. Curry loves playing in the Garden. It's where he was hoping to land in the 2009 draft.

So when he managed just 13 points on seventeen shots in his latest trip to New York, it was clear something was up. Tired. Uninspired. Slumping. Whatever the reason, he looked listless on the court.

In hindsight, it was predictable he would explode in the next game, February 3 at Washington. He and his buddy John Wall, co-endorsers of Degree deodorant, usually put on a show when they face off. Plus, the defending champion Warriors were set to visit the White House.

So Curry blitzed the Wizards from the outset, turning the visiting crowd into his cheerleaders. He scored 25 in the first quarter. He made his first five 3-pointers and missed just one of his 10 shots over the opening twelve minutes.

After a Draymond Green layup put the Warriors up 13, Curry knocked the ball away from Wall before he could get past half-court. Curry chased the loose ball toward the sidelines. Wizards forward Jared Dudley dove for it, sliding across Curry's path. Dudley's foot kicked the ball up to Curry, who was facing the sidelines as he grabbed the ball out of the air. Curry turned and shot it right from where he stood, which was two steps behind the 3-point line on the left wing.

The crowd, which featured a strong Warriors contingent, erupted after it went in. Curry just stood still, taking a moment to soak it all in. Once he realized the Wizards had inbounded the ball and were bringing it up court, he turned to hustle back on defense. But a Washington timeout halted play, and the sound of the whistle stopped Curry before he could fully get going. The momentum spun him around, and so Curry went with it. With the arena abuzz in D.C., Curry hopped in a circle in place, like a boxer getting warmed.

"He was, to use slang . . ." President Barack Obama would say the next day during the Warriors' visit, "he was clownin'." The President even mimicked Curry's hop.

The Baby Faced Assassin is known for clownin'. Both having fun and looking to show dominance. If he's fouled and makes a 3-pointer, he celebrates by counting to four on his hand—guaranteeing he'll make the free throw. The "shimmy" is a regular part of his celebration repertoire, beginning in February 2012 as an ode to his coach Mark Jackson, who was known for shimmying in his playing days.

Curry's second MVP campaign was laced with "clownin'" moments, authored by his alter ego. He got fouled on a jumper in New Orleans in November and, while seated on the hardwood, danced to a beat in his head. A buzzer-beater from half-court against visiting Indiana was followed with Curry taking out his mouthpiece for a double-shimmy, each punctuated with him yelling "Boom!" as Oracle went nuts. Against the Hawks in February, he hit a 3-pointer from the corner and turned to shimmy in front of the home team's bench, a taunt he said was directed at friend and former teammate Kent Bazemore.

But Curry's trademark is the look-away. You can't be a superstar in the NBA without a signature. Not after Michael Jordan—with his wagging tongue, baggy shorts, and fashionable sneakers—showed the world how to be a sports superstar.

The NBA is now full of routines, all aimed at producing the same kind of style points Jordan made popular. Dunks are followed with screams. Most 3-pointers are followed with some kind of gesture—holstering or shooting an imaginary gun, a three-finger salute, or keeping the follow-through pose held high. Three-point plays are punctuated with muscle flexes and scowls.

But only a few can forge signatures that really tout a unique prowess. At the height of his powers, Jordan would shoot a free throw with his eyes closed. It was the kind of bragging that added to his legend. It was skill-flexing that flaunted his work ethic as much as his natural talent.

LeBron James, he's got the chase-down block. LeBron hunts fast-break layups like a lion does a cheetah, hiding out of sight then pouncing in a display of sheer power. Just when his opponent thinks he's got an open layup, LeBron soars out of nowhere to swat it away. He punctuated the Cavaliers' Game 7 win in the NBA Finals with the chase-down block of his life on Andre Iguodala.

Extraordinary leapers like Vince Carter and Blake Griffin get so high, they don't even dunk it in the traditional sense. They just throw it down into the hoop, scarcely even touching the rim, if at all.

Allen Iverson, like Tim Hardaway before him, had the crossover move. But while Hardaway's was founded on quickness, and he used it to get by his defender, Iverson's was a deceptive drag designed to embarrass. It was more about making his defender look foolish, duped by Iverson's magic.

And in twenty years, when Curry's story is retold in barbershops and at picnics by ol' heads who aren't impressed by the latest up-and-coming stars, his look-away will be the point of emphasis. It will be the unbelievable part of the story that will force a fifteen-year-old to YouTube it for proof.

And they will see clips of Curry in the 2013 NBA Playoffs shoot a 3 from the corner and then tauntingly stare at the Denver Nuggets bench before the net splashes. They'll see the highlight from March 2015—in the Warriors' sleeved charcoal jerseys with red and yellow accents to celebrate Chinese New Year—when Curry took a 3-pointer from the left wing against Milwaukee and turned to let the crowd's reaction tell him if it went in or not. They'll see him pull up from 3 against Sacramento in January 2016, turning to stare at the Kings bench—which featured his brother Seth—as the shot went in.

Inevitably, they'll come across the time he did it in the 2016 playoffs against Oklahoma City. In Game 2 of the Western Conference Finals, he pump-faked as Thunder forward Serge Ibaka flew by him. Curry reset, stepped in and took a 3-pointer, and turned to look at Ibaka while the ball was in the air.

It's the height of NBA swagger, a taunt too difficult for most to mimic. Curry has such a mastery of shooting he can treat it with the monotony of a free throw. And the alter ego in him, the one born of constantly being the prey, is just fine returning the favor. Anyone who knows Curry finds him to be the opposite of brash. But on the court, when he is an assassin, he plays a style that is as cocky as they come.

The very type of shots he takes is arrogant, as only one with excess confidence would dare take. It's like how Kobe Bryant would shoot over two defenders because he was convinced he had a better chance of making it than his wide-open teammate. Curry mocks the game with long-range bombs and the kind of ill-advised hoists that would get most other players benched.

That was the genesis behind his former coach, Mark Jackson, saying Curry was bad for basketball. It was a backhanded compliment to his former star and biggest supporter, and Curry didn't like how it was worded even if he understood the point Jackson was trying to make.

But Jackson's sentiment was pointing at the audacity of Curry's alter ego. Jackson's worry was that Curry inspires young players to pursue shots that are bad for mere mortals. He makes shooting look so easy, he normalizes attempts that are anything but. And gyms across the nation are full of players pulling up for 3s in transition and jacking up bombs while curling off screens.

The Baby Faced Assassin, though, is less concerned about setting examples for children than making examples out of his defenders. This personality is necessary for his success. It's the drive that makes him conquer the limitations that are supposed to beset him. It's the Buddy Love to his Sherman Klump. It's how Curry rises to the challenge, beats the obstacles, silences his naysayers. And those never seem to stop coming, even at the heights he's reached in the game.

On February 25, 2016, NBA legend Oscar Robertson gave Curry more fuel. At the time, Curry was averaging 31.9 points on 50.7 percent shooting—largely thanks to 4.9 3-pointers per game. But Robertson attributed part of Curry's dominance to the softness of modern defense.

"He has shot well because of what's going on in basketball today," Robertson said on ESPN's *Mike & Mike* radio show. "In basketball today, it's almost like if you can dunk or make a 3-point shot, you're the greatest thing since sliced bread . . . There have been some great shooters in the past . . . But here again, when I played, if you shot outside and hit it, the next time I'm going to be up on top of you. I'm going to pressure you with three-quarters, half-court defense. But now they don't do that. These coaches do not understand the game of basketball, as far as I'm concerned."

Robertson's analysis suggested Curry's success wasn't because he was a revolutionary player; instead he was taking advantage of an inferior era. Robertson, a legend, became the typecasting for yesteryear stars throwing shade on the Warriors and their star.

That night, Curry put 51 on Orlando with eight assists and seven rebounds. And he did it all in thirty-four minutes of action. He laughed openly after a buzzer-beater just inside of half-court to end the third quarter. He said his reaction was from the craziness of the shot, which he didn't expect to go in when he heaved it. But it banked in off the glass anyway. His laugh looked more like that of a villain who'd just revealed his evil plot to destroy the world.

"It's starting to get a little annoying just because it's kind of unwarranted from across the board," Curry said after Robertson's breakdown went viral. "For the most part, you don't hear us talking about, you know, comparing ourselves to other great teams and 'We could beat this team, we're better than this team.' We're living in the moment."

Cedric Ceballos, a vet from the nineties, followed Robertson's comments with more Warriors shade. He said his 1993–94 Suns would beat the Warriors easily. That Phoenix squad was No. 3 in the Western Conference and lost in the second round of the playoffs. But Ceballos said they would have handled the defending champions, who were 52–5 at the time of his comments.

Isiah Thomas echoed Robertson's sentiments the next morning. He acknowledged Curry is a shooter like the NBA has never seen, but he also said perimeter defense is its worst ever.

The night after these comments, Curry scored 46 against Oklahoma City in overtime, tying a record with twelve 3-pointers—his last a buzzer-beater from thirty-seven feet in overtime to beat the Thunder.

The crazy part: even after winning the unanimous MVP, and leading the Warriors to seventy-three wins, Curry entered the 2016–17 season harboring the same slights.

It was a grueling 2016 playoffs for Curry, who sprained his foot in the first game of the postseason and returned only to sprain his knee. He was out two weeks, returning in time to dispatch Portland in the second round. He had enough to overcome a rough go against Oklahoma City, closing the series with a bang. But in the Finals, after an epic Game 4 that seemed to end the series, Curry sputtered the rest of the way.

He needed one more big game to put away LeBron again. He needed one more big game to thwart off the greatest collapse in NBA Finals history. And he couldn't get it.

He didn't play well. He didn't live up to the expectations he had pushed to legendary levels. When the most people ever were watching him, including millions of casual fans who were expecting to see the modern marvel they'd heard about, Curry was average. Compounding his plight, LeBron James was anything but mortal. The contrast made Curry look all the more inferior. The slights poured in. Emboldened by the eleventh hour vindication, the contingent of Curry critics grew louder.

The dialogue wasn't about an all-time great and champion who came up short. The dialogue was more like "See, told you he wasn't all that." The only NBA greats to make the Finals and not lose are Michael Jordan and Bill Russell. Everybody else, from Magic Johnson to Larry Bird to Wilt Chamberlain to Jerry West, they all know the sting of losing in the Finals. It is a rite of passage, practically.

Yet, for Curry, losing in the NBA Finals was an indictment in the eyes of many, especially in the inner circle of current and former players. It was evidence of his unworthiness. Even James, who too has lost in the NBA Finals, to Curry, didn't embrace Curry as a worthy foe with whom he relished battling. He didn't treat Curry as he did the San Antonio Spurs stars, a foe he honored in defeating. James joined, if not led, the charge in mocking Curry and the Warriors. In his subliminal way, he egged on the teasing of the Warriors while the cool kids laughed at the newcomers.

Again, Curry's reaction looks different, just like his NBA takeover did. Phase one in Curry's response was something most stars of his caliber wouldn't do—embrace another star.

The Warriors had been planning to go after Kevin Durant for years—before they became an NBA juggernaut, before Curry became MVP and a renowned baller. At the time they started plotting to at least make Durant possible, the Warriors were but a team on the rise. Durant had the Thunder among the NBA's elite, occupying a status the Warriors dreamed of reaching. They signed Andrew Bogut and Andre Iguodala to contracts that declined in salary, making them easier to trade if needed. The rest of their moves—Shaun Livingston, LeAndro Barbosa, Marreese Speights—were set up so they would expire in 2016 or the Warriors could get rid of them if needed. They even passed on signing Festus Ezeli to a contract extension though he figured to be their center of the future. The prize was always Durant.

But in that three-year span, the Warriors leapfrogged the Thunder. And Curry joined Durant as one of the elite players in the NBA, even supplanting Durant in terms of popularity and success. Then the Warriors eliminated Durant's Thunder from the 2016 Western Conference Finals, with Klay Thompson going berserk as the Warriors stormed back from a 3–1 deficit to make a second-straight NBA Finals. It seemed an epic rivalry had brewed.

But the context didn't change the Warriors' desire for Durant. And Curry was all in. He played a key role in recruiting Durant, who said his biggest concern was whether Curry would welcome him to the Warriors. Durant knows how territorial NBA stars can be. He had to be sure Curry wanted him there before he took this gigantic leap. And Curry was emphatic in his embrace.

He headlined the Warriors contingent that went to the Hamptons to recruit Durant. Part of the Warriors' presentation was a players-only meeting. Curry, Draymond Green, Andre Iguodala and Klay Thompson holed up in a room with Durant, away from the executives and the prepared lines, for some real talk. After the meeting, on his way to a Warriors camp in Hawaii, Curry reiterated his embrace of Durant with text messages for emphasis.

Undoubtedly, part of Curry's welcoming of Durant is the point guard in him. The unselfish team player who relishes the idea of playing with and feeding a player of Durant's talent. With that said, better believe the Baby Face Assassin was helping type those text messages luring Durant. Better believe Curry's embrace wasn't solely because he is friendly with Durant, but because he was envisioning the supremacy they could forge.

Some consider it weak for Curry to invite a player onto the team who might dim his glow, render him second fiddle. But that's not how his alter ego thinks. Curry probably doesn't even believe he is conceding anything. He might score fewer points and lose attention, but that would just be a chance to grow in other areas people said he couldn't. He'd be simply dominating in another fashion.

But from the perspective of the Baby Faced Assassin, what Curry did gain was a co-star who could help his game soar to another level, giving him a freedom he rarely gets to experience. What he did gain is a great chance to rack up championships and yank out the tongues of his critics.

There is a lesson it seems the NBA hasn't quite learned: these slights feed Curry. Players knew not to talk trash to Kobe so as not to awake the monster. Looking at Jordan the wrong way could be misconstrued by him as a personal attack and unleash his killer instinct. On the court, Curry is cut from that same cloth.

Off the court, though, he's a choirboy. He doesn't throw shots in the media. He refuses to make personal slights about fellow players, past and present. And when what they say is brought to him, he declines to address it.

Inwardly, though, he's saying, "I'll show you."

Game Changer

o   o   o

"I've spent more time thinking about Golden State than I have any other team I've ever thought about in my whole career. Because they are really fun. I'd go buy a ticket and go watch them play."

—Gregg Popovich

CHAPTER 2

When Curry first came into the league, the question was whether he was a point guard or a shooting guard. From the start he was bent on proving he was the former. But many NBA experts, analysts, and connoisseurs scoffed at the notion, informed by the abilities and style of a long list of great point guards. Curry didn't seem to fit that mold.

Point guards tend to be physically imposing in some way or another—with quickness, explosiveness, strength, height. Most of all, even the ones who aren't physically gifted impose with traditional point guard strengths: court vision, basketball IQ, leadership. They control their team with a unique instinct and understanding of the game, being an extension of the coach on the court and playing chess while other players dabble in checkers. Their control is unmistakable. The best ones combine their physical attributes with their cerebral game.

Magic Johnson. John Stockton. Jason Kidd. Steve Nash. Chris Paul. They carry the banner in a lineage of floor generals. Curry never seemed cut from their cloth. He wasn't physically imposing. He wasn't a domineering leader, especially not in the first three years of his career when he deferred to guard Monta Ellis. Curry's reputation as a point guard suffered from his glaring, head-scratching turnovers, the kind "true point guards" wouldn't make, the kind that still hamper his game.

Assist-to-turnover ratio has long been a barometer for point guard–ness. Curry's never quite stacked up. Three assists to every turnover is a standard goal for a point guard. Curry usually hovers around two-to-one when he's playing well.

Still, he sought to prove naysayers wrong. He has been known to cram his game into the traditional mold. He sometimes picks his spots with his shots, passing up open looks in favor of running the offense and trying to get his teammates going. This has long been a thing for Curry.

In high school, his coaches begged him to shoot more. Shonn Brown, the head coach at Charlotte Christian, is convinced Curry could have averaged thirty per game. But shooting too much felt selfish.

Brown spent the early part of Curry's prep career trying to convince him that not shooting more was being selfish. Not only was he their best chance of scoring, but forcing the defense to bend to him was the best way for others to get good shots.

Brown and his staff even sat Curry down and gave him goals to reach. He was all but ordered to take five shots per quarter. They really wanted fifteen or sixteen shots from him at minimum, but they set his minimum goal at twenty because they expected him to have a hard time putting up that many shots.

"He made such a high percentage, we had to convince him we were better if he was taking more shots," Brown said. "He struggled with it until his teammates were like, 'Why aren't you shooting?' He wanted to make sure his teammates thought highly of him."

After his breakout season in 2012–13, when Curry showed he could take over, his growth has been in figuring out when to look for his shot and how to get it within the offense. Curry was prone to leaving Warriors fans wishing he would take over. But he was also intent on improving himself as a point guard. He became more dogged about penetrating, forcing himself to the rim instead of settling for jumpers. He shows off his court vision and passing skills whenever he can, using touch and anticipation to pull off the same types of gorgeous passes executed by revered NBA point guards. He even gets into trouble on occasion trying to make the spectacular pass, attempting the kind of dimes that would demand respect for his point guard skills. When they don't work, they become "what is he doing?" turnovers.

In the early years, his goal of being a good NBA point guard came at the expense of being a great NBA player. So many of his turnovers were a result of him trying to master the craft, make the pass he was supposed to make. But he would misjudge the length and speed of defenders, or make casual, predictable passes.

Conformity to traditional standards limited his capacity. He averaged fewer than fifteen shots per game in his first three seasons, and posted mediocre player efficiency ratings. Even Mark Jackson would have to tell Curry to just shoot it if he found himself in trouble, because that had a higher percentage of success than forcing a pass under duress.

The silver lining: Curry shoehorning his skills into the desired box developed key areas of his game. Instead of limiting himself as just a shooter, he got stronger to help him protect the ball better and deal with pressure from physical types like Chris Paul. And he had to brace for being challenged on the defensive end. He elevated his ball-handling and worked on manipulating screens as a way of forcing himself to the basket.

Still, the truth is that Curry was both a point guard and a shooting guard. The knock on him coming into the league was that he was a 'tweener—a player caught between two positions. A combo guard is what it's commonly called, a moniker for players who combine attributes from both positions and can play either. Usually it is given to small guards who are best at scoring, a description used even on Hall of Famers Isiah Thomas and Allen Iverson. Implied in being a combo guard, typically, is that the player isn't good enough to start at one of the positions full-time. The situation dictates which role he fills, and usually it means coming off the bench when a team has a "true" point guard or shooting guard. Combo guards tend to live an unstable existence in pro basketball.

But Curry's game has grown to shatter the ceiling placed on it. He is a point guard who can light up the scoreboard with the best of shooting guards. He is a shooting guard with all the skills of a top point guard.

Curry could be a really good player either way. But the secret to him becoming MVP was the ability to be either at any given moment. His strength is that he is a star at both. Not because he can switch back and forth between the positions, but because he presents the threats of both point guard and shooting guard at the same time, at all times.

Defending Curry means guarding the outside shot and protecting against the drive. It means having to rotate properly because he'll find the open man, and not making mistakes because he will see them and take advantage.

Often the best scorers in the league aren't as good when it comes to setting up teammates. Usually the best passers can't put 30 points on the board. Curry came to be one of the handful of elite players who could do both—in the same game. He has three games in his career where he's scored 30 points and dished 15 assists, the same number as Michael Jordan, John Stockton, and Gary Payton.

But maximizing this ability of Curry's required looking at the game a different way. When Curry came into the league, the question was who would he defend. He was too small to defend traditional shooting guards, but not athletic enough to keep up with top-level point guards. That meant an immediate diminishment in his value.

At the same time, the best teams in the league were employing three-guard lineups or playing a small forward with skills of a guard. Having more players on the court who could shoot and handle the ball allowed for the offense to be initiated by multiple people.

So the Warriors, believing they had a special talent, started figuring out how they could surround Curry with a roster that played up his strengths while hiding his weaknesses. He came into the league playing next to a guard of the same stature in Monta Ellis, which exposed Curry's defensive limitations. Most of his first three seasons were spent with jaded veterans and NBA Development League call-ups. He lacked a supporting cast who could cover up the holes in his game.

Even Magic Johnson had Michael Cooper to defend the best point guards. Magic also had an array of finishers capable of handling his magical passing. Even Michael Jordan's career only took off when he started trusting his teammates, which required having teammates worth trusting.

But Curry entered the prime of his career with a blend of cohorts that fit his game, and a unique philosophy that emphasizes skill as much as size and athleticism. The Warriors embraced what Curry could do instead of being deterred by what he couldn't.

It is a rare thing in the NBA for a superstar to get the supporting cast he needs and a system that maximizes his strengths. LeBron James left Cleveland because he couldn't, taking matters into his own hands and plotting the union with Dwayne Wade and Chris Bosh.

In 2011, the Warriors started from scratch building the Warriors around Curry. They hired a legendary point guard in Mark Jackson to be the head coach. They surrounded him with defensive-minded players and shooters. They made sure to have a starting-quality point guard on the roster, allowing Curry to play off the ball in a three-guard lineup.

They eventually fired Jackson and brought in Kerr, in part to better maximize Curry's skills. Jackson's offense relied heavily on post-ups and isolations. It proved a limiting style for the Warriors' roster as Curry was the only real isolation player. The Warriors haven't had a proficient post player since undersized power forward Carl Landry. So Jackson's coaching not only didn't match his players' strengths, it forced Curry to work hard to make offense happen. Curry did become great at the pick-and-roll under Jackson. But he spent a lot of time playing shooting guard, and the lack of playmakers around him allowed defenses to key on him.

In came Kerr, whose motion offense created a flow that played right into the hands of Curry and his cohorts.

Then, in the 2015 playoffs, the Warriors learned they could turbocharge the pace of the game by going with a small lineup and not give up too much on defense. Replacing the center with Andre Iguodala, the Warriors became too fast for most traditional lineups. It worked against Memphis, a bruising half-court team that had the Warriors in a 2–1 hole in the 2015 Western Conference semifinals. The Warriors went small in the starting lineup in Game 4 of the 2015 NBA Finals after Cleveland had successfully slowed down the game.

But that was just scratching the surface. And the start of 2015–16 had seen them weaponize this gimmick. It grew from an option to be used against big, slow teams to being the Warriors' best lineup. What was once a countermove became a knockout punch. What was once their reaction to being bullied became their method for bullying. That idea took life on November 19, 2015, against the Los Angeles Clippers—a team that in theory it should not have worked against.

The point of the small lineup is to sacrifice size for a speed and quickness advantage. But the Clippers had two big men in Blake Griffin and DeAndre Jordan who could run with anybody. So going small not only failed to give the Warriors a significant quickness advantage, it also figured to leave them at a size disadvantage—which only fuels Lob City.

In hindsight, the Clippers, spearheaded by Chris Paul, were the perfect test for the validity of the Warriors' small-ball style. Their best five players rivaled any in the league as far as talent. They presented a challenge on both ends.

The Clippers loved to get up and down the court, and punctuated fast-breaks with thunder. They were called Lob City because they'd make highlight reels with Paul just throwing it up and letting Griffin or Jordan go get it. And for a time they owned the Warriors.

Golden State was just good enough to hang with the Clippers. But eventually a Los Angeles surge would happen and the Warriors would get overwhelmed. The Warriors cut their teeth on the Clippers, who punished them for turnovers, exposed their need for ball-handlers, and feasted on the Warriors' interior.

In the 2014 playoffs, the Warriors took the Clippers to Game 7 with their small lineup. Both of their centers, Andrew Bogut and Festus Ezeli, were injured and missed the series. And Jermaine O'Neal, the third string, was playing hurt. The Warriors were down to David Lee and Draymond Green as the big men. And they almost won. But eventually, the size of the Clippers was too much.

During the 2014–15 season, the Warriors tilted the scale against the Clippers. Curry's game grew to the point he could outplay Paul. A healthy Bogut and Green offset the Clippers' size. This was how the 2014–15 Warriors could dominate—they could play big and small, fast or in the half-court. They had the components for an explosive offense centered on Curry, and the defense to back him up.

The Warriors went on to win a championship without facing the Clippers in the 2015 playoffs. The following season, it was the Clippers gunning for the Warriors. If the small lineup could score with a team as explosive as the Clippers, and defend against their size and athleticism, then the Warriors' small lineup could be more than a gimmick.

The small lineup was where Curry was most dominant. Curry is impossible to defend in wide-open, up-and-down games. And the attempt to guard him in that setting scatters opponents so much his teammates benefit. The question about the small lineup is, always, whether it can defend. So even though the Warriors had passed up the Clippers on the NBA totem pole, Paul's team was still a measuring stick for where the Curry-led Warriors were headed. And the revelation came in the first meeting between the teams after the Warriors won a championship.

Warriors guard Shaun Livingston didn't get to play in that pivotal showdown early in the 2015–16 season against the Clippers. A hip flexor strain had him confined to the bench in street clothes, trying to limit his movements to avoid the sharp twinges when he moved the wrong way. The visiting bench at Staples Center, like most NBA arenas, is especially crammed, fifteen behemoths sitting on padded lawn chairs, scrunched together so the hosts can sell more courtside seats. So even though the six-foot-nine point guard is thin enough to hide behind a stop sign pole, the scarcity of legroom made watching the game from the bench painful for Livingston. He added a thick cushion to his seat to alleviate some of the discomfort.

"I was like Phil Jackson," Livingston said, referencing the legendary coach who had a custom chair on the bench because of hip problems.

Watching the game from the locker room wasn't an option for Livingston as he didn't want to miss any of the hyped affair. The atmosphere at Staples Center is always charged when these teams meet. But it was especially so this Thursday night, three weeks into the season.

Dub Nation, the Warriors' fan base, took up what seemed like half the arena. Seven months earlier, Golden State fans had been so loud at Staples Center that Blake Griffin chided his home base after the game, saying his Clippers don't have a home court advantage.

"It's kind of like when we play the Lakers," Griffin told reporters after the Warriors won in April 2015. "Maybe worse."

Griffin's comments were before the Warriors won the NBA title, their first since 1975. As reigning champs, their fan base grew exponentially. The cheers when the Warriors took the court for warm-ups made Staples Center feel like Oracle Arena's guesthouse. Curry jerseys were everywhere and chants of "M-V-P" rang out with a colosseum's passion.

Normally, when the opposing team goes on a run, it silences the crowd. But with the Warriors in town, the cheering factions warred with each other, creating a back-and-forth between Clippers and Warriors fans that raised the energy of the building.

The friction was high on the court, too. The previous three seasons had seen a rivalry brew between the Clippers and the Warriors: on-court skirmishes, trash talk, off-the-court run-ins, a heated seven-game playoff series in 2014. Andrew Bogut and DeAndre Jordan were like bighorn rams in the paint. Draymond Green's toughness and defensive prowess were the yin to the yang of Blake Griffin's offensive explosiveness.

The Chris Paul and Curry matchup was more than a clash of two of the best point guards in the game. Paul was trying to take his torch back from Curry.

Paul, like Curry, is a North Carolina native. He was the star prospect when Curry still had to double-knot his basketball shorts to keep them up. Since then, Paul has been a standard bearer for Curry, whose motivation to win the matchup with the game's best point guard fueled him to get better. And the last time the Warriors were in this building, Curry orchestrated a viral moment that punctuated the seismic shift in the NBA point guard landscape. A double behind-the-back crossover move, capped with a baseline jumper, buckled Paul and flooded the Internet with memes. It was the ultimate from a season of highlights that concluded with Curry winning the league MVP and the Warriors winning the NBA title—while Paul has accomplished neither.

When he faced Paul for the first time after he won MVP and a title, Curry reaffirmed his supremacy. In Oakland, the fifth game of the 2015–16 season, Curry scored 13 straight points over a five-minute stretch in the fourth quarter, his seventh 3-pointer of the game putting the Warriors up for good in a nail-biter on national television.

They met again, two weeks later, but on Paul's turf. The Warriors were 12–0 and the nation was catching on. Their superiority was continuing into the new season, though many expected the loaded Western Conference to pull the Warriors back to the pack like crabs in a bucket.

Clippers coach Doc Rivers was partly responsible for the Warriors' surge to start the season, as his comments highlighted a narrative that powered their bent to validate their championship.

"You need luck in the West," Rivers told Grantland.com in October 2015. "Look at Golden State. They didn't have to play us or the Spurs."

All the Warriors needed to hear was the word *luck*. The beef was set: Rivers was dissing their ring.

"If we got lucky," Klay Thompson responded, "look at our record against them last year. I'm pretty sure we smacked them."

The Clippers' coach later clarified his comments, emphasizing that he never called the Warriors lucky. His point was that getting the breaks is necessary to navigate the deep Western Conference. But the Warriors weren't buying Rivers's explanation. He is an expert at the verbal body blow, and even better at explaining it away. He has been a central part of the rivalry between the Warriors and the Clippers because of his willingness to step into the banter and trade shots. While most coaches play it down, Rivers seems to appreciate the entertainment value of subliminal disses and the layers of subplots that add complexity to the games.

The Warriors came to learn over the years that Rivers knows exactly what he is doing. And to dish it right back.

"We've got a ring," Andrew Bogut said when asked about Rivers's comments. "We did all the hard work. We know what it takes. We don't need any more motivation, but if they want to throw some at us, we'll definitely put it on a little board and be aware of that."

The layers and layers and layers of the Warriors-Clippers rivalry made this game early in the 2015–16 season a must-watch. Which is why Livingston was sitting on the bench, toughing out the discomfort as if he were in a middle seat on Southwest.

His suffering was amplified by what he watched on the court. The Clippers had their way with the Warriors. Paul, clearly determined to shift the momentum of his matchup with Curry, scored 18 points in the first quarter. He masterfully weaved around screens and ripped jumper after jumper, each one an exclamation of his eliteness.

The Clippers were clicking and the Warriors seemed overwhelmed. The Warriors fell into a 23-point hole in the second quarter. A minute into the third quarter, they were still down 18. That's when Livingston saw the switch flip.

It wasn't an obvious shift. Noticing it requires intimate knowledge of this team's makeup. Livingston couldn't even pinpoint when it happened, but suddenly he felt it coming, like a mountain climber sensing the avalanche before feeling the rumble. One moment, the game felt like an inevitable loss. Out of nowhere, his inner voice was whispering "uh oh."

For those without that sixth sense, the rumble began at the 6:52 mark of the third quarter.

First, Curry stuck a jumper to cut the Clippers lead to 13, prompting the hosts to call a timeout. After the stoppage, he scooped up a Paul Pierce miss on the run and was off on the fast-break. A crossover helped him blow by Paul and glide in for a finger roll as Staples Center oooooh'd. Under the basket, Curry ran in place for a second before heading back on defense, like a cartoon character building up momentum before taking off.

The Warriors were finally getting started, revved up and ready to shift gears on the Clippers. It was still an 11-point deficit. But the defending champions had decided they wanted to win.

That they were going to win.

What happened over the next eighteen-plus minutes turned this sure loss into a seminal moment in what would turn out to be the best start in NBA history. And eventually the greatest regular season in history. And perhaps the blueprint to the NBA's newest dynasty.

A Curry hook in the lane, after Green fed him on a backdoor cut, and the lead was down to single digits. The Staples Center crowd was now on to what Livingston had already felt. A drive-and-dish by little-used guard Ian Clark led to a 3-pointer from the left corner by Green as the horn went off to end the third quarter. The Warriors were down by six and the Clippers were in a world of trouble.

A hot streak from Harrison Barnes early in the fourth quarter cut the Warriors' deficit to a point. But back-to-back dunks by DeAndre Jordan and Josh Smith capped a run to push the Clippers' lead back to nine, prompting Curry to re-enter the game for his final stretch. A 3-pointer by Paul had the Warriors down 109–99 with just under six minutes left in the game.

The Warriors had seen this movie before in Staples Center. Many times. Their turnovers fuel the Clippers' transition game, activating Lob City. This is what the Clippers are known for, blitzing opponents with *SportsCenter*-worthy dunks, rattling their foes with a wave of energy and pressure. The Warriors have fought valiantly before only to have their composure crushed by the frenzy from Clippers highlight plays.

But the Warriors were in the process of experimenting with their own game changer.

With 5:41 left in the fourth quarter, and the Warriors down 10, Festus Ezeli came running off the court and Iguodala checked in. The Warriors were back to their championship-winning lineup: Curry, Thompson, Iguodala, Barnes, and Green. They had used this lineup nine times during the twelve-game win streak. But never down like this, against a team this good.

The Clippers folded like starchless shirts. An Iguodala corner 3, set up by a pick-and-roll with Curry and Green, cut it to 7. Then Green posted up Paul for an easy layup. Then Iguodala hit a wide-open 3 from the right corner. In between baskets, the Warriors' defense made up for lack of size with activity. Klay

Thompson ended up switched onto Griffin, but a double-team took away Griffin's size advantage.

After a timeout, Griffin tried to post again to no avail. Thompson followed with a step-back 3-pointer. In fewer than three minutes, the Warriors scored 11 straight points and erased the Clippers' 10-point lead, completing a coup of Staples Center as Warriors fans went bananas in another team's house.

Jamal Crawford dropped in a 3-pointer, trying to re-settle the Clippers. But it was a sandbag against a tidal wave.

Curry answered right back with a 3-pointer. After Paul missed a contested jumper, the Warriors turned to one of their trademark out-of-bounds diversions: using Curry's gravity to draw attention away from the basket, leaving the rim exposed. This time, Griffin jumped out at Curry, leaving Green an easy path to the basket. Iguodala, the passer, playfully shuffled all the way to half-court, where he waited to celebrate with Green.

Coming back from a 23-point deficit had become an illustration of the might in their new knockout blow. It was an epiphany revealing the new level they had reached. It was clear their championship wasn't a pinnacle, but the start of something greater. And they knew it after what they did to the Clippers.

And how they did it, going with a small lineup, would have an impact on basketball that is still being felt. And the reason it works is because of Curry. He is the axis on which the Warriors spun circles around teams.

The first six years of Curry's career were marked by trying to find the delicate balance of getting the most out of his crazy skills while minimizing the detriment of his weaknesses. But the Warriors found the answer by giving in whole hog to the lineup and style of play that best fits Curry's game. And it left the league dazed. In that sense, Curry was the pioneer of a basketball revolution, the missing puzzle piece in a decades-long basketball riddle.

For the longest time, small ball was the reason the Warriors couldn't win. Never able to get his hands on a good enough big man, former Warriors coach Don Nelson tried to outscore teams. Instead of playing a traditional center, which for the Warriors usually meant a player who brought little more than height, Nelson would play with an extra perimeter player to increase the skill quotient in his lineup. He'd much rather play a six-foot-four guard who could run well and shoot than a seven-footer who plodded up the court and could only score if the opportunity was created for him.

The Warriors could get their hands on guards. Quality seven-footers who could dominate were rare gems. The ones that were established had no interest in playing for Golden State. But perimeter players were easy to find.

Nelson loved forwards who could dribble like guards, allowing him to invert the game and have the "big men" play on the perimeter. This opened up the floor, preventing defenses from leaving their center near the rim and giving his skill players room to operate. The result was a high-scoring offense.

The famous Run TMC era was built on these principles. The Warriors won fifty-five games in 1991–92 with five guards—Chris Mullin, Tim Hardaway, Sarunas Marciulionis, Mario Elie, and Vincent Askew—ranking in the top seven in minutes. The other two players were Tyrone Hill, a power forward thrust into the center role to handle the dirty work duties, and Billy Owens, a forward with the skills of a guard who Nelson used to run the point.

But small ball, for all its offensive fireworks, was never taken seriously among the NBA's most credible. Because defense wins championships, and forfeiting size also meant forfeiting rebounding and rim protection and interior offense. Nelson's Warriors never made it past the second round of the playoffs. They were eventually thwarted by teams with traditional lineups and legitimate NBA big men. Teams that played good defense.

The Run TMC Warriors, who became legend for their run-and-gun style of play, and the We Believe Warriors, who pulled off (at the time) the biggest upset in NBA playoff history in 2007 by beating the top-seeded Dallas Mavericks in six games, were flashes in the pan. Both of those blips of brightness in Warriors history relied on "small ball" only to learn it wasn't sustainable. Winning requires playing defense, and Nelson's scheme sacrificed defense.

When new management took over the Warriors, they went away from the stigmatized style of play for which the franchise was known. They traded away star guard Monta Ellis in 2012, upsetting a large portion of the fan base who loved Ellis, to roll the dice on Bogut. Getting a quality center was so important, and so hard to do, that the Warriors traded their leading scorer for a guy who was rehabbing from his second season-ending injury with an indefinite return. Months after the trade, the Warriors drafted a center prospect in Festus Ezeli. Suddenly, they were stocked with two sizeable men, both physical and imposing, setting the Warriors up to compete in the traditional sense.

That's partly what made the Warriors' NBA Finals–changing adjustment as revolutionary as it was ironic. They changed the tide of the 2015 NBA Finals by benching Bogut, the very player who gave them the credibility of a contender. Their small lineup dominated Cleveland and paved the way to the title.

And then it became the kill shot as the Warriors blasted out of the gates the following season. The Warriors' small lineup was the most potent in the game. After that comeback against the Clippers, it started being called the "Death Lineup."

Curry is the Death Lineup's biggest weapon as one of the primary purposes of going small is to create what the modern hoops lexicon refers to as "pace and space." And he is a master at it. Pace—or playing faster—crams more possessions into the forty-eight minutes of an NBA game and provides more opportunities in transition, before the defense is set. Space—or spreading the players out on the floor—uses shooters to draw the big men out of the paint and gives the offense more room to work, especially near the basket.

"Pace and space" is the environment where Curry is most dangerous. His shooting, his ball-handling, his court vision are highlighted when the tempo is fast and the defense is spread out. He has room to dribble and probe. The chaos of transition leads to open shots. And with more possessions, he has more chances to bomb 3-pointers.

But Curry is not alone. The Death Lineup featured five players who are all able 3-point shooters, including Klay Thompson, Curry's brother of splash. He, too, thrives at a faster pace, when the defense can lose sight of him and set up clean looks from 3. He's the deadliest shooter in the NBA not named Curry. He's even better at catching-and-shooting than Curry.

Green, the center in the Death Lineup, made all three of his attempts from behind the arc against the Clippers. Opposing big men either had to come out of the paint to defend the 3, which leaves the rim unprotected, or stay in the paint and give the Warriors' open looks from deep. Often, even if the plan was for power forwards and centers to come out of the paint to challenge, it was easier said than done. Their defensive instincts were to stay inside, and old habits die hard.

It's such a tough choice for most opponents. If they leave in their traditional lineup, their big men are forced to defend on the perimeter, chasing smaller players around and running constantly. That's usually not a sustainable style for big men. That's why most teams have to take out their big men and put in smaller players who can keep up, sacrificing their size advantage over the Warriors' lineup.

But it wasn't enough to just roll a quintet of guards and forwards out there and hope to match the Death Lineup. The Warriors' lineup was so multidimensional, it was hard to contain and difficult to duplicate. Much like their championship run in 2015, and their MVP, the Death Lineup is an organic concoction that has turned out to be magical. Lightning in a bottle is hard to replicate.

It's hard to find another Green. He's the reason the Death

Lineup works. It was effective because despite being small, that five-man unit can defend and rebound in addition to scoring. And Green is the anchor on that end.

He is listed at six-foot-seven, but he becomes the center when the Warriors turn to the small lineup. He not only holds his own but often dominates. He's got a seven-foot-one wingspan that he wields with the expertise of a swordmaster. He's got a leathery toughness developed in Saginaw, Michigan, a sheer will that compensates for his lack of height. He's got tremendous defensive expertise played out in his understanding of leverage and angles and timing. And he is an extremely smart player, who picks up on tendencies and preys on weaknesses.

Green is the backbone of this lineup as he's the rim protector and post defender. He's the presence in the middle who opponents feel. He inhales rebounds, especially in traffic. And because he has skills like a small forward, Green makes himself a special force by being able to get the rebound and go. Who else has a center that can lead a fast-break?

A small forward coming out of the draft, Green's strength has always been his diverse skill set. He made up for his lack of size and athleticism with his ability to dribble, pass, rebound, see the floor, and do all the little things that add up to winning. And over the first few years of his career, Green improved his shooting. He stretched his range out to the 3-point line, making him an even more versatile player.

But the Death Lineup works well because, in short stretches, the Warriors don't lose much on the defensive end of the court with Green playing center, allowing them to have offensive potency and defensive sturdiness.

In the first quarter of the sixteenth straight win, setting the record for best start to a season, the Warriors' coaching staff found themselves discussing a decision that would illustrate how the small lineup works. Midway through the first quarter against the Los Angeles Lakers, it was time for Iguodala to enter the game. Usually he came in for Barnes in the first quarter. But during the timeout, at the 5:19 mark, they wrestled with another option: going with the small lineup early.

Barnes had run off 8 points in a four-minute stretch. He was clearly in a groove, and bringing him out might have killed it. However, Iguodala replacing Bogut presented a concern.

The Lakers started Roy Hibbert at center. He is a seven-foot-two, 270-pound giant. Was he too big for Green? Was that asking too much of him?

The coaches put their money on Green. They'd been down the alley with him before.

Sure enough, the moment the Lakers recognized that Bogut had not emerged from the huddle, they quickly hustled forward Brandon Bass into the game and took out Hibbert. The Warriors were willing to put their undersized power forward against the biggest guy in the arena. But the Lakers blinked first.

"Who is six-seven and can guard centers?" Warriors assistant coach Bruce Fraser said. "Draymond's a crazy piece because he's so versatile and for his size he can guard those bigs. And then they've got to guard him. This is a guy that also has such fight in him. He's such a winner. When we need that rebound, he's in there. He's getting that ball. That's like an intangible he has. It's not just his defense or his ability to stop this guy in the post on this play. It's that rebound. All the little things he does."

Green had been known for his intangibles, but his impact started showing up in the statistics almost immediately. And all of what he had become was on display in win No. 24 at Boston. A double overtime victory revealed the best of Green: 24 points, 11 rebounds, 8 assists, 5 steals, 5 blocks. Even more than the numbers will show, it was the grit required, the toughness necessary. The Celtics' green was a form of kryptonite for the Warriors. Boston's scrappiness contrasted the Warriors' finesse; their length and athleticism warred with the Warriors' rhythm.

But Green gives Golden State excellence in those areas, allows them to be more than just fast-breaks and 3-pointers. The Death Lineup could claw with the best of them, grind as well as any. It's not just Green, but he sets that tone. He does the dirty work that sets the table for the pretty basketball they play.

Another hard-to-replace component of the Death Lineup is Iguodala. If Curry is the star, Green is its base. And Iguodala is the analyst.

He instinctually calculates percentages and measures angles. He's got ten years of experience being a star player and defensive stopper, feeding his algorithm with data that repeatedly guides him into the right position. He doesn't swarm and smother as would Tony Allen when he's amping up the defense. But Iguodala plays the percentages and takes away strengths. His defensive style is preventative medicine, removing the options for harm with swift closeouts and instinctual reads.

Physically, Iguodala is a prototypical defensive specialist. He's six-foot-six with a wingspan that stretches out five inches wider. He's on the other side of thirty, but he is still a special athlete, chiseled and agile even if some of his explosion has tapered off over the years. But what makes him a weapon for the Warriors' defense is his brain.

On top of his defense, Iguodala is a calming presence on offense. He was one of the few advanced ball-handlers the Warriors had. In the Death Lineup, he became a second point guard on the floor.

A former front-line star, Iguodala averaged at least 17 points in four of his eight seasons in Philadelphia. He was never a natural scorer, more of a playmaker with the ability to handle the ball, pass, and finish at the rim. His scoring production tapered off, but his skills made him a reliable floor general, giving the Warriors the flexibility to turn Curry into a shooting guard and take advantage of his 3-point stroke.

And in 2015–16, Iguodala became a master at his role. But initially, he didn't accept it.

The first 758 games of his professional career, Iguodala was a starter—a revered position in basketball. But when the Warriors hired Kerr in the summer of 2014, he turned Iguodala into a reserve. Iguodala's array of abilities makes him a chameleon who can enter a game and blend into the flow, adapt to what his team needs. For Kerr, that made Iguodala a better sixth man—the first player to come off the bench—than Harrison Barnes, who came off the bench under Mark Jackson. Iguodala can fill in with the top players or run the show with the second unit. Barnes, much younger but less skilled, was best when surrounded by the Warriors' strongest players.

But that logic didn't make it an easier pill to swallow. Iguodala said all the right things, but he wasn't feeling the move. He was definitely taking one for the team and biting his tongue. But he didn't buy in all the way. Not at first.

A couple of months into Kerr's tenure, Iguodala was benched late in a game, which prompted him to voice his irritation. He and Kerr, both University of Arizona alums, had a text message exchange that covered Iguodala's displeasure. That led to more discussions about his role and what Kerr wanted from him.

"And then he came out and basically said screw it," Fraser explained. "Like an F you to Steve—in a good way. He started to really get going. Once he got going, he started to buy in . . . Andre is skeptical about life, people. Also, once he accepts things, he's loyal. He's all in."

One of Iguodala's personal favorites on the roster is Thompson. Since he joined the Warriors in 2013, Iguodala took a liking to Thompson and took him under his wing. Iguodala even lobbied for Thompson when it was time for him to get a contract extension.

Interestingly, Thompson's game has grown noticeably. Formerly a one-trick pony, living and dying by his shooting ability, he grew into a well-rounded player. His offensive repertoire grew enough to allow him to create his own shot. Thompson came into 2015–16 with an improved post-up game, much more comfortable taking his defender off the dribble, and an automatic mid-range jumper he turned to when the 3-pointer wasn't open.

But he made himself critical to the Warriors' core with his defense. Thompson has good lateral quickness for a player his size. He's not just tall, he's thick. He isn't especially ripped, like some of the exceptional athletes at his position. But he is not little. Strong legs give him a sturdy base, allowing him to hold his ground. Long arms help him take up a lot of space. It works together to irritate opposing point guards.

To most NBA point guards, Thompson's smothering makes life difficult. Thompson has never been a stellar defender when it comes to reading the offense and making the proper rotations on time and carrying out three or four assignments on a possession. He's gotten better over the years, but his focus still betrays him.

But if you tell him to do one thing—go guard that guy—that's when Thompson is great. Jackson would do that to opposing point guards, dispatch Thompson on them like a hungry Rottweiler, and it became his thing, a specialty. They can't shake him because he covers so much ground. His size advantage allows him to track guards down from behind even when he gets beat. His presence must feel like a wet peacoat they can't take off.

In win No. 23 of the streak, Monta Ellis got to feel Thompson's weight. Thompson spent his rookie season as Ellis's backup with the Warriors. On December 8, 2015, Ellis was now the focus of Thompson's relentlessness on defense. Ellis, quick as they come and usually aggressive, looked disengaged and frustrated. He finished four of eleven against his former team, totaling just 9 points.

And really showing off his two-way prowess, Thompson also scored 39 points. He scored 17 points in the first quarter and went on to make ten of sixteen 3-pointers.

"Klay is really one of the great, complete players on this planet," said Duke coach Mike Krzyzewski, Thompson's coach on Team USA. "He's more than a shooter. He's an outstanding offensive player who loves to play defense and really never seems to get tired. He has a great motor."

Harrison Barnes rounded out the Death Lineup. The youngest of the pack, Barnes was valuable filler. He had the ability to make open shots, of which he received a lot. His best attribute was also on defense. At six-foot-eight, 210 pounds, Barnes was the most explosive of the five players. He is big and strong enough to guard bigger players, yet athletic enough to defend smaller players.

His ability to bang with power forwards and compete inside, then turn around and outrun them, was critical to the Warriors' ability to play fast and yet still play defense.

After playing that role during the championship season, Barnes bulked up a bit. He didn't want the grind of playing power forward to take away his legs again. Facing the prospect of locking horns with Zach Randolph and fighting for position against Serge Ibaka, Barnes sought to get stronger.

It cost him on offense, where he perennially struggled with consistency. He couldn't impose his will on the defense, and the extra bulk took away some of his quickness. It probably played a role in his early season ankle injury, and it could also explain the drop in his shooting percentage.

But the fact is Barnes's role in the Death Lineup wasn't to be a dominant scorer. He was a finisher, not a creator. His ball-handling wasn't yet good enough to attack complex defenses, and he thinks more than he lets his instincts take over.

Barnes was the most criticized player on the Warriors' roster because he never met the expectations birthed by his talent. He's been a prodigy since high school in Ames, Iowa. He arrived at North Carolina pegged a surefire NBA star. He was drafted by a Warriors franchise who felt blessed he fell to them at the seventh overall pick in 2012. Barnes was supposed to be a perennial all-star. Instead, he wound up a role player feeding off the other stars.

Still, Barnes had great value to the Warriors. Before joining Andrew Bogut and Seth Curry in Dallas, Barnes played a pivotal role in the grooming and developing of one of the most unique talents in NBA history.

Curry's ascension to Hall of Fame status is at least part a function of manufacturing. His unique skills were allowed to flourish because they were given the right setting and the right complementary pieces to develop. Curry likely would have been great no matter what, with his shooting ability and work ethic. But the Matrix likely wouldn't have been decoded if Curry had been forced to exist in a traditional NBA setting and surrounded by typical NBA complements.

The Warriors' 24–0 start showed how Curry could dominate with the right cast around him, elevate from superstar to unstoppable force. He changed the game.

In the core of the Warriors, he has a big guard next to him who can defend well enough to switch with Curry when a superior athlete gives him problems. With this core, he has the defensive support behind him to allow him the freedom to be aggressive on defense. He has other playmakers who can take advantage of opponents double-teaming him. He has shooters to open up the floor, give him room to work and targets to find. Curry even has another point guard–type good enough to run the show and allow him to be aggressive with his scoring.

And then for the 2016–17 season the Warriors doubled down on this Death Lineup.

Warriors general manager Bob Myers was a nervous mess. They had planned for years to get Kevin Durant. Now it was time to make their pitch. Myers was like a National League manager in the playoffs, manipulating his roster to get the win.

Marketing was working on the PowerPoint. Steve Kerr handled the basketball strategy. Joe Lacob was on the future of the franchise and the new Chase Center in San Francisco.

Draymond Green's assignment was to call Durant, use that personality of his to make Durant smile. Myers didn't have Curry call. Instead, he leaned on his point guard's text message proficiency.

They all had a role to play in the recruitment of Durant and converged on the Hamptons, where Durant was listening to pitches.

"Draymond is [the type to] hit you over the head with a bat. 'Come play for us!'" Myers said. "Steph is not. He'll give you like a text a day, maybe. But it's going to be powerful. And it's going to be real. Andre is like an older brother that says, 'Look, I got you. Trust me. I left a team, too. I chose to come to the Warriors. They beat us in the playoffs, too.' Different situation. But we beat Denver and he came. 'I took a risk.' Because he was the only one that really came as a free agent, Andre. And then Klay is just, I don't know what Klay is . . . 'Klay, are you alive?'"

There was a reason the Warriors' rampant success didn't temper their desire for Durant. Even though they ousted the Thunder, and came oh so close to a second straight title, Durant still represented the future.

What the Warriors learned in the playoffs was that the elite teams were creating their own Death Lineups to rival the Warriors, who created the new millennium blueprint. In the Western Conference Finals, the Thunder's version looked even better than the Warriors' did. Durant played the role of Barnes, and Serge Ibaka, a six-foot-ten superior athlete and defensive specialist, took Green's role. And the Thunder's version dominated the Warriors' through the first four games of the series. Some of that was the fact that Curry wasn't himself, still feeling the effects of his knee injury in the first round. But it also had to do with the Thunder's small lineup being bigger than the Warriors' version, with even more length than the Warriors' version, and more athletic.

Thompson and Curry, especially Thompson, went bananas from 3-point range and saved the Warriors. But Cleveland followed with a similar model. Tristan Thompson was a bigger power-forward-playing-center than Green, with the same ability to run the floor. LeBron James was a matchup nightmare on both ends of the court at power forward, especially on defense. And point guard Kyrie Irving was an elite scorer who started buckling down on defense. J. R. Smith and Iman Shumpert gave the Cavaliers three guards who swarmed the perimeter and spread the floor with their shooting.

Curry was injured, to be sure. Fully healthy, the Warriors still could best Oklahoma City's and Cleveland's small lineups. But there was no denying the model was being successfully duplicated. Curry made combo guards en vogue. He went from being knocked for being more of a scorer than a point guard to creating a model for other franchises to follow. The Thunder and the Cavaliers followed it with success, using Russell Westbrook and Kyrie—two other guards who have been criticized for looking for their own shot too much for a point guard.

What the playoffs also showed was that the model for the Warriors only works because of Curry. But in order for the Warriors' version to be better than the other vaunted small lineups, they needed to turn it up a notch.

Durant represented the upgrade, a new model designed to keep the Warriors a step ahead. In the process, they presumably broke up the Thunder's small lineup and theoretically became more equipped to take down Cleveland's, which is anchored by LeBron James. And by getting Durant, the Warriors are able to continue pursuing championships in the heart of Curry's prime.

The Warriors got a championship and a regular season record for wins out of building around Curry and helping his game blossom. Durant is the key to sustaining that.

Wardell II

o   o   o

"People ask me all the time if Curry is as good a person as he seems. My response is always no. He's much, much better."

—Rick Welts

CHAPTER 3

hirtless, Curry sat bent over at his locker, sandwiched by a
Gatorade fridge and Draymond Green, his elbows resting
on his knees and his chin pressed against his chest. One hand
scratched the top of his wooly mane as he gazed at the ground.
Between his feet, resting on the shades of gray carpet in the visiting locker room of Chesapeake Energy Arena, was a single sheet
of paper. On it: the autopsy report from the Warriors' 118–94
loss in Game 4 of the 2016 Western Conference Finals at Oklahoma City.

It wasn't the destruction they endured in Game 3. But the
impact was much more jarring. The Warriors gave up 77 first-half
points and trailed by 19 at the half. The roar of the Thunder fans,
dressed in white, rolled onto the court like an avalanche as Oklahoma City crushed the visitors in the second quarter. It rattled the
defending champions, foiled their game plan, shook their core.

They rallied back into the game as Klay Thompson caught fire.
He scored 19 straight points in the third quarter, the last coming
on a layup off a feed from Curry that cut the Thunder's lead
to 6 points. The defense held Oklahoma City to 7-for-23 shooting in the third quarter. It looked as if the championship resolve
had kicked in. The Warriors appeared to be back to themselves.
Another Thompson 3 to start the fourth quarter, and the Warriors
were within 9 with a full quarter to play. Nine points had been
nothing for them all year.

And then it all crumbled. Again. A 7–0 run by Oklahoma
City stomped that fire out quickly. Later, a Russell Westbrook

3-pointer with just over three minutes left prompted coach Steve Kerr to wave the white flag, pulling his starters with a 23-point deficit.

The Warriors were down 3–1 in the series and the locker room felt like it. They got destroyed in Game 3, trailing by as much as 41. But they wrote that game off like lost change. That beatdown merely got their attention. But Game 4, that was a crippling body blow. And afterward, they were collectively slumped over in spirit, grappling with the brink of historic disappointment.

Curry also had to wrestle with the emotions of his unclutchness. He was 6-for-20 shooting, missed eight of his ten 3-pointers and had more turnovers (six) than assists (five). He looked nothing like the two-time MVP, and nothing piles onto the agony of defeat for Curry like him not playing well.

The whole locker room felt like the life had been sucked out of it. For the first time all season, the postgame atmosphere was somber. No one was laughing, which was unusual even after losses. Frustration, usually visible in deep sighs and random shouts of expletives, was also absent. Instead, there was silence. Enough to hear the hum of the refrigerator filled with sports drinks, water, and nutrition shakes. Enough to hear tape being peeled off ankles. Enough for Curry to hear his phone vibrate.

He shook his head slowly, still in disbelief, as he finally tore his eyes away from the stat sheet to grab his phone. He'd gotten a text from Ayesha, his wife. It was a video. He pressed play and the precious voice of his daughter Riley boomed from his iPhone.

"I'm sorry you lost the game, Daddy. I love you. I love you. I can't wait to see you again."

Instantaneously, Curry was revived. He sat up in his chair, smiling at the love smiling at him. He unwrapped the tape from his knee and stood up to take off his game shorts. Suddenly, he was singing as he wrapped the towel around his waist, then removed his tights.

"Are you worried?" Curry was asked as he made his way

toward the shower. His initial response was a confused look. His head snapped back, his brow scrunched, and his lip turned up as if he'd heard something ridiculous.

"Worried?" he replied with the same facial expression from a mural in West Oakland that merges his likeness with Bay Area rapper Mac Dre. "Have you not seen this team before? Why would I be worried?"

He finished singing as he walked into the shower. Suddenly, he had a pep in his step. His newfound energy clashed against the lugubrious ambiance.

It was vintage Curry. As fast as he can change directions on the court, as quickly as he can transition from dribbling to shooting, Curry can regain the perspective at his core. It's how he handles all this—the rapid ascendance to cult figure status, the steady stream of opportunities and obligations, the pressure of such rarified air. It all works for him because, at his foundation, Curry is just a guy.

See, Steph is the excitable, intense, competitive kid-at-heart who wears his emotions on his sleeve. He is the guy chewing his mouthpiece, taking trick shots, and doing the salsa on the bench in honor of his Brazilian teammate's highlight. He is the persona that revels in the challenge of breaking down the defense, enjoys heated battles with fellow stars around the league, and punches his head after a dumb mistake.

But he can flip to Mr. Curry, the executive, the pitchman and mogul, the billion-dollar brand who can flash the charm. That's the persona that says yes too much, coaxed by his mission to expand his kingdom. The part of him that is acutely aware of his image and his associations. This is the guy who comes out when it's time to rub shoulders with the CEOs, rap stars, and anonymous power brokers, or when he's thrust into character as an international celebrity.

Holding Steph and Mr. Curry together is Stephen, the boring guy who better fits the mode of supporting cast in a network sitcom. That's what his mother and wife call him, Steffan. He is the contradiction to the superstar. The common man trapped in an abnormal existence thanks to his supreme talent. He impresses people who know him best with his allegiance to this regular guy at his core.

Stephen meets people and asks questions that suggest he genuinely cares about the answer, and he will remember the answer in the next encounter. He sees and appreciates the thankless efforts of the people in the shadows, the very spirit that prompted him to mention Warriors security man Ralph Walker and equipment manager Eric Housen in his first MVP acceptance speech. He is a silly guy who pranks his teammates and dances with Oracle Arena security guards before every home game, mimicking the two-step from the "Jones BBQ and Foot Massage" commercial on YouTube.

It's Stephen who leaves people floored by the superstar's normalcy. The bigger his star rises, the more shocking his down-to-earthness. Those who are closest to him even shake their heads at how much he hasn't changed.

"My definition of success is what's sitting here in front of you. It's the people that know you the best that love you the most," Warriors general manager Bob Myers said, addressing Curry directly during the press conference of his second MVP. "And I know you're loved by a lot of people that don't know you. But the ones that know you love you the most, and that's a true testament. Because there are a lot of people that are well known and have accomplished a lot of things, but their family doesn't love them or their friends don't love them. You are the antithesis of that. You are someone that it is very hard not to like you. I find it impossible."

The trappings of his stardom—the fame, the access, the adoration—prompt him to cling even closer to Stephen. He hedges himself inside his values. He tethers himself to his faith and his family, keeping him grounded despite his meteoric rise.

He is arguably basketball's greatest show on the court, and off it he can be as ordinary as a neighbor. Sure, he gets to golf with the President and appear on popular talk shows. He has millions of fans to go with his millions of dollars. But all of that gets compartmentalized and eventually pressed beneath the part of him that's been groomed from birth. And the constant struggle is to enjoy the spoils that come with being Mr. Curry, courtesy of the accomplishments of Steph, without losing the essence of Stephen.

That essence is best exemplified, and maintained, through his relationship with Ayesha. It is impossible to really know the NBA star without being confronted with her importance. She is the assurance that Stephen never leaves, and he cherishes her role in keeping that part of him prevalent.

That's why the best portrait of Wardell Stephen Curry II, the person behind the star, can be found in his marriage. And the public image of their marriage—the happy couple that has endless fun together—pales in comparison to how they are away from the spotlight.

"It's so beautiful. I just really look and say, 'Ugh,'" Steph's mom, Sonya, said, playfully pointing her finger down her throat before breaking into laughter. "Sometimes, I'm just like, are you serious? Seriously? They're so perfect."

One balmy night in Oakland, still buzzed from the Warriors' Game 1 win over Houston in the first round of the 2016 playoffs, the couple had dinner at Ozumo, a Japanese restaurant. Curry had gotten the first of his two playoff injuries that night. At the time the injury to his right foot late in the first half seemed like a minor blip to wrapping up the championship season, so they went and enjoyed nightlife in the ever-popular Uptown. It was at dinner they learned about the Kirk Franklin concert going on down the street at the Paramount. They immediately searched the Internet for tickets, to no avail.

After dinner, they took their sweet time walking to the car. The seventy-nine-degree day had left some warmth for the evening air. The soothing breeze was like a whisper in their ears as they held hands walking down West Grand Avenue. It was the perfect setting for their own impromptu concert. They didn't get to see Kirk Franklin live, but they could do Kirk Franklin live. Right there on the sidewalk, they broke out singing "Lean on Me"—a "We Are the World"–type collaboration featuring R. Kelly and Bono. Ayesha, ever the actress, put some feeling into it when they got to Mary J. Blige's part.

One walker-by even shot them a crazy look, like the Currys were weirdos, until she realized who they were and gasped in shock.

A typical night for the Currys. Stephen and Ayesha are a real, live romantic comedy. Sappy and silly and touching. Surprisingly regular while incredibly rare. They're that couple best described by the millennials' favorite four-letter word for attractiveness, youthfulness, and anything that provokes warm and tingly: cute. Actually, the Currys are soooo cute. The Kennedys of the emoji generation. The NBA's Cory and Topanga. The embodiment of #RelationshipGoals.

They give many glimpses into their life on social media. Dancing videos. Funny pictures. Captures of quality time together. It may look staged to a jaded audience that's been force-fed Brangelina and Bennifer and Kimye.

But when you know their love story, it is clear their appearance isn't a PR concoction.

"They started perfect. It's going perfect. They have perfect babies," said Chris Strachan, who's been a close family friend since he roomed with Seth Curry at Liberty University. "They have perfect parents. They were perfect kids. It's a perfect relationship."

How this relationship came to be, and how it operates, is a vivid picture of Stephen. It started in 2002 when Dell Curry retired and moved back to Charlotte. The family settled on the Central Church of God as their home congregation. The Curry kids took part in the youth group. That's where Stephen met Ayesha. Kinda.

She hardly talked to him. But she definitely liked him. A Toronto native, Ayesha would visit Canada with her family and come back with candy from her home country. Curry loved the Maynards Fuzzy Peach, which he'd eaten when he lived in Toronto, sugar-sanded gummies that triggered his love for Sour Patch Kids.

"That's how she would flirt with him, in a way," said Stephen's sister, Sydel Curry. "She would find him after church, barely say two words, and like walk away. I would look at her like 'God, she's so lame.' He clearly liked it. It left an impression."

Ayesha is a mix of a little bit of everything: African-Polish-American-Chinese-Jamaican. She has two brothers and two sisters. Eventually, her family relocated to Charlotte to be near her maternal aunts who were doing residency in the medical field. Her dad was a road manager whose résumé included touring with Rick James and teen rappers Kris Kross. But that life was too much for the Christian family, so he gave it up and switched over to real estate. The suburbs of Charlotte proved to be a good fit.

They visited a number of churches and settled on the same one as the Curry family because it reminded them of Agincourt Pentecostal Church, their family's congregation in Canada. Ayesha would sit in Wednesday night Bible class with Stephen. They'd talk on the phone here and there.

"It was that shy middle school, high school stuff," Curry said, describing their phone chats. "We didn't talk much."

In March of 2008, he became a national star. He was the most prolific scorer in college basketball, and everybody knew it after he tore up the NCAA tournament, leading Davidson to the Elite Eight.

That's about the time Sonya Curry said she had a revelation. For years she had been praying, fervently, that her teenage son would focus on school and basketball, and "stay away from girls, stay away from girls, stay away from girls." But one spring morning, she woke up and prayed. Before she even got to "Amen" she realized her prayer had suddenly changed.

"I said, 'Dell, oh my gosh. I'm praying for Stephen's significant other," Sonya recalled telling her husband. "He said, 'Whaaaaat???' I said, 'I know. I'm freaking out.'

"I was ready for him to find someone."

That summer, Stephen was invited to the ESPYs. He was nominated for Best Breakout Athlete, which required a trip to Los Angeles.

"Oooooh. L.A.," Curry thought. "That's where Ayesha is."

Ayesha—who attended Weddington High, a twenty-minute drive from Curry's school—had graduated a year early. At seventeen, she moved to Hollywood to pursue her acting career, which was promising enough for her to be accepted to Arts York, a renowned program in Canada that counts Hayden Christensen as an alum. Ayesha landed cameos in Disney Channel shows like *Hannah Montana* and *Good Luck Charlie.*

They hadn't talked much over the years. But Ayesha stayed somewhere in Curry's mind. She was pretty, sweet to him, ambitious, and bright. He was fond enough to take to Facebook and set up a reunion.

Ayesha maintains she wasn't really interested in Stephen at the time but relented.

"I ain't buying it," Sydel, his sister, said. "She was feeling him."

Stephen and Ayesha hit the Hollywood tour spots: the Walk of Fame, the Kodak Theater, the whole deal. The entire time, his dad was waiting for him in the hotel room. They were supposed to go to a party hosted by Eli Manning, but, to borrow a line from the movie *Good Will Hunting*, Stephen had to see about a girl.

Next thing Sonya knew, her eldest son was bringing Ayesha to the house. Sonya had eight of her friends over for a women's Bible study. Stephen, blindsided by the activity at his house, walked Ayesha past the study and into the kitchen. All the women sized up Ayesha, checking to see if she was good enough for the church's darling son.

"She came into kind of a hostile thing," Sonya said.

Sonya surprised the women's group by vouching for Ayesha.

She didn't think the timing was right for them, but she had no doubts about her son's choice.

"Y'all, I feel it in my spirit that this is the one," she told the study group. "She's the one."

Sydel wasn't so sure. Actually, she was certain Ayesha was not the one. No girl was, not for her big brother.

Sydel is the baby of the three Curry kids, with her father's eyes and her mother's spunk. She took pride in her role as the annoying little sister. So every time Stephen brought home a girl he liked, Sydel made it her mission to throw shade.

When Stephen and Ayesha watched a movie together later that evening, Sydel made sure to join them. She wanted to sit between them but settled for a spot on the other couch. While they watched the movie, she watched them.

Sydel's disdain didn't last. She tried, but Ayesha won her over in about a week. She now describes Ayesha as "best friend" and the "sister I never had."

Ayesha moved back to Charlotte while Stephen was in his junior season at Davidson. Bryant Barr, Stephen's best friend since they were freshmen on the Wildcats, knew things were serious because Stephen was often "AWOL." No time for the fellas. He spent his spare time with Ayesha.

"She was there so much," Barr said, "people thought she went to Davidson."

Curry was now a college basketball star and serious NBA prospect, and he loved how that didn't seem to impact Ayesha at all. Whether he scored 30 points and his highlights were on *SportsCenter* or he had a bad night shooting and Davidson lost, she didn't change how she interacted with him. At a time when everyone swooned over Steph for his basketball skills, Ayesha was simply into the man and not his game.

"That meant a lot to me," Curry said. "She didn't care about basketball or the NBA or none of that. She didn't just let me do whatever I wanted, and I liked that."

When Stephen got drafted, he moved to an apartment in Oakland near Lake Merritt while Ayesha stayed in Charlotte. To help him prepare for life on his own, she taught him and Chris Strachan—who moved to the Bay Area with Stephen—how to make chicken pasta. Neither of them knew their way around the kitchen, and she wouldn't be there to cook for her man. So she walked them step by step through cooking the chicken, preparing the noodles, and making the sauce.

That's when Strachan knew Ayesha was the one. Curry had already decided he wanted Ayesha to be part of his NBA life.

The NBA comes at a man fast. Bright lights. Big checks. Bold women. Many men would jump at the spoils. Though it was all enticing, Curry's desires were already shaped by New Testament teachings. He wanted to be sanctified, keep his nose clean. His goal was to start early being the kind of man and father he wanted to be. So he leaned on Ayesha. They prayed together in the mornings, shared the details of their day in the afternoon, laughed at random stuff in the evening. It was the kind of talking they'd never done as teenagers.

"That whole year," Strachan said of Curry's rookie campaign, "Steph walked around on FaceTime or on his computer with Ayesha. If he wasn't playing or practicing, he was talking to her."

Less than two years later, they were back in Charlotte. On July 30, 2011, at the same church they ran around during Vacation Bible School. Stephen stood at the altar, the nervous tension inside him warring with his smooth appearance. In a smoke-gray tuxedo with black piping on top of a black vest and a silver tie, he was cooler than a polar bear's toenails. But in a blink, he melted.

The doors to the auditorium opened, and light as if from heaven pierced the church. Ayesha, in a strapless white taffeta dress and a veil that seemed like curtains draped from her halo, came into view. The sight blew Stephen away.

"That was the best part of the ceremony," Stephen told *Carolina Bride*. "I still have that picture of her in my head."

Their union does seem like a divine orchestration: a great love story, now two beautiful daughters, exploding careers, likable in-laws.

They have their issues like every couple. They've had to navigate family concerns, their young marriage, a schedule more crammed than a Louis Vuitton satchel.

They have toddlers, so clearly every day isn't a magazine photo shoot. Riley, their oldest daughter, famous for crashing press conferences, runs their house. Ayesha's first year of motherhood was a whirlwind. Mr. Curry was blowing up and being pulled in every direction. They went through pregnancy for the first time and parenting for the first time and stardom for the first time—all at the same time.

As a gift, Stephen created a picture book that chronicled Riley's first year. It was all handmade and clearly took him plenty of time he didn't have. He made it happen, though. Because that year was so hectic, went by so fast, Ayesha didn't get to fully enjoy it. So he captured the memories. And they went back over the moments together.

"She knows I don't really do stuff like that," Stephen said of his arts and crafts skills. "So me taking the time, that really meant a lot to her."

Stephen and Ayesha are so nauseatingly ideal that Strachan doesn't even accept their counsel on his love life.

"They try to give me advice all the time," he said. "But I'm like, 'Please, please. Y'all don't understand.' They can't tell me anything about this crazy stuff that I have to deal with. They know nothing about the difficulty of finding someone out here. Everything about their relationship is abnormal. They have a TV fairy tale relationship. And they don't even know that."

But the Currys are exceptional because they maintain the ordinary parts of them. Despite all of their access and extravagance, they cling to the simple. Yes, they are moguls. It has been nothing short of savvy how they have maximized their platform and crafted their image. Don't think for a second they aren't brand aware and business minded. Yet, privately, they relish the less-glamorous aspects of their life. Carpet time with the kids. Family dinner. A small circle of like-minded friends. Battles over board games.

Oh, they get down on board games.

Hanging out with friends and family usually leads to a spirited game of Hedbanz. The Wheel of Fortune matches between Stephen and Ayesha on Nintendo 64 can also be intense.

"She doesn't want to win for the sake of winning," Curry said. "She wants to win because she knows I hate to lose. Making me upset is more important than winning to her."

They are still kids at heart, even if responsibility forces them to be grown. They still crack up laughing. They still share a gazillion inside jokes. They still find delight in randomness.

Such as Ayesha, in the hall after Game 2 against the Rockets in 2016, a game Curry sat out with that same injury, illustrating how she would sing the national anthem. She stopped suddenly, then took a dramatic step forward like there were an invisible stage. Her expression switched to serious as she threw one arm to the side, cutting off her husband's path, while with the other arm raised an invisible microphone to her mouth. She slowly elevated her head, revealing her widened hazel eyes and unveiling her best breathy baritone. Right there in the hallway that leads to the Warriors locker room.

"Ooooooooooh saaaaaaay," she oozed from her diaphragm before abruptly snapping out of character. "That's as far as I've gotten."

Ayesha almost instantly shifted gears to how hungry she is, Stephen's signal to stop chatting and get going.

Yes, Stephen is a two-time MVP and NBA champion. He is the face of sports apparel giant Under Armour, one of his many endorsements. He's a multimillionaire. But that doesn't fly with Ayesha. He still gets the business. Like every other husband. Ever.

Let him not take out the trash. Or take too long to respond to a text.

"She doesn't care about that global superstar stuff," Strachan said. "He is just Stephen. She will bite his head off at any minute. She is going to keep it real."

Stephen likes the normal he gets in his relationship with Ayesha. He can just be the man he is, not the idolized basketball phenom or the shot-calling empire head, but the homebody who binge watches golf and listens to Christian rap and pushes his mother into the pool at family gatherings.

He and Ayesha grew up together, experienced life moments while holding hands, weathered storms in each other's arms. Each is the other's first serious relationship, so they caught each other before baggage could pile up and facades formed. So they can truly be themselves around each other.

Which means lots of singing. And self-deprecating videos, like Ayesha's Gina Jamaica alter ego on Instagram. And soaking up every surreal moment—backstage with Lecrae, in the White House with the Obamas, cheeseburgers with Drake—then going home to laugh about it together like the fantasy it is.

"Their personalities just connect so much," Sydel said. "She is like the goofiest person you'll ever meet. And so is he. They like the corniest things. They have this need for adventure. They have the same base support: God, family. Their priorities are right in line. You don't come across people like Stephen. You don't come across people like Ayesha. And they have each other. It's perfect."

This relationship is critical because it is Stephen who keeps this ride on the rails. His wholesome aspirations, his something-greater perspective, anchors the whole operation in the midst of the tornado that has become his life. He is diligent about not getting lost in the persona, so he goes extra hard to keep Stephen's voice inside him prominent.

That's why he spends as much time around Ayesha as possible. That's why he surrounds himself with family. His entourage is his parents, siblings, in-laws, and just about whoever else on the family tree is trying to roll. He crams his business obligations on the road to avoid robbing the family of his physical and emotional presence.

That's how Riley became a national celebrity as a preschooler.

After Game 1 of the 2015 Western Conference Finals, in which Curry scored 34 to hold off James Harden's Rockets, Curry was headed to the postgame interview podium. He left the locker room, and as was normal, Ayesha was standing in the hall waiting for him. They shared a kiss. Ayesha was less than two months from having the couple's second daughter, Ryan, and asked her husband to take the reins on the rambunctious, almost three-year-old Riley.

"Sure," Curry said. "I just have to . . ."

Before he finished explaining he was due up for postgame interviews, Ayesha had already squatted down to look Riley in the eye and ask, "Would you like to go with Daddy?" Riley said yes and it was done. Curry was then making the trek to the interview room, near the visitors' locker room at Oracle, with Riley in his care.

Curry wasn't sure how Riley would react when facing down a room full of media and cameras. But he knew it could get interesting. She's been with him before in interviews at his locker, dancing in his chair behind him while he stood and answered questions. Two weeks earlier, Riley had stolen the show behind the scenes of Curry's MVP announcement. After his speech, a photo shoot was set up behind the curtains for Curry and his family. But before anybody could hop in, Riley went vogue on 'em. The then two-year-old delighted the entire private audience with a series of poses, unleashing enough cuteness to stop a heartbeat.

That same showstopper wound up at the podium after the playoff game, becoming an instant celebrity on May 18, 2015. Undeterred by the setting, Riley did what she does. Explored. Interjected. Interacted. It didn't matter how far past bedtime it was, she was present and more awake than anyone else in the room.

Everyone who knows the Currys knows Riley runs the show. She is the party. She has a presence unbecoming of one her age, combining the energy of a toddler with the kind of wit and personality that suggests an older person lives inside.

Curry can tell Riley stories all day. The Stephen side of him loves it. Being a dad. Having her around. Playing a background role in the movie starring his wife and daughters.

That side of him is also why Riley didn't make a podium visit during the 2016 playoffs. The regular dad in him led to Riley's appearance being shut down. Her celebrity status had attracted some weirdness and negativity.

There is a Riley Curry on social media. But he is a twenty-nine-year-old former college football player. He received some of the mean tweets and Instagram posts people thought they were directing at the NBA star's daughter. It compelled him to speak out during the NBA Finals, seeing some of the venom people directed at a preschooler.

Even members of the media were critical of Riley's podium appearances, deeming her a distraction from their interview and a form of disrespect to the profession. But the presence of Riley told more of the story the media was tasked with seeking. It was a glimpse into the life of Stephen, which is the foundation of the star that has grasped the media's attention.

Riley became famous because her dad put the needs of his pregnant wife first, because he embraced his role as a father above his role as a basketball star. Because this entire ride is a family deal, just like it was when he was a kid around his NBA dad. He and Warriors general manager Bob Myers probably talk about fatherhood and family more than basketball.

"The conversations that we do have when you want to talk to me," Curry directed at Myers during his second MVP speech, "we talk about family and we talk about parenting and we talk about the challenges of what we do for a living, and it's refreshing to get that kind of advice from somebody that's in the same kind of situation, that is away from the family a lot and has two daughters. I'm a young parent and want to be the best dad that I can be, and to be able to have somebody to bounce that off of is definitely special."

The portrait of Curry isn't complete without this part of Stephen, and it is perhaps the most glaring example of his mother's influence.

Curry is the spitting image of Sonya. Her coffee-with-lots-of-cream complexion. Her piercing pastel eyes. Even the way her nose scrunches when she laughs. He is his mother's son. But that extends past looks, to levels deeper than the physical. A great case can be made that Sonya is most responsible for producing this NBA great.

The most common, and sensible, connection is made to his father, Dell, a sixteen-year NBA veteran. The easy explanation for Curry's success is the genes passed down from his sharpshooting dad. This magical journey to two-time MVP status was even traced by ESPN writer David Fleming back to Grottoes, Virginia. That's where Dell's dad, Wardell "Jack" Curry, put a hoop up in his backyard for his only son. Wardell Stephen Curry spent hours shooting on the rickety backyard court in the woods of the northern parts of Virginia. The jumper he developed on that court helped turn him into a McDonald's All-American from Fort Defiance High and a star at Virginia Tech.

Dell was then selected by the Utah Jazz in the 1986 draft, No. 15 overall, and after one season was traded to Cleveland in a four-player deal that included Darryl Dawkins. Five months later, while Dell was in Madison Square Garden scoring 15 points off the bench against the Knicks, his wife delivered their first child in a hospital back in Akron. The next night, Dell flew back to Cleveland to see Wardell Stephen Curry II, then went to Chicago and scored 12 points off the bench as Michael Jordan torched the Cavaliers for 38.

Per his mom, their first child attended his first basketball game at the Richfield Coliseum, halfway between Cleveland and Akron. He kept his eyes open the entire game and went right back to sleep after the game.

The Charlotte Hornets and Miami Heat franchises were set to join the league for the 1988–89 season. The Cavaliers made Dell Curry eligible for the expansion draft in June of 1988. The Hornets took Dell second in the draft, which turned out perfect because Charlotte was an hour flight home for him and his wife, who also was raised in Virginia.

The Currys settled roots in Charlotte, which was the right mix of country and city. It had the small town feel both Sonya and Dell grew up with but also some of the metropolitan access and luxuries Dell could enjoy with his NBA income.

Charlotte became home on the court, too. After the expected disaster of the inaugural season, Dell's game started taking off his second season in Charlotte. He averaged 16.0 points in 1989–90, earning a four-year contract extension. The 3-pointer became a key part of his game as he took and made a career high. He made fifty-two 3s that season. He had made sixty-four combined his first three seasons.

His sweet outside stroke was becoming a greater weapon. His release was such he could get his shot off in a blink. The way he could curl off a screen, catch and fire in one motion—and with a suavity that made it look easy—is evident in his son's game. And if he had time to set his feet, the defense was going to pay.

As the Hornets drafted well, the roster started to come together, and Dell's ability became even more valuable. Young front-court studs Alonzo Mourning and Larry Johnson gave the Hornets an inside game that set up Dell's outside touch.

From 1991 to 1994, he set a career-high in 3-pointers made and total points scored as the Hornets grew into a playoff team. Dell was known around the league for his sweet shooting. He won NBA Sixth Man of the Year after the 1993–94 season. In 1994–

95, he missed thirteen games and took nearly four hundred fewer shots than his award-winning season. Still he set a new career high in 3-pointers made (154) and 3-point percentage (42.7).

Dell lasted sixteen seasons in the NBA, mostly as a reserve. He made more than twelve hundred 3-pointers at a 40 percent clip. His best years came in Charlotte, where he averaged 14.0 points in 25.1 minutes over ten seasons with the Hornets.

Anyone who has ever watched Dell play, whether in his day or on YouTube highlights, could see the origins of Stephen Curry's game. It seems as if he was destined to be the best shooter ever when you watch his dad's shots barely move the net. It was Dell who molded the 3-point shot that would change the NBA.

And ten minutes with Dell would explain his son's mild demeanor and easy charm. They are men of few words. But they don't need many to establish their presence in a room. Like his dad, Curry looks you in the eye while talking. He doesn't have his father's drawl, but he shares the ready smile and welcoming expression. They smoothly engage in small talk and are always down for a good laugh.

But while he and his pops are peas in a pod, Curry is a testament to his mother. He has been built on a foundation established by Sonya. And her story reveals the pillars that hold up Stephen Curry the player, the persona, and the person.

"If you spend any time around Sonya Curry," Warriors president Rick Welts said, "it all starts to make sense."

Sonya's story starts in Radford, Virginia, on the family tree of John and Eliza Snell, free blacks who settled in Patrick County in the middle of the nineteenth century. The Snells were aplenty as Sonya's great-great-grandfather had eleven children.

The matriarch of the current Curry empire was groomed in the country, a small town given its life by the New River that flowed from Claytor Lake and given its personality by the railroad industry. Not many pennies to go around, and each one was earned.

The Snells were a big family in a small town. They produced a heritage of athletic prowess, work ethic, and religion. Candy Ann Wyms was a daughter of the Snells and injected all those traits into her three children: Clieve, India, and Sonya.

"Candy did not play," said John Pierce, Sonya's volleyball coach at Radford High and Virginia Tech.

Sonya's first impression is usually her striking attractiveness. It's one of Curry's greatest irritations in life, people going overboard commenting on his mother's beauty. One of the rare times he's shown his anger publicly was after a Warriors game at the New Jersey Nets. Before he could be asked about the game, Curry was asking reporters the name of the broadcaster with a scowl on his face. He wanted to find the person who he was told said on air, "The only thing prettier than Stephen Curry's jumper is his mom, Sonya." He's been hearing about his hot mom since he began playing competitive basketball.

What most don't know, though, is that Sonya's lasting impression is her fight, her infectious fun-loving spirit, and her faith—all of which she harnessed in Radford, Virginia.

Sonya developed a competitiveness growing up around the many athletes in her family. Her mother's strictness produced a rigid discipline. She also adopted Candy's no-nonsense approach to life.

Once in class, a girl called Sonya the N-word. She warned the classmate not to call her that, but the advice wasn't heeded. Sonya beat up the girl right there in class.

"Sonya was tough," said Santa Clara assistant men's basketball coach Steve Snell, one of the many cousins Sonya grew up with in Radford. "She would battle with us. She didn't back down."

The intangibles evident in Stephen Curry's game were first present at Radford High School, where Sonya was a dominant volleyball player. She was a superior athlete crammed into her petite frame. Pierce said she was one of the three best athletes he's worked with in his four decades of coaching. But he revered her for her grit.

In the 1984 regional championships, Sonya's senior year and

last chance at a state title, she tweaked her back in the warm-ups before playing defending champs John Battle High. She was worried enough to pull coach Pierce to the side and tell him.

Both were worried. Both knew they didn't stand a chance without her. They sat together and prayed, right there in the gym at Abingdon High. She then went out on the court, blocking out the pain.

"There was no way she wasn't playing," Pierce said.

Radford, with her on the court, won the game and went on to beat Jefferson Forest for Radford's first state championship.

Sonya continued her volleyball career at Virginia Tech in nearby Blacksburg, where Pierce had established the school's program while simultaneously coaching at Radford High. Sonya was the team's best setter and server, and one of the top defenders.

Her competitiveness helped elevate Hokies volleyball. They didn't win big, but they did upset the University of Virginia once, and Cincinnati, and Sonya was named All-Metro Conference as a junior. Pierce would play pepper with her in practice, firing spikes while she dug them out and the whole gym watched. It was at practice where her life would change.

The volleyball players would have to wait for the men's basketball team to finish on the court before they could practice. That's how she first saw Hokies star guard Dell Curry. Pierce said when she first laid eyes on Dell, Sonya said, "I'm going to marry him," then ran off to warm up for practice.

Some three years later, she dealt her coach a tough blow when that prediction came true.

"Her senior year, she came in and said 'I need to go,'" Pierce recalled. "She said she was getting married and moving. I tried to talk her out of it, get her to finish school. But she knew what she wanted to do. It was definitely hard for her to stop playing volleyball. She was so competitive and she was good. But she knew she wanted to marry Dell and start a family."

The couple wed in August of 1988, five months after Stephen

Curry, their first child, was born. The family of three came to visit Pierce as Sonya brought her family to watch a Virginia Tech match. Curry weighed just nine pounds when Pierce got to hold him.

The coach wondered if Sonya regretted giving up her passion. But one look at the family and it was obvious she didn't. No doubt she missed volleyball. But growing up in Radford, family is everything. Sometimes the only thing. So all her competitiveness was channeled into making her family work.

Just days before their second anniversary, their second child, Seth, was born. The reigning NBA Sixth Man of the Year had his third child in October 1994. At the height of Dell's NBA career, Sonya was a mother of three keeping the house afloat.

They for sure had means. But NBA players weren't paid in the nineties like they are today. Dell made about $5 million over his first six seasons. It wasn't as if life were a traveling fantasy.

NBA wives, during the season especially, are like single mothers. The fathers are traversing the nation while the wife is holding down the empire. Sonya would occasionally travel with the kids to road games on long trips to make sure they didn't go too long without seeing their father.

"Not having my dad there was hard for us," Sydel said. "I kind of knew it would be hard not having her husband around. That's one thing I really admire about her now, how she handled all that. Especially having three young kids. We would visit my dad all the time. I don't know how she did it, traveling with three kids, especially having two older boys who fought with each other. Me and Seth were the sneaky ones. Stephen was such a Goody Two-shoes. It's annoying."

In 1995, Sonya opened up the Christian Montessori School of Lake Norman in Huntersville, North Carolina, about fifteen minutes from Davidson College. Her children attended her school, which became a place where her faith and Radford-bred work ethic shined. It was an extension of her home.

And like her mom, Candy, Sonya is known for not messing

around. Her basketball-addicted sons got court time yanked for not doing homework, got their video game hijacked on numerous occasions. Their chores were posted on the wall in chalk. Curry once had to sit out a middle school game because he didn't handle his.

Sydel was sixteen years old, knocking on the door of college, when she got her last spanking from Sonya. Sixteen.

Stephen still gets calls from his mother. Once during an ESPN telecast, the replay heading into commercial showed Curry celebrate a 3-pointer by screaming an F-bomb. It was in slow motion, too, so it was pretty clear what he said. Caught up in the moment, he didn't even know until he got a call from Mom.

It wasn't all tough love from Sonya. Such is most evident in how all three of her children, each so different in personality, adore her. Even her relentless corny jokes.

"She thinks she's hilarious, though," Seth said with a smile. "That's all that matters."

First and foremost, she is ride-or-die. Their biggest advocate is Sonya Curry. And everyone who deals with them knows the mother hen is present. The same woman who guided them into walking a fine line is the same woman first to go to bat for them. She is always there. Even when all three of her children's sports overlapped, she found a way to make their games, and was wrapped up in each game. The same woman fans remember screaming at Duke games or dancing at Warriors games watches Sydel's volleyball games with gritted-teeth intensity.

Plus, Sonya knows how to have fun. Her party heart has been tamed by her church roots, but it is still there.

Even now, at fifty.

"She is all about the turn up," Sydel said after they celebrated her mom's birthday in Las Vegas before the 2016 NBA Finals. "She loves to get with her cousins and my aunt. They probably turn up more than I do, and I'm the twenty-one-year-old."

All the Curry kids have an understatedness to them, a smoothness siphoned from Dell. Seth is the most like his too-cool-for-school father. Yet they all buckle under their mom's glare. Each of them seeks Sonya out for advice and feels comfortable opening up to her, especially now that her tough love and parables are producing fruit in their lives. She still sends them Bible verses and makes sure they hear the hard thing they need to, in case no one else is willing to tell them.

They confide in Sonya. Even the daughter who once clashed with her mother's molding now can hardly find enough words to praise her mom. Even the youngest son, who had to forge his own way from the shadows of his older brother, drops his swag to declare his mother's impact.

Even Stephen, one of the most popular people in the country, and head of his own household, has utmost reverence for Sonya. He doesn't need her like he once did, because Ayesha fills that void. But most of his life has been guided with wisdom infused by his mother and his faith.

In the hall outside the private family room at Oracle, after the Warriors clinched win No. 73, Sonya was expressing her amazement over Stephen and Ayesha. There was commotion all around her as guests of Warriors players hung out. But Sonya was serious, face frozen by reflection, gazing as she took a second to reminisce about how her son found his wife. She remembered the time Stephen, still in college, first told her he was getting serious about Ayesha.

"He was like, Mom, 'I want to ask her parents' permission to court her.' Where does 'court' come from?" Sonya said, reacting with the same confused look she gave to her eldest son. "I don't understand. Can you define 'court'? I don't get that. Me and your daddy hooked up. We didn't court."

So much about Stephen is the product of Sonya. Get close enough to both, the similarities become obvious. His intense competitive spirit and overt emotion on the court, that's Sonya.

The devoutness of his faith, rooted in scriptures etched into his psyche, that's Sonya. Since college, Curry has written two Bible verses on his shoe. One is his favorite verse—Philippians 4:13: "I can do all things through Christ who strengthens me." The other is his mother's favorite verse—Romans 8:28: "And we know that all things work together for good to those who love God, to those who are the called according to His purpose."

His emphasis on home life, being present despite his hectic schedule and including his family in his journey—that is all a by-product of watching how his mother served as the glue in his childhood. His view that all of this is a part of his ministry to the world is a result of Sonya's emphasis on faith.

That is why he jumps on random acts of kindness. The responses of genuine appreciation from the people he touches strengthen his resolve to remain Stephen.

Just before the 2015 training camp, after a whirlwind off season as champion and MVP, Curry was eager to focus on basketball. By late September, he was done with the media tours and endorsement obligations. It was time for hoop. Yet when the Warriors told him about Taliq Davis, Curry made room for an impromptu Make-A-Wish Foundation fulfillment. Normally those things take a year or two to work out. This one came together in a couple months, with Taliq and his family flying to the Bay Area from Texas. The Warriors star consoled the overwhelmed boy, who was crying well before actually meeting Curry. He laced Taliq with gifts and even played a little hoop with him.

"This is what it's all about," Curry said.

The day after Christmas, Curry and his family, including his parents and siblings, continued their tradition of personally handing out food and toiletries at Beebe Memorial Cathedral in Oakland. It began before Steph's game took off and Curry became a household name. Before the Warriors were regulars on the NBA's ever-popular Christmas Day games. But his hectic schedule wasn't going to stop him from showing up on 39th Street and Telegraph Avenue to distribute boxes with his own hands.

On February 24, 2016, before the Warriors took on host Miami, Curry interrupted his pregame ritual to meet with Shaun Kennedy, a Niagara Falls, New York, native who is living with a rare brain cancer. The four-year-old got the shoes Curry warmed up in, with "keep being brave" written on them, and a conversation with the MVP. Curry obliged the request from his head coach, who had gotten an email about Kennedy.

Countless moments, Curry has used his celebrity to make others feel good. Numerous times he has violated the wishes of his security people to sign more autographs and take more selfies. On several occasions, behind the scenes, he doled out gifts to unexpected recipients.

These are the things that keep him grounded, centered on the person and not the star.

Even after the gut-wrenching end to the NBA Finals, in which the series spiraled out of control and Steph couldn't stop it, and Mr. Curry suffered a major blow to his reputation, it was Stephen keeping him grounded. He didn't have time to sulk because he had to focus on his wife.

The summer proved to be huge for Ayesha, who debuted her cookbook. It was a *New York Times* bestseller that required a massive national push. And Stephen was along for the ride with Ayesha, helping her become a mogul. Her Food Network show, *Ayesha's Homemade*, debuted three days before the start of the season.

When Curry took his annual Asia tour for Under Armour, he brought his wife and made time for dim sum and spring roll lessons in Guangzhou, China. When Ayesha was the grand marshal for the IndyCar series at Sonoma Raceway, Curry was there with her, in his firesuit, using his pull to draw attention to his wife's ventures.

This is the man behind the star, the person Sonya raised him to be, the figure at the center that makes all of this work.

St3ph

o   o   o

"For deep range, I don't know if there's anybody better. What a weapon a shooter like Curry is with the green light. Missing one or two means nothing to him. He just goes back deeper. He can make you look bad in a hurry."

—Larry Bird

CHAPTER 4

Even before Curry started breaking records, the NBA had been shifting to a 3-pointer-heavy league. The Miami Heat, coming off its first championship with LeBron James in the 2012 NBA Finals, signed one of the greatest shooters of all time in Ray Allen. Even at his advanced age he helped them go from twentieth in 3-pointers made to third, winning sixty-six games and capturing a second straight title. The San Antonio Spurs, which lost to the Heat in the 2013 NBA Finals, led the NBA in 3-point field goal percentage on their way to the 2014 NBA Finals win.

The average number of 3-pointers per game in the NBA hovered around eighteen for five years, starting in 2007–8. But then it jumped to twenty in 2012–13 and has increased each year since. The Houston Rockets set a record for 3-pointers made in 2014–15 as the league on average hoisted 22.4 3-pointers per game. The Warriors broke that record the following season by making 1,077.

The NBA, once a league that coveted size and athleticism to get closer shots, has been moving away from the rim to take advantage of the bonus point. And Curry has been in on this shift since his college days. He finished the 2012–13 regular season with 272 3-pointers made, breaking Allen's seven-year-old record (269). Two seasons later, Curry topped his own mark with 286 3-pointers. He then made an NBA record 98 3-pointers in twenty-one playoff games as the Warriors won the 2015 NBA Finals.

In 2015–16, Curry went from participant in a trend to an anomaly of basketball modernity. Even in an era where the 3-pointer is so common it's monotonous, Curry made it spectacular again. Though its aura as basketball's magic trick has been washed away by a flooded market of shooters, Curry brought the marvel back to the 3-pointer.

This six-foot-three guard has forged his way into the elite in a league of big men because of his 3-point mastery. He has become a force because his incredible skill is worth 50 percent more than every other shot. And he has figured out how to use that to become one of the most efficient scorers in NBA history. He can get more points with fewer shots, and that ability creates a ripple effect that benefits everyone on the court with him.

In 2015 he came out of the gates firing from deep and hasn't stopped. He took twelve 3-pointers in the season opener, scoring 40 points on the night the Warriors got their championship rings. Four nights later, in New Orleans, he took fourteen, putting into action a plan he had been working on through the NBA Finals and his summer workouts. He figured out how to take 3-point shooting to an entirely new level.

And in Oklahoma City on February 27, 2016, Curry made his 287th 3-pointer, breaking his own single-season record with twenty-five games left in the season. He tied the NBA record for 3-pointers made in a game, his twelfth being a legendary dagger that finished off the Thunder.

With the game tied at 118 in overtime, Curry calmly dribbled past half-court with 3.7 seconds left. The end goal was to put the ball in the basket, but the artistry was in the how. In those precious seconds, with the nation watching on ABC's new Saturday evening NBA showcase, Curry was seeking inspiration and direction, letting the moment guide him. And two steps past the dividing line, Curry made up his mind. He had figured out the how, and the final moment would illustrate his revolutionary impact on basketball.

With 3.2 seconds left, Curry had already begun his shooting motion, crouching as he two-stepped into his shooting stance with one last left-hand dribble.

"I got a good rhythm dribbling up," Curry said, "and I found a spot to take off from."

Anthony Roberson, the six-foot-seven small forward who is in the NBA for his defensive prowess, drew the Curry assignment. He's a good athlete, with a six-foot-eleven wingspan and good defensive instincts, so the logic was that he should be able to, at the very least, get a hand up on a Curry shot attempt. The only problem was that defending Curry requires violating decades of basketball indoctrination.

Roberson, as he would in every other situation, hustled back to get set up on defense. He backpedaled until his back foot was just outside the 3-point line. That's good positioning against every other 3-point shooter in the world. He was guarding the 3-point line. But against Curry, that was too far back, though Curry was still miles away from the 3-point line.

Draymond Green, the Warriors' all-star forward who finished second in the 2014–15 Defensive Player of the Year voting, was on the same wavelength as Roberson. His expectation was that Curry would dribble into a reasonable shot. His instincts were jarred by the sight of Curry pulling up from just past half-court.

"Why would you take that shot from that far with three seconds left?" Green recalled thinking. "Just absurd. But hey, he's Steph. It's just beyond crazy to me."

Anthony Morrow, the Thunder's sharpshooter who started his NBA career with the Warriors, was on the bench for the final seconds. He was standing up on the sidelines, screaming at Roberson to press up closer on Curry. But it was too late. Curry had already sized up the shot. He had already gauged distance of the rim and what kind of arc and touch he needed from that far. His pregame warm-ups include near-half-court shots so he can get the feel down in case he needs to hoist from long range.

With 2.8 seconds left, Curry was halfway through his form. He had already caressed the ball into his shooting pocket, gliding it subconsciously until the grooves lined up how he likes. And, according to ESPN's tracking, he was 38.4 feet from the basket. With 2.3 seconds remaining, before Roberson realized what was happening and lunged toward Curry, the ball was in the air. It hadn't even reached its apex and Oklahoma City big man Enes Kanter was seen on the bench shrugging, his hands falling to his side in exasperation.

Kanter was right. Curry's 3-point hoist snapped the nets with .6 seconds left, breaking the heart of the Thunder and assuredly prompting a yell from most of the 3.98 million viewers.

"BANG! BANG!" sports broadcast great Mike Breen yelled over the ESPN airwaves, capturing the shock of the moment by turning up the octaves and repeating his trademark moniker. "Ohhh, what a shot from Curry!"

It was a climactic end to a performance that encapsulated how much Curry had revolutionized the NBA into a now 3-point obsessed league. With the performance in Oklahoma, he became the first player to make ten 3-pointers in consecutive games, having dropped in ten the game before in Orlando. In two games, Curry totaled 97 points on fifty-one shots. No player in NBA history had topped 90 points over two games on so few shots. But Curry scored 66 of those points from the 3-point line.

"What he's doing right now," Warriors coach Steve Kerr said, "it's never been done before in terms of his style, the types of shots he takes. Whether you're talking about Michael Jordan or Kobe or Kareem or Larry Bird or Magic—he's having that kind of impact on games. But he's putting his own signature flair on it."

It was Curry's fate to be here, in this position as the face of an era, even if his many detractors couldn't see it. He was groomed for this. The hindsight view of his journey illustrates vividly how he was fashioned for this role as the flag bearer for the 3-point revolution in basketball.

The 3-point shot has been on a long journey for acceptance in basketball. The road from carnival trick to a respected element in the sport has been more than fifty years in the making. What

Michael Jordan was to the dunk, and Magic Johnson was to the assist, Curry is to the 3-pointer. He's not the first to do it, but the one to make it mainstream, to commercialize it and ingratiate it into pop culture.

More than its popularity, the 3-pointer has altered how the game is played, how players are evaluated, how statistics are kept. Efficiency is now part of the basketball lexicon because of the 3-pointer. It has helped expand the game and aided in basketball's global growth by making it possible for more people to be successful—since 3-point shooting isn't dependent on size. It might eventually be what allows the first woman to play in the NBA.

And on the legacy of the 3-pointer's impact on basketball, Curry is the pinnacle. It sure feels like this was his destiny when considering the history of the 3-pointer.

October 13, 1967. That is the day the American Basketball Association played its inaugural game.

The NBA had been up and running for eighteen seasons, twenty-one including the three seasons when it was the Basketball Association of America. The league was an established brand boasting plenty of greats: George Mikan, Hal Greer, Neil Johnston, Paul Arizin, Bob Pettit, Bob Cousy, Dolph Schayes, Bill Russell, Wilt Chamberlain, and Oscar Robertson.

Before the ABA debut, the NBA had concluded the season with Wilt Chamberlain winning his first championship. The Philadelphia 76ers dethroned the Boston Celtics in the East, denying Russell a ninth straight championship and breaking the monotony of green-and-white dominance. That set the stage for an epic championship round.

Guard Hal Greer dominated as the 76ers soared to a 3–1 series lead in the 1967 NBA Finals. But Rick Barry led the Warriors to a surprising Game 5 win in Philadelphia. That set up a riveting Game 6 in San Francisco, played before a sellout crowd of nearly sixteen thousand at the Cow Palace, and another four thousand plus watching on closed-circuit television.

Basketball nation watched Chamberlain hang on for a nail-biter, 125–122 championship clincher, staving off 44 points from Barry.

That's the climate in which the ABA was born. Granted, the basketball market in the sixties was miniscule compared to now. But whatever that market was, the NBA was atop it. And a wave of young stars—such as Barry, Willis Reed, Jerry Lucas, and Dave Bing—solidified the NBA's viability moving forward. So the start-up ABA needed something to garner attention from an audience groomed by the credibility of the NBA. And the 3-point shot was going to be its game-changer.

"Their whole thing was banking on the 3-point shot," said Warriors legend and franchise ambassador Al Attles, who played with Chamberlain before losing to him in the '67 Finals. "The NBA, we turned our nose up at it. We were all about getting the ball inside. That was the right way to play. I was spoiled. I played with Wilt. I played with Nate Thurmond. Why would you want to shoot the ball from way out there? Get it inside to those studs."

The ABA wasn't the first to use the 3-point shot. A 1945 college basketball game between Columbia and Fordham experimented with a 3-point shot from twenty-one feet away. The teams combined to make twenty of them. And the ABA wasn't even the first professional league to use it.

Former owner of the Harlem Globetrotters Abe Saperstein's American Basketball League, which debuted in 1961, was the first professional league to use the 3-point line. But that league folded in the middle of its second season. The Eastern Professional Basketball League, also known as the Eastern League, which later became the CBA, adopted the 3-point line in the 1964–65 season. But this league never made much of a ripple on the national stage, which the NBA monopolized.

But George Mikan, the Hall of Fame center from the Minneapolis Lakers who cofounded the ABA and served as commissioner, had every intention to rival the NBA. The plan was to open up the game, countering the NBA's rigid and methodical style of play and making it inviting for smaller players. The ABA—with its red, white, and blue ball—encouraged faster play. It welcomed flashy players, high flyers, and fancy dribbling. It played in college towns, especially in the Southeast, and had teams play at multiple sites in their region.

And the foundation of this new style, which would distinguish the brand and challenge the NBA's stranglehold, was the 3-point shot.

"We called it the home run, because the 3-pointer was exactly that," Mikan said in the book *Loose Balls: The Short, Wild Life of the American Basketball Association*. "It brought fans out of their seats."

And that was the environment around the ABA's inaugural game. The Anaheim Amigos had a point guard named Lester Selvage, a six-foot-one rookie out of Truman State University. He was quick enough to be dubbed "Lightning Les" and was known for the range on his jumper. Because he was a little guy, going inside was a tall order. So Selvage developed his outside shot since it was the one he could get easily. He was exactly the kind of player the NBA didn't value. That he needed a 3-point shot meant he wasn't good enough to play at the highest level.

"What is it but an admission that you are dealing with inferior players who can't do anything but throw up long shots?" Eddie Gottlieb, of the NBA rules committee, asked in a 1967 *Sports Illustrated* article. "Is length the only criterion for excellence? I would say that out of every 40 or 50 shots, at least 20 are more difficult than a simple long shot. If it is worth three points to make a standard long jump shot, well then, a twisting, driving hook, going full speed to take the pass, cutting between two big defenders—why, that must be worth six points. You encourage mediocrity when you give extra credit to this sort of thing."

For the ABA, though, Selvage was perfect. And in the first-ever ABA game, Selvage made four 3-pointers. There were ten made in total as the teams combined for 263 points in four quarters. Oakland Oaks guard Andrew Anderson, a rookie out of Canisius College who was drafted by the Celtics in the eighth round, led all scorers with 33 points. He made two 3-pointers.

This groundbreaking game took place in the same arena Curry now calls home.

The ABA kicked off at the Oakland-Alameda County Coliseum, which is now known as Oracle Arena. A half a century ago, the 3-point revolution was conceived in earnest under the same concrete roof that now looks down on Curry bombs. See? Destiny.

The ABA merged with the NBA in 1976. Part of the agreement included four ABA teams joining the NBA. But the 3-pointer didn't come with them. Not at first, anyway.

"When the leagues merged, the NBA moguls didn't want the 3-point shot," Angelo Drossos, owner of the San Antonio Spurs—one of the teams to cross over from ABA to NBA—said in *Loose Balls*. Red Auerbach hated it and said the Celtics would never go along with it. He had everybody up in arms against the play. Of course, a few years later Red drafted Larry Bird and suddenly he was all for it."

It was in Bird's debut that the first NBA 3-pointer was made. On October 12, 1979, nearly twelve years to the day since the ABA's first game, Boston Celtics guard Chris Ford made one at Boston Garden with 3:48 left in the first quarter of a win over visiting Houston. Later that evening, Washington Bullets forward Kevin Grevey also made a 3-pointer.

That season, San Diego Clippers point guard Brian Taylor made an NBA-high ninety 3-pointers. He also took the most attempts (239). Taylor took 176 3-pointers over his four years in the ABA.

Ford made seventy 3-pointers that year, making 42.7 percent of his attempts. That percentage was second only to Downtown

Freddie Brown, the Seattle SuperSonics guard who made 44.3 percent from deep.

Just over a month later, Western Carolina guard Ronnie Carr made the first 3-pointer in NCAA history. Western Carolina was in the one conference the NCAA sanctioned for the experimental use of the 3-pointer, from twenty-two feet. Since they had a great shooter in Carr, the Catamounts wanted to start playing first to give Carr a better chance at making history. The school's sports information director, Steve White, said in a 2007 article on Rivals.com that he talked the school into tipping off their game against Middle Tennessee State a half hour early.

Much like Selvage, Carr, a six-foot-three guard, was accustomed to shooting from that range even before it was worth 3 points. Carr made a 3-pointer from the left corner with 16:09 left in the first half, two minutes, six seconds after he missed one from the top of the key.

Oh, and that first conference sanctioned by the NCAA to use a 3-point line? The Southern Conference—the same conference Curry starred in while at Davidson College, when he used the 3-pointer to take the mid-major Wildcats on an epic run to the Elite Eight of the NCAA tournament. Destiny. Again.

By the 1986–87 season, the last of the major conferences in the NCAA had adopted the 3-point line. Providence guard Billy Donovan led the nation with ninety-seven 3-pointers. Donovan is now the coach of the Oklahoma City Thunder, whom Curry foiled with a game-winner from near half-court. Curry took the shot right in front of Donovan, who stood with his arms folded as the ball sailed in the air.

In 1987–88, Celtics guard Danny Ainge became the first player in NBA history to make more than one hundred 3-pointers in a season. In 1993–94, guard Dale Ellis, at the time with the Spurs, became the first player with one thousand career 3-pointers made. That same year, an eighth-year shooting guard from the Charlotte Hornets started really taking advantage of his shooting. Dell Curry knocked down 152 3-pointers, 57 more than the career-high mark he'd set the season before. For the first time in his career, more than half his shots were from the 3-point line. Destiny.

In 1994, with hopes of giving the league a boost in scoring, the NBA shortened the distance of the 3-point line to a uniform twenty-two feet around the basket. Before, it was twenty-two feet from the corner and twenty-three feet, nine inches everywhere else. With a shorter 3-point line, New York Knicks guard John Starks became the first to make two hundred 3-pointers in a season, connecting on 217. His record lasted a year as Orlando Magic forward Dennis Scott made 267 in 1995–96. Dell Curry made a career-high 164 that season. The next season, Reggie Miller became the third straight player to make at least two hundred 3-pointers.

The NBA returned to the original distances for the 1997–98 season, the same year Miller became the league's career leader in 3-pointers made, becoming the first to surpass the fifteen hundred milestone. He would be the king for twelve years.

In 2001–2, sixth-year Milwaukee Bucks guard Ray Allen led the league in 3-pointers (229) for the first time. It was also Dell Curry's last year in the NBA, after playing for the Toronto Raptors for three seasons. His family moved back to Charlotte from Toronto and Curry enrolled in Charlotte Christian School.

Steph had dominated middle school basketball in Toronto even with his small size. He was already a good shooter, but he had developed a slingshot-like form to compensate for his lack of strength. To get the ball to reach the rim, he'd squat a tad and sling it from his waist, using momentum to compensate for his power shortage. Even if the pass came high, he would have to bring the ball back down so he could push it from his hip. It was effective, but wouldn't work against the type of players he'd face in high school and beyond.

Curry played junior varsity his freshman year at Charlotte

Christian, getting a call up to varsity late in the season. In garbage time of a playoff loss, Coach Shonn Brown gave Curry some minutes. It was revelatory.

Curry got the ball with a defender on him, smoothly executed a dribble move, and pulled up for 3. After it went in, Brown turned to assistant coach David Houseton and declared Curry was the future of the program. Off one shot.

"He had never been in a varsity game. He was as flimsy as a wet noodle," Brown said. "But he never missed a beat. He came down and took that thing like, 'This is what I do.' You watch a freshman at Duke get in for the final minutes. If the ball comes to him, he's getting rid of it like a hot potato. But for Stephen, the moment was nothing for him."

After his freshman year of high school basketball in Charlotte, his father asked him about how serious he wanted to take basketball.

"Are you sure you want to put in the work?" Dell asked his oldest son.

The sixteen-year NBA veteran had been relatively hands off his son's athletic career up until this point. But Curry had fallen in love with basketball and was ready to make it his primary sport, Dell's cue to get hands-on. And their first project was fixing the rising sophomore's shooting form.

Curry had already become a special marksman for someone so young. But his father knew the real problem Curry had: getting his shot off.

"I got my shot blocked a lot," Steph said, reminiscing on his younger days.

So with assurances from Steph that he wanted to continue to keep growing as a player, his father gave him some drills to work on, changing his release point to above his head. And Curry got it down through repetition. He'd spend hours in his backyard, working to make this form second nature. The weak muscles in his scrawny arms burned. Early on in this process, he'd head back into the house after a session with his arms feeling like logs.

Curry thought about quitting. It wasn't fun. The joy of watching the ball go through the hoop was replaced by pain. An experience that was once thrilling was now torturous. And Dell, honoring his son's desire to become the best player he could be, didn't let up.

The worst part: the new form wasn't working. At least for the first few weeks, Steph couldn't make a shot outside of the paint. And when he played with others, he couldn't make shots anymore, robbing him of his primary strength.

"That had to be one of the worst summers of my life," Curry said. "I was at basketball camp and people were like, 'Why is he even here?' It looked like I didn't even know how to play."

Curry likely couldn't see it at the time, but the end result was a much cleaner and less blockable shooting stroke. Because Curry endured, he now has the most efficient shooting form in basketball. No wasted motion. Succinct. Easy for him to replicate. Easy for him to execute quickly. Easy for him to get it off from multiple angles.

The higher release point also gives him more arc on his shot. Higher arc, in essence, makes the rim a bigger target.

Curry's constant practice also helped him with many of the other elements: feet shoulder width apart, hips facing basket, making sure his shooting elbow was in close to his torso and the ball stayed off his right palm, eyes focused on the rim, sharp flick of the wrist to follow through. His dad, after all, made more than twelve hundred 3-pointers in his career.

Curry was born with some of the other intangibles, making him a good shooter almost out of the womb. He has incredible hand-eye coordination and depth perception, which helps him to accurately gauge where he is on the court and the distance and angle to the rim. Curry also has what the basketball world knows as touch, a term that oversimplifies a difficult-to-explain skill. Touch is how a shooter determines how much strength is needed, how much loft is necessary to make the ball fall softly, how much spin is required to make it break at the desired angle. Touch is what allows a player to miss a free throw off the back iron and on the second know how to take just enough off to get it perfectly in the center of the rim. Curry apparently has Spider-Man senses in his fingertips.

After enduring his dad's training, he went into his sophomore year at Charlotte Christian with a new, more efficient shooting form. And his new higher release point helped him get it off quicker. Curry no longer needed so much time and space to shoot his deadly 3. His quick release has continued to evolve, so the shots we are seeing him take now seem to happen instantaneously. The time elapsed between the moment Curry starts to shoot and the moment the ball is out of his hands is so diminished that it is almost impossible to guard. The defender just doesn't have time to react without excellent instincts or a thorough understanding of Curry's tendencies.

His slingshot was now a sniper rifle. And the nation got its first glimpse during the 2008 NCAA Tournament. In his sophomore year, Curry led Davidson to the Elite Eight with a shooting display that forecast his current greatness. He made twenty-three 3-pointers (tied for third most in tournament history) in four games. No one has ever averaged more 3-pointers per game in a single tournament.

But it was the next year Curry added to his arsenal. With Davidson starting point guard Jason Richards graduating, Curry passed on entering the NBA draft so he could hone his point guard skills. He returned for his junior season and developed his off-the-dribble shooting. Because he was the primary ball-handler, and coming off his epic tournament run, all the attention was on him. Open looks would be scarce.

Curry was naturally comfortable going left, so it wasn't too difficult for him to learn to knock down shots of the dribble in that direction. Going right, though he is right-handed, is a bit awkward. Squaring up to face the basket requires contortion since the shooting hand is facing away from the basket. But Curry's minimalist shooting form makes it a seamless adjustment.

"We used to run plays at Davidson where there would be a screen here and a screen there," Curry said, pointing to spots on the Warriors practice court. "I could go left or right off the screen and the defense didn't know which way I was going. So I had to be able to come off those screens either way and shoot."

His 3-point totals and percentage dipped his junior season. He shot 38.7 percent on 3s his third year at Davidson. The 130 he made was thirty-two fewer than the previous season, when he shot 43.9 percent. But he picked up along the way a new repertoire in the variety of ways he could get his shot off, forced to do so under the weight of hype and smothering defenses. Staying an extra year in college became the lab work he needed for the NBA.

Curry didn't always wield his 3-point prowess with the Warriors. Though he shot 43.9 percent from deep, he only took 380 3s his rookie season. Lester Selvage took 461 in his rookie season for the Anaheim Amigos, the inaugural season of the ABA, and he made just 31.9 percent.

Curry didn't have the freedom, initially. He hit the all-star break of the 2009–10 season making fewer than two of his four 3-point attempts per game. His attempts were mostly of a catch-and-shoot variety. But after the all-star break, with star guard Monta Ellis out with an injury and coach Don Nelson giving the reins of the team to the rookie, Curry offered a glimpse of what was to come. With the ball in his hands, he lit up the second half of the season. After the break, he averaged 22.1 points and 7.7 assists, up from 14.8 points and 4.9 assists before all-star. And part of the boost in his production was his 3-point shooting. Curry made 2.7 of his six 3s per game after the break.

With Ellis back and playing eighty games, and the offense centered on him, Curry took fewer attempts his sophomore season in the NBA. In his third season, ankle injuries limited him to twenty-six games.

Over the first three seasons of his career, Curry was just one of several good shooters in the league. The 3 ball wasn't the epicenter of his game but a weapon used to keep the defense honest. That changed in 2012–13. Ellis was traded to Milwaukee for Andrew Bogut, an excellent screener. The Warriors drafted another excellent screener in the 2012 draft in Draymond Green, and a forward in Harrison Barnes who became integral to the Warriors' small-ball style of play. Another major acquisition in the summer of 2012: point guard Jarrett Jack.

With this cast, especially later in the season, Coach Mark Jackson looked to pick up the pace. He would let Jack run the offense and run plays for Curry, taking advantage of his shooting prowess. He played Barnes at power forward to make the Warriors quicker as a unit. The pace favored Curry, who was harder for defenses to attach to, and having another point guard on the floor freed him up to look for his own shot.

Over the last thirty games of 2012–13, Curry made 123 3-pointers—an average of 4.3 per game. And he did it at a 47.4 percent clip.

This was an explosion. A 3-point barrage like we hadn't seen from him. And it wasn't just him chucking 3-pointers. It was him using his 3-pointer as a way of throwing defenses off their strategies and taking over games. He was running off screens like Reggie Miller and pulling up for 3 off the dribble like Ray Allen and drilling 3-pointers on fast-breaks like no one before him.

For most of his career, Curry had been a point guard who could make open 3s when he took them. Some games he'd get more looks than others, depending on how defenses played him. But his primary job was attacking off the pick-and-roll, setting up his teammates, and getting the team going in transition.

The breakout moment came on February 27, 2013, at Madison Square Garden. Under the biggest tent of all. With the Warriors down 11 after the first quarter in New York, Curry took off his point guard hat and put on his dominant star crown. He stopped running the offense and became the offense. He stopped taking what the defense gave him, but instead began manipulating the defense for what he wanted.

And what Curry wanted—especially since the Warriors were playing without David Lee, who had been suspended a game after an altercation in Indiana the night before—was to maximize his impact, knowing that was the Warriors' best chance to win. He needed to produce enough for two players. And the best way for him to do that was the 3-pointer.

Over the next three quarters, he scored 50 points, finishing with a career-high 54. He took twelve 3-pointers in three quarters. He made 11 of them.

This was the formula being proven: an aggressive Curry looking for his 3-pointer is the key element. If he's making them, he's scoring at a higher rate than anyone else in the league. Even if he isn't, the defense is now terrified of him catching fire, and that reality opens up a warehouse of options for Curry and his teammates.

This is the answer to the popular nineties strategy of packing the paint and daring an offense to enter. But while defenses are accustomed to building a fortified wall in front of the rim, Curry catapults firebombs over the wall from deep.

Curry went on to set the 3-point record that year, besting Ray Allen's mark. He made forty-two more in twelve playoff games despite playing on a sprained ankle. The next season, Curry slumped from 3, by his own standards, making 261 3-pointers and shooting a career-low 42.4 percent from 3. The Warriors lost Jack to free agency and didn't have a viable point guard behind Curry. And after his big splash the previous seasons, defenses were focused on him with a desire to rough him into missing.

In the postseason, the Warriors pushed the Clippers to seven games despite being down two centers. Golden State played with a small lineup and looked to outrun the Clippers. Though exhausted and swarmed, Curry flipped a switch in his mind and started relentlessly attacking the Clippers, who had stolen a game at Oracle and led 2–1 in the series. He took the fight back to Chris Paul, the league's top point guard, whose tactic of over-powering Curry worked well in their matchups. Curry countered by looking for his shot. He took fourteen 3-pointers in Game 4, making half. The Warriors blew out the Clippers as he scored 33.

The Warriors lost the series, but the plan was much clearer. An aggressive Curry changes everything. The Warriors just needed a second player on the floor with Curry who was comfortable handling the ball and making decisions, giving the Warriors the option to move Curry off the ball.

The Warriors went out and got Shaun Livingston, a veteran point guard who is as steady as they come. Center Andrew Bogut, one of the best passing big men in the NBA, was used as a hub, a seven-foot floor general, in new coach Steve Kerr's motion offense. And Andre Iguodala, the veteran swingman, was used as a point guard with Curry on the floor instead of as the backup point guard spelling Curry.

The result: 286 3-pointers, a new record. Then a record 98 in the playoffs.

Over his first three seasons, Curry totaled 843 attempts from behind the arc. In 2014–15, he took 878 3-pointers over the course of 101 games, combining postseason and playoffs, and made 43.7 percent of them. It was the greatest 3-point season the NBA had ever known. And it turns out that was just the prelude.

As Chris Webber once said on a TNT telecast, providing a voice for the helpless defenders, "I have no words for it. Off the pick step back. As a big man, how are you supposed to come out and show? As a guard that's checking him, how are you to send him one way? Because the way that you send him is preferred. He doesn't care: right or left."

But beyond Curry's ability to shoot 3s from any angle, he has added the further complexity of being able to successfully hoist the ball through the hoop from as far away as the moon. He really put that together in the fifth game of the 2015–16 season.

He was facing the Pelicans. He had burned them already for 40 in the season opener, including four 3-pointers in a 24-point first quarter, and they were determined to stay glued to him. Pelicans head coach Alvin Gentry had his players hugging up on Curry near the 3-point line, taking away his clean looks and forcing him to drive, where defensive help was waiting. It can be done, but it requires an attuned defense. Curry's man had to be diligent enough to stay close to Curry. And if he got screened, the other defenders had to be alert enough to switch onto Curry quickly. Being late a half a second would give Curry enough time to shoot.

In theory, New Orleans had the pieces to make this game plan work. Rather, the perfect piece. Anthony Davis is an NBA anomaly. He is six-foot-ten with a seven-foot-five wingspan and a small forward's athleticism. A defender at heart, Davis has impeccable timing and instincts.

Since the Warriors run a lot of pick-and-rolls with Curry and Green in half-court settings, Davis found himself switched onto Curry a few times during the 2015 NBA playoffs. Davis's length and agility made it harder for Curry to get a clear look at the basket and harder for Curry to get around him. Beating Davis required Curry to reach into his bag of ball-handling tricks with elaborate crossovers to create space or get by Davis.

After a disappointing showing at Oracle Arena in the season opener, the Pelicans were locked into the game plan on Halloween Night in New Orleans. In the opening minutes, every time Curry touched the ball, a defender was in his face. If he got a screen, his man would follow him closely around the screen and a big man was ready and waiting on the other side. More than four minutes into the game, Curry hadn't even taken a shot.

It appeared as if he finally had some daylight on a fast-break with just inside of eight minutes left. Green rebounded a miss and pushed it up the court, dishing a jump pass to Curry, who was running down the right side with him. Curry caught the pass in perfect position to step right into a 3-pointer a step behind the line. But Davis, who had missed the shot that started the break, left his man to jump on to Curry. Davis's presence forced Curry to pump fake, as Curry knew one lunge from Davis and his long arm would interfere with the ball's trajectory.

Just like that, the window to shoot quickly closed. The fast-break opportunity gone, Curry held the ball and waited for the offensive play to develop. Davis inched closer and swiped at the ball, knocking it backwards.

Curry retrieved the ball and turned back toward the basket. Davis? He didn't move. He held his ground, his toes on the 3-point line. Back then, it was great defense by Davis, one of the best defenders in the league. But in a split second, Curry decided to experiment.

He was thirty-one feet from the basket. There were sixteen seconds left on the shot clock. Yet, with Davis back at the 3-point line, Curry had all the space he needed. He decided to take the shot. Surprised, Davis tried to lunge in time to block it. He was too late. Too far back. Even the New Orleans crowd gasped.

Curry laughed as he ran back down court. It was silly to take the shot, comical that it actually went in. After the game, Curry called it a dumb shot. What he didn't know yet, or didn't want to share for the sake of sounding arrogant, was that it was actually brilliant.

"That's when I first thought about it," Curry said months later. "He's so long it's hard to get space. And I had it, so I thought, 'Why not?' I know I can shoot from out there."

What Curry has done since that game is elongate the court. Now the space between 3-point lines on each end of the court isn't just a transition area. Not when he is on the court. Defenses now have to come out farther to guard him because his range extends past the usual limits. The farther out the defense extends, the more open space is left behind its front line. That leaves the defense vulnerable.

"Honestly, I don't know exactly where I am, so it's not like I'm calibrating in my head, all right, thirty-eight feet, thirty-seven, thirty-six," Curry said. "Just literally, you've got a sense of—I've shot the shot plenty of times. You're coming across half-court and timing up your dribbles, and you want to shoot before the defense goes in. And that was pretty much my only thought."

The NBA 3-point line, at its deepest point, is twenty-three feet, nine inches. Curry finished the 2015–16 regular season having taken forty-five shots from at least thirty feet—ten more than he had taken the previous two seasons combined.

Shots from that distance are usually last-second heaves to beat the buzzer or the shot clock. In 2013–14, Tony Wroten led the league with twenty shots from thirty feet or farther. In 2014–15, Jamal Crawford topped the NBA with twenty-two.

The crazy part isn't just that Curry took forty-five from so deep. The reason it works is because he made twenty-one of them. Twenty. One. That's 46.7 percent, which is insane from that distance. Clippers center DeAndre Jordan shoots a lower percentage than that from the free throw line.

There is a relatively new stat called effective field goal percentage. It's a shooting percentage that factors in a 3-pointer being worth more. Curry's effective field goal percentage from thirty feet or farther is 70 percent. In essence, if Curry took forty-five shots from 2-point range and made all of them, he would have scored 90 points. Because of the 3-pointer, he scored 63 points in those forty-five shots—70 percent of what was possible without the 3-pointer.

LeBron James's effective field goal percentage inside of five feet for 2015–16 was a league-high 68.0. So Curry shooting from thirty feet was a more effective shot than LeBron shooting from five feet.

And that's Curry's secret weapon. He can score more points in fewer shots because of his mastery of the 3-pointer. He finished with 2,375 points, his first time breaking the 2,000-point barrier in a season. Curry is the thirty-fifth player to do it. It was the seventy-eighth time in NBA history a player scored more than 2,300 points in a season. Only Shaquille O'Neal, Adrian Dantley, and Karl Malone have reached that plateau in fewer shots—and they all took at least twice as many free throws as Curry.

But even more impressive was Curry breaking the mark of four hundred 3-pointers in a season. It cements him as one of the immortals among elite athletes across sports. Like Ted Williams batting .400 for a season, or Wayne Gretzky eclipsing 200 points, or Eric Dickerson rushing for 2,100 yards. Curry does his damage with the 3. Jordan had the fade-away jumper. Kareem Abdul-Jabbar had the sky hook. Curry has the mastery of the deep ball.

Curry entered the last game of the season with 392 3-pointers. He had made at least eight 3-pointers in fifteen games before the finale. But the Warriors were hosting a depleted Memphis team who, with the Warriors pursuing seventy-three wins, were in for a destruction. It was unlikely Curry would even play a full game.

He took nine shots in the first quarter. All of them were 3s. Of course he was going for it. Curry made six 3s in the first quarter, turning his goal from a reach to a formality. He got number four hundred early in the third quarter, turning to the crowd with both arms in the air, each hand holding up three fingers.

He finished with a number that will make him a legend for his 3-point prowess: 402.

In the sixth game of the 2016–17 season, Curry went 0-for-10 in a loss to the rebuilding Lakers. It was the first game he went without making a 3-pointer since November 11, 2014.

Back in April 2013, when Curry set the NBA record for 3-pointers made in a season, the Atlanta Hawks tweeted out a playful congratulations to Curry. "Talk to us when you've made a three in 73 straight games, Steph Curry," the tweet said. It was their way of touting Kyle Korver's record, a playful competition when there was a question of who was the game's best shooter. Korver went on to make a 3-pointer in 127 straight games, breaking the record of 89 set by Dana Barros. Eight months after Korver's streak ended, Curry started one of his own. It lasted nearly two years and ended at 157 games, 30 more than Korver's.

If you count playoff games, Curry made a 3 in 196 straight games. Even more ridiculous: from November 13, 2014 to November 4, 2016, Curry made 865 3-pointers at a 44.2 percent clip.

Fittingly, in the next game after snapping his streak, Curry set another record: most 3-pointers in a single game. He made 13 of his 17 3-pointers against New Orleans, eclipsing the record of 12 set by Kobe Bryant in 2003 and tied by Donyell Marshall in 2005.

His new teammate, Durant, was still in awe after the game.

"He can light up the scoreboard really, really quickly and it was fun to see," Durant said afterward. "It's kind of crazy, now that I'm on his team it just happened so quickly, I saw it against Portland when he poured in 23 so quick and then tonight with the 13 threes. It was just phenomenal."

It is a safe bet that by the end of his career, Curry will own every relevant 3-point record, including Ray Allen's career mark of 2,973. That is clearly his destiny.

Curry Appeal

○ ○ ○

"He's this generation's Jordan. We all wanted to be like Mike, and children today will grow up seeing Steph."

—Jason Kidd

CHAPTER 5

The final seconds ticked away, and the crowd in Toronto's Air Canada Centre came to its feet. With victory in tow, his team up 20 points, Curry was torn about his next move. The classy thing to do would be to dribble out the clock. But the crowd wanted him to shoot. It was, after all, the 2016 All-Star Game.

Kevin Durant came over to get the ball. If Curry wasn't going to take the last shot, he would. But Curry didn't give it up.

"Yeah, it was a little imaginary tug-of-war for that ball and the decision of whether to shoot or not," Curry explained. "I think KD wanted it at one point, and then the crowd got into it and wanted me to shoot. Coach Popovich wanted one of us to shoot."

In the end, Curry decided to heave it. TNT had cut away to Kobe Bryant, who was wrapping up his last all-star game. So millions didn't see Curry hoist from a step inside the half-court line. They didn't see Draymond Green throw his hands in the air, signaling the 3-pointer was good before the ball even began its descent. They didn't see Durant get hyped when it splashed all net. They didn't see Curry run back the other way, holding up three fingers on either hand as the crowd gasped at his range.

While all-star games are replete with dunks and no-look passes, Curry's long-distance shooting was on the must-see list. He'd dominated the first half of the 2015-16 NBA season with his spectacular shooting. So it made sense for him to end the annual showcase with his best trick. A fitting end to an all-star game in which Curry was a marquee attraction.

Only Bryant's farewell tour rendered the reigning MVP second fiddle. Bryant, in his twentieth season, was the biggest draw. Even after the game, Curry was part of a contingent of players seeking to have their final moments with Kobe. In the locker room, Curry took off his red No. 30 jersey representing the Western Conference and had Kobe sign it. In this moment, the hottest name in basketball was just an admirer.

Curry looked like a fan after the game, too, when he did his postgame interview—which happened to be at the same Toronto Raptors practice court on which he and his brother Seth played as kids. He wore a black Under Armour hooded jacket over a white hooded sweatshirt with the Canadian leaf on the chest. The bill of his all-black baseball cap was curved perfectly, as if he'd molded it to block the sun at a baseball game. The only thing missing was a backpack.

But a moment illustrating Curry's enormous appeal happened before he addressed the media. In a private area behind the podium, where players waited until it was their turn to answer questions, a father approached Curry for a picture with his two daughters.

"My girls love you," the father said with a grin.

Curry immediately granted the request. He took off his hat and greeted the girls with a big smile, and all three assumed the photo-with-a-celebrity position. The shorter of the sisters, Gianna, three months shy of her tenth birthday, held a basketball with both hands as the Warriors' star rested his right hand on her shoulder. Her unzipped puff coat revealed her red Western Conference All-Star jersey. The older sister, Natalia, her puff coat zipped all the way up and her knit cap already on, prepped for the frigid temperatures awaiting outside, was tall enough for Curry to rest his left arm on her shoulder.

With beaming smiles, the girls posed while their dad, a few steps away, worked to get the perfect angle on his phone's camera. He leaned backward, trying to get a full body shot of his princesses with Curry.

After the picture was taken, Curry chatted with the girls and shook their hands as their dad walked over to thank him. The two men shook hands and pulled each other in for a half-hug.

The girls' dad? Kobe.

It was his all-star game. He's the reason the 2016 installment will be remembered. He was serenaded at every turn, current and former players laying verbal roses at his feet all weekend. Yet his daughters wanted to see Curry, and Bryant, wanting to impress his beloved girls, found himself on the other side of the fishbowl.

Two months later—after the Warriors trounced Memphis in the season finale, clinching their record-breaking seventy-third win of the season, and Curry topped four hundred 3-pointers on the same night—Matt Barnes made his way to the Warriors' locker room. Crowded with camerapeople and reporters, front-office personnel and equipment staff, the Warriors' locker room was a sweltering mess. Curry's locker, sandwiched between Harrison Barnes's and Klay Thompson's, was overrun with media checking out the jersey Curry had autographed by his teammates, the game-worn shoes from his record-breaking performance, as well as the net from the Oracle Arena hoop.

Suddenly, maneuvering through the crowd was Matt Barnes, then the Grizzlies' six-foot-seven bad boy with his twin sons, Carter and Isaiah.

"I appreciate this, Steph," Barnes said as Curry took a photo with his boys. "They are bigger fans of you than they are of me."

Though both Barnes kids had met Curry before—in September 2015, the Barnes and Curry families ran into each other in Cabo San Lucas—Isaiah was still acting nervous. He's a diehard Curry fan. When their school had them come dressed as someone they admired, Carter wore his dad's jersey and Isaiah wore Curry's jersey. Barnes had to give his star-struck son an extra nudge to break through the timidity.

Curry has become the favorite NBA player of the children of NBA players. His regular-size magnetism has attracted millions, and seemingly out of nowhere. Normally, these megastar athletes are visible a mile away. Especially in the current generation, the masses are introduced to phenoms while they are teenagers. LeBron James, Kobe Bryant, Kevin Garnett—they were still in high school when they were anointed as future stars. Prodigies are definitely on the radar by the time they are finished with college.

Curry gained some name recognition in college, leading Davidson on an improbable NCAA tournament run. That was but a flash as Curry, drafted by one of the NBA's most irrelevant franchises, spent four years in the NBA off the grid, save for people in the Bay Area; Charlotte, NC; and among NBA diehards who recognized his potential. Whatever luster was on him after college was dulled by the Warriors' futility and his spree of ankle injuries.

But when Curry broke out, he soared. He didn't just become one of many stars. His rise didn't stop at that tier popular enough to get a shoe deal and be stalked by TMZ. Curry's appeal was so blistering that in a span of two years he was the most popular player in the league, leapfrogging several established players and crossing over into the mainstream.

In February 2013, Curry was an all-star snub. It was David Lee who broke the Warriors' sixteen-year all-star drought. Curry was hoping to get voted in by the coaches as a reserve, but instead they chose Lee, pegging Curry as a level below the studs.

An electric playoff run in 2013 boosted Curry into a rising young star, an underground gem touted by knowledgeable NBA fans. Just before the next season started, rap superstar Drake helped Curry become a household name.

> *I been Steph Curry with the shot.*
> *Been cookin' with the sauce*
> *Chef, curry with the pot*

By February 2014, Curry was the leading vote-getter among all guards in the all-star game—although Bryant was injured, siphoning away some of his votes, and Curry was aided by campaigning in China.

In February 2015, Curry had risen to the leading vote-getter among all NBA players, not just guards. And he led the NBA in jersey sales.

When the all-star game rolled around in 2016, Curry was on top of the league. He'd supplanted LeBron James as the face of the NBA. His game had taken off on the court and his star rose dramatically off it. In three years, he'd gone from all star–caliber, the hope of a disregarded franchise, to a household name. The boundaries of the NBA couldn't contain him. Curry had crossed over. He wasn't a basketball player, but a sports star, a pop culture celebrity.

His off-season was crazy after the Warriors won the title, officially hijacking King James's crown. Days after winning the title, Curry led boxer Andre Ward's entourage into the ring for his fight at Oracle Arena. He held Ward's title belt while wearing his Warriors' championship hat.

Curry golfed with President Barack Obama, who had previously invited Curry to the White House in February 2015 to discuss his work with malaria. Curry, a skilled golfer who could play professionally if not for his basketball jones, shot a 76 in a two-on-two, he and his dad against the President and former sharpshooting NBA guard Ray Allen. Curry attributed his score, in part, to the intimidating presence of the Secret Service and Obama's trash talk.

"He was talking through my back swing," Curry said with a smile. "But he's the President. What are you going to say?"

Curry did the talk show circuit: Jimmy Kimmel, Stephen Colbert, Kelly Ripa and Michael Strahan. He danced onstage with Grammy-winning Christian rapper Lecrae at a concert in Oakland.

And things didn't slow down when the 2015-16 season began. The Warriors started 24–0, Curry came out of the gate dominating, and his fame got crazier.

In December 2015, in the first game after their record streak was snapped, the Warriors blew out Phoenix to get back to their winning ways. After the game, Curry and his wife hung out with Drake. They were spotted at In-N-Out in Alameda.

In February 2016, Curry was an honorary member of his hometown Carolina Panthers during the Super Bowl. He wore a white No. 30 Panthers jersey with "Curry" on the back and did the traditional pounding of the Panthers' drum.

In March, Prince did a pair of sold-out concerts at the Paramount in Oakland. In a surprise, he added another concert the following weekend at Oracle Arena. Part of his motivation, in addition to his shows getting rave reviews: Prince wanted to see Curry play. The music legend, a Minnesota native and well-known basketball fan, sat courtside in a shimmery purplish-blue coat in dark shades and a gold cane as the Warriors beat Oklahoma City on March 3. Prince died exactly seven weeks later.

On March 30, 2016, Curry was signing autographs after his pregame warm-up. The crowed was so crammed and eager for an encounter, the railing broke and three kids fell over. None of them was seriously hurt, and Curry gave all of them autographed gear for their troubles. This was in Utah.

It seemed everybody wanted a piece of Curry. Celebrities were enamored. His fan base grew exponentially. The Warriors' public relations team had to rein in his interviews and hire extra security. The team's head of security, former Oakland police officer Ralph Walker, became Curry's body man.

Companies were lining up to have him represent them: Degree, Kaiser Permanente, JBL, Brita, Fanatics. That's in addition to his main endorsement, Under Armour, in which he is a shareholder who gets royalties on his shoe sales. By the end of the season, Under Armour's shoe sales had jumped 64 percent over the first quarter of 2016, largely due to Curry's sales.

Curry's popularity got so ridiculous, the Charlotte Hornets held a Curry night. Officially, they were honoring his father, Dell

Stephen Curry—seen here scoring on West Charlotte High School his senior year, his brother, Seth, on the bench—was clearly a prodigy in high school. But it was hard to get over his baby face and frail physique. His high school coach, Shonn Brown, didn't help. He ordered new uniforms when Curry was a sophomore, but he didn't order any small sizes. *Courtesy of Charlotte Christian High School, December 29, 2005*

While the ACC schools weren't feeling Curry, Davidson was all over him. Coach Bob McKillop, whose son Brendan played baseball with Curry when they were ten, recruited him harder than anyone. "I wouldn't be here if it wasn't for you," Curry told McKillop at the Coaching Corps Game Changer Awards ceremony in 2016. *Courtesy of Davidson College/ Tim Cowie, DavidsonPhotos.com, March 21, 2008*

Curry is a global sports star. His wife, Ayesha, is a lifestyle icon and celebrity chef. But neither of them are the most beloved in their house. That honor goes to Riley— their adorable and boisterous elder daughter. She steals the spotlight in every room she is in. And they love it. Note: Younger daughter Ryan may be coming for the crown.   *Jose Carlos Fajardo/Bay Area News Group, May 30, 2016*

Curry, flanked by his NBA dad, Dell, and mom, Sonya, on Draft Day, did not want to be drafted by the Warriors. He even refused to work out for Golden State, and Curry's agent practically begged Warriors general manager Larry Riley not to select Curry. The Warriors, though, had no intention of letting Curry get past them. *Golden State Warriors/Getty Images, June 29, 2009*

When Stephen Curry dropped Chris Paul with the crossover seen 'round the world, it was the unofficial passing of the torch. *AP photo/Danny Moloshok, March 31, 2015*

Warriors assistant coach Bruce Fraser has worked with Michael Jordan, Reggie Miller, and Steve Nash. And now he's responsible for sharpening the Warriors' star. Fraser helped Curry create his complex and popular pre-game routine. *Alex Lopez/AlexLopez Images.com, April 5, 2016*

One of the signature moments of his career came in Game 4 of the 2016 Western Conference Semifinals. Curry scored a record 17 points in overtime at Portland, his first game since spraining his right MCL two weeks earlier. "I'm here! I'm back!" he screamed after a dramatic 3-point dagger. *AP photo/Craig Mitcheldyer, May 9, 2016*

Curry's first three years were spent in tumultuous locker rooms, led by disgruntled players wanting to leave Golden State. But Curry used some Davidson style when he became the locker-room leader. Along with veteran David Lee, he orchestrated team outings, gave gifts to his teammates, and made sure to be one of the biggest cheerleaders whenever he was on the bench.   *Alex Lopez/AlexLopezImages.com, April 5, 2016*

Curry has the NBA record for 3-pointers made in a season, 3-pointers made in a game, 3-pointers made in a playoff series, and consecutive games with a 3-pointer. When he's finished playing, every 3-point record imaginable might have his name at the top.   *Derick E. Hingle, USA Today Sports*

As a Christmas tradition, the whole Curry family shows up at Beebe Memorial Cathedral in Oakland to personally deliver food and toiletries to people in need in the community. Even though Stephen and Ayesha have become iconic figures, they still make it a point to be present. *Alex Lopez/Alex LopezImages.com, December 26, 2015*

Russell. Chamberlain. Abdul-Jabbar. Malone. Bird. Johnson. Jordan. Duncan. Nash. LeBron. Curry. That is the complete list of players who have won back-to-back NBA Most Valuable Player Awards. This alone assures that Curry will be in the Hall of Fame and no other Golden State Warrior will ever wear number 30. *Daniel Gluskoter/Icon Sportswire, May 10, 2016*

Curry went to the White House twice to meet President Obama, once to speak about his work fighting malaria and once after the Warriors' 2015 championship. They've also played golf together. Curry said the President talks a lot of trash. First Lady Michelle Obama, when the two were on *Ellen*, gave Curry tips on talking trash back. "If you're putting, you want to say, 'The shadow from your ears is really messing up my putt.' Try that one." *Official White House Photo by Pete Souza, February 25, 2016*

Kevin Durant was drawn to the Warriors, enticed by the team's spirit and bond. Certainly, the talent quotient and title shot helped. But the sentimental things caught his eye and eventually his heart. That as much as anything points to Curry's influence. The tone he sets as a superstar, his presence in a locker room, has helped establish a culture of unselfishness that attracts players. *Jane Tyska/Bay Area News Group*

Curry. But nobody was fooled, considering how it was strategically planned for the one night the Warriors came to town. They'd managed to capitalize on Curry's popularity in Charlotte. Warriors' officials behind the scenes had to tip their cap at the Hornets' clever tampering.

Even Curry's warm-up has become a sideshow. Like a Barry Bonds batting practice, like Odell Beckham Jr. practicing one-handed end zone snags, Curry's pregame routine is a must-watch display. Two hours before tip-off, the arena is abuzz with people marveling at his skills, thousands of smartphones pointed at him.

"It's definitely weird," Curry said. "I've learned to block it out."

His pregame routine is a microcosm of the Curry phenomenon and how wild it has gotten. It is an illustration of how his status has reached a new level. It went from opposing arenas featuring a healthy share of No. 30 jerseys to a traveling spectacle with people cramming to get a peek—of him practicing. Non-sports reporters and international media began showing up early, unable to resist Curry's magnetism.

Within his warm-up are also illustrations of why people can't seem to get enough of him. It's flashy, the kind of sparkling display that captivates. It's extensive work, which makes him a dream for every coach and teacher who's tried to share the value of effort and diligence. It's infused with a fun-loving spirit, the kind of playfulness that delights young people.

About an hour and a half before tip-off, Curry takes the court to a round of applause in a practice shirt and often low-top sneakers, instead of his usual mid-tops and ankle brace. Oracle's ovation is usually hefty, and Curry immediately props his feet up on a seat on the bench and tightens his shoes. Then he takes his position on the baseline, just left of the paint, a basketball in either hand. That's where the show begins.

Usually before he starts, he'll chat with his routine partner, Warriors assistant coach Bruce Fraser, or with Warriors staffers. Oracle security guard Curtis Jones is one of Curry's favorites. Stationed right where the Warriors enter the court, Jones has become a fixture in Curry's game days. It's fitting, too, since Jones is a bona fide hoop junky. He's been a Warriors fan since the mid-sixties. He has a prediction with a breakdown before every home game. After each game, he makes his way to the media room to get a copy of the game's stats. A point guard in his recreational playing days, Jones has a special appreciation for Curry's game, part of the reason he is protective of Curry's process. He cuts off access to the superstar and keeps his dialogue with Curry short and sweet, suppressing his own perk to help Curry get into the necessary zone.

Often, Curry will take a few seconds to survey the landscape. He loves moments. He loves pausing time and absorbing the now. The humming of the crowd in conversation. The song blaring through the sound system. The squeak of shoes. The thump of balls on the hardwood. It's partly because he's a typical millennial with a hyper attention span, and stopping to linger on the moment slows his mind down, helps his focus. It's also partly because at his core, Curry appreciates all of it. The suddenness of his climb hasn't obscured the anomaly of it. Though he's still shy of thirty, and on top of the sports world, Curry has the advanced maturity that has long figured out it's the little things that will survive time. The details are what make a journey precious.

Then, in a blink, he'll start his routine, squatting down suddenly to dribble both balls. There is a rhythm to it as he picks up the pace, like a boxer on a speed bag. After seconds of syncing each ball so they bounce off the court simultaneously, he switches it up so they alternate, a subtle shift that is much harder than it looks. Next, another level of difficulty: he bounces the ball to the opposite hand. The short, quick crossovers emphasize his ambidextrous handle—bounce, switch, bounce, switch, bounce, switch. As a wrinkle, Curry eventually starts switching one of the balls between his legs.

He's not above a stumble at this juncture. But once he knocks it out seamlessly a few times, he goes back to the rapid dribbling, executing a series of complex dribbles. At this point, he's not looking at the balls, but scoping the scene around him, or talking to Fraser, letting instinct and feel guide the basketballs. Side-to-side in front of him, back-and-forth on either side of him, fluctuating between in-sync and alternating dribbles.

After about a minute, he'll take a short break. More people-watching and chatting. Then he resumes, this time standing more upright, freestyling a mix of crossovers and between-the-legs dribbles all around him. It looks random, complex, one ball behind his back and the other in front. One ball bouncing straight up and down, the other being whipped around his leg and back to its original spot. Curry looks more like a juggler than a point guard.

It looks fancy. Any person who's ever tried dribbling a ball can grasp the difficulty of his display. In basketball vernacular, this is called "handles"—a slang way of identifying a player's dribbling expertise, or ability to handle the basketball.

There are two types of handles in basketball. Cleveland point guard Kyrie Irving, one of the other elite ball handlers in the NBA, has the slippery, innate kind of handles. His are so much more about feel and instinct. The ball is only part of a scheme of misdirection that is as much about body control as ball control. Irving leans and zags and shifts in a way that gets the defender to commit, creating an opening he can exploit with his quickness. Irving doesn't dribble. He glides, slithering between cracks and slicing at invisible angles. He has a unique ability to get his defender leaning one way and zipping back the other, to slink around screens and intuitively maneuver around defenders.

The kind of handle Irving has can't be acquired. You have to be born with it. You can't teach his level of improvisation, or coach the way he understands when to spin off or juke left or step back.

Curry has some of those intangibles, too, but his handle is less natural and more a product of work ethic and focus. Curry has a bag of tricks, a mastery of moves that his perfectionism has practiced until they're second nature. For his kind of handles, the ball is the carrot. And if the defender takes the bait, by reaching for or leaning toward the carrot, Curry snatches it away and is off the other direction or pulling up for a jumper. Or, he can mesmerize with a series of dribble moves, freezing his defender long enough to be victimized.

Curry's style of handle is much more showy in a practice setting. Irving's brilliance is best revealed by confused defenders and seeing him emerge from the traffic jam in the paint, whereas Curry's is as obvious as watching a three-card monte expert. His pregame routine exemplifies how he has the ball on a string, and also how he got it there. This dribbling exhibition is how he gets warm. He practices at high degrees of difficulty so it feels natural in the heat of competition.

Next, he ditches one ball and passes the other to Fraser. Curry becomes a receiver, crouched to invite the pass. Fraser zips it to him, Curry catches and immediately goes into random dribbling moves, staring down the invisible defender in front of him, then passes it back. Fraser bounces it again to Curry for another series of crossovers, between-the-leg and behind-the-back dribbles. After a few back-and-forths, Curry is done. He's warm and ready to move onto the court.

Curry gives the ball to Fraser and walks toward the free throw line area. Curry walks at the pace of a grandfather with a toddler on his back. When he's not running, Curry saunters, his head drooped, arms dangling like he doesn't have the strength to hold them up. It makes sense in the middle of the game, when Curry slugs his way to the free throw line, or to the bench on timeouts. It's a smart way to conserve energy, save all of his juice for the action. But when he does it while cell phone cameras are recording and thousands are watching, it's just teasing.

This is the part people came to see. His dribbling is the appetizer, his shooting is the entrée. And he starts this portion with lazy left-hand layups off the glass. It's not as exciting as what's to come but just as important, as Curry is working on touch. Those high-arching flip shots he drops in the lane aren't luck. He has a relationship with the ball and the backboard and the rim that he has worked religiously to develop. It's evident as he scoops it, then hook shots it, both effortlessly off the glass.

After five makes, he moves to the left elbow of the key. From there, he shoots left-handed. The first makes are runners off of one foot. Then, when he catches the pass, he goes into a crossover and lofts a push shot with his left hand. After making three of those, it's on to the right side, where he does the same process but shoots with his right hand. He ends this portion of the drills with a one-footed runner over Fraser, who plants himself in the lane and jumps to impede Curry's vision.

Curry then takes it to the perimeter. Most NBA players look like good shooters in warm-ups. Uncontested, pressure-less jumpers are nothing to most players at this level. But Curry's mastery is clear once he starts chucking. He makes them at a rate that drops jaws even for practice.

Curry starts by making fifteen shots at five spots around on the court: the right corner, the right wing, the top, the left corner, the left wing. He shoots until he makes five set shots, followed by five pull-ups off the dribble, then he steps back behind the 3-point line. Curry, part trying to make it fun for himself and part trying to prepare for in-game situations, complicates matters by taking difficult fadeaways or putting extremely high arc on some of his shots. You get the sense he could knock down fifteen easily, but that would be boring to him. So he rolls out the fancy dribble moves or adds in an exaggerated step-back, or takes the shot off one foot, or launches it high enough to scrape the rafters so it rips the net when it drops. When he gets to the top of the key, he doesn't take the 3-pointer from right behind the line like everywhere else. Instead, he backs all the way up to the team logo. Each bomb he drops in solicits oooohs and aaaaahs from the crowd.

When Curry misses too many, the frustration bubbles to the surface. He'll smirk if he misses two in a row. If he misses a third at the same spot, you might see him shaking his head. By the time he completes his around-the-world drill, he's made seventy-five jumpers, ninety-seven when you count the lefty and righty floaters and scoops he began with. And he still isn't done.

He goes back to the elbow for one-on-one action with Fraser. He starts with his back to the coach, leaning on him and using the defender as leverage. Fraser bumps, swipes, and pressures Curry while he works on step-back jumpers. Three from the left and three from the right. He follows with ten made free throws before the catch-and-shoot portion. He runs along the perimeter, catching passes from Fraser and hoisting 3s. Often, the Warriors will move Curry to off guard and let him evade his defenders around screens. It's all designed to give the best shooter in the game a fraction of a second of freedom to release his shot. But this requires him being ready to catch and shoot from many angles and body positions. Unlike most, Curry doesn't have to square up and have his feet set to be an effective shooter. He can catch the ball facing away from the basket and have the shot in the air without having to line everything up perfectly—which is born out of the necessity of his height. That's because of practice, because of countless hours of running along the perimeter and working on shots. On one part, he starts at the top, runs along the 3-point line, pirouettes into a backpedal, and receives the pass on his way to the corner, where he catches, turns, and shoots. He caps his pregame routine on the same side he started, backpedaling into the corner and dropping a skyscraper 3-pointer.

At home games, Curry has a final trick to end his pregame warm-up. He walks up the tunnel toward the Warriors locker room and faces the basket. Much of the crowd moves over to the seats near the tunnel, where they can get a closer picture of

Curry and watch his trick from the close-up angle. Former Warriors guard Monta Ellis originated this tunnel shot. Curtis Jones challenged Curry to try it years ago, and it has become a staple of his routine.

"Steph is a kid at heart," Steve Kerr said. "He's always trying crazy stuff."

While Curry waits in the hall, Jones underhands a pass to the Warriors star. Curry catches and lofts it, in essence from the stands. It's too far for him to shoot it normally, so he steps into it and heaves it from his hip. He gives himself three tries. When he makes it, the crowd roars like he hit a buzzer-beater, then he signs autographs for the fans dangling over the rails.

The Warriors started opening the doors early in December of 2015 so fans could watch Curry's warm-ups. Shortly after, Comcast SportsNet Bay Area, which televises Warriors games locally, started airing its pregame show earlier so it could broadcast Curry's routine live.

In March 2016, with Curry well on his way to a second MVP, he came out to cheers from a surprisingly large crowd. Two hours before the game, the arena was electric. Roughly nine of the sections in the lower level were already full. Even the security guards were watching intently. This was in Dallas.

The Mavericks also let fans in early to watch Curry. The next night in San Antonio, the only team within spitting distance of the Warriors, a father and a son decked in Spurs gear argued with a staffer at the ticket booth of the AT&T Center. Their ticket wasn't in a section permitted to enter the arena earlier than normal. The Spurs fans missed Curry's warm-up.

Curry's wide-ranging appeal is undeniable. In pretty much two years, he has established himself as a bona fide force in sports. Global soccer superstar Lionel Messi sent Curry an autographed jersey. Golf star Jordan Spieth met him as a fan in Dallas after a Mavericks game, and Curry immediately negotiated how many strokes Spieth would give him on a golf course matchup.

Curry's appeal isn't random, more of a perfect storm of qualities.

First off, Curry is six-foot-three, 180 pounds. That's considerably taller than the average man. But in the NBA, Curry looks like a regular-sized human.

Technically, Curry isn't unusually small for his position. He's not big by any means, but many point guards are smaller than him. But the appeal isn't based on his size relative to other players as much as on his size relative to his dominance. Little guys succeeding in the NBA is by no means new. But the novelty is in a little guy taking over the league.

Most NBA players are winners of a genetic lottery. They either reach heights of rarified air or have been blessed with exceptional physical gifts, trending them toward basketball success. The great ones are usually endowed with both: size and talent. See LeBron James in the dictionary.

Curry, on the other hand, could blend into the line at a Starbucks, and yet he bends the game to his will. And he isn't freakishly athletic in the traditional sense. He isn't a high-jumping, blazing-fast, muscle-bound anomaly. He represents everyone who is small in stature yet has the biggest of dreams. Curry is proof regular packages can be extraordinary gifts.

This explains in part why kids adore Curry. They can relate to him in a way they cannot with most other megastars. In a relative sense, he is them. His looking-up perspective in the NBA is similar to the existence of the young people who cheer for him. In that way, his success is inspirational, fodder for their imagination.

Perhaps nobody embodies Curry's appeal to young people more than Jaden Newman. The twelve-year-old is a basketball wizard (Google her), and she loooooves her some Steph Curry. In the Newman household, located in Orlando, Warriors games are often family events. And when there is no game, she is not above rewatching old ones on the computer. Over and over.

You should've seen her when Curry hit the game-winning 3-pointer at Oklahoma City in February 2016.

"She went nuts," said Jamie Newman, Jaden's dad and coach. "Screaming. Going crazy. Jumping up and running around the house."

For Newman, who has been an Internet sensation since she was nine, Curry is the cutout for her proverbial vision board. She has been playing varsity for Downey Christian High School girls basketball since she was in the third grade, dominating at four-foot-seven.

Curry is validation for what Jamie Newman has been instilling in his children—including his son Julian, who was playing varsity at eleven years old—about how ball-handling and shooting unlocks hidden levels of basketball. Every day, Jaden spends three to five hours mastering her game. She does strength and conditioning. She spends an hour doing ball-handling drills, some including two and three balls. She also does a shooting regimen that suggests she is already Steph Curry: three hundred made baskets—one hundred 3-pointers, one hundred mid-range, fifty off-the-dribble 3s from really deep, and fifty free throws.

"If you can shoot the ball with unlimited distance and handle the ball and shoot it off the dribble, you're unstoppable," Jamie Newman said. "That's what we're seeing with Steph. It's just crazy to be able to do it. You don't see anybody that just pulls up from deep. If you can possess that . . . Jaden can pull up from thirty feet off the dribble."

Which underscores another major factor in Curry's magnetic appeal: shooting. His special talent is the part of the game that's universal. His superpower can be mimicked even if only in hope. Watching Blake Griffin soaring through the air doesn't make onlookers say, "I think I can do that." But anybody can at least trick themselves into thinking they can shoot like Curry.

Basketball, at its core, is about putting the ball in the basket. It is compelling in its simplicity. Its essence is centered on humans' time-honored obsession with hitting the mark. The challenge of, and satisfaction from, making the shot is attractive. We shoot balled-up socks into dirty clothes hampers, crumpled paper into wastebaskets, grapes into mouths. That lure of making it in is what draws many to basketball, and watching Curry shoot tickles that desire.

We marveled at how Jordan and Kobe flew through the air. At LeBron's combination of power and speed. Shaq's massiveness. Magic's intuitiveness. Hakeem's footwork. But those abilities are obvious in their rarity. It is clear normal people can't even try to do what they do.

Curry's skill is hardly something anybody can do. But it is certainly something anyone on a court can try to do. And most everyone has at least taken a shot before. They've been drawn to the task, been struck by its difficulty, maybe even pricked with the fulfillment of making it.

Anyone who has ever made a shot, especially three or four in a row, has bonded with Curry in a shared experience. A small percentage knows what it's like to soar above the rim. But many know the adrenaline of making shots, the confidence boost of seeing the next splash, the sensation that comes with drilling one from deep.

But Curry isn't just a shooter. He is what basketball circles call a shot-maker, someone who specializes in making difficult attempts. He makes the kind of shots people daydream about.

Ever see a kid dribbling an imaginary ball, then playfully pull up for an imaginary shot over the lengthy imaginary defender? The kid then holds his follow-through to enjoy the imaginary swish and the cheers of the imaginary crowd. Curry does it in real life, and it's hypnotizing.

The NBA became the first organization to surpass two billion loops on Vine and has 1.8 million followers on the app—the most of any other league. A big part of that is because of Curry and his highlight-heavy style of play. He is among the NBA leaders in did-you-see-that? plays.

When Curry came out of college, some NBA insiders saw his

potential, even called him the black Steve Nash. Like the two-time MVP, Curry was a point guard with a great outside shot.

But Nash was a wizard at point guard who could also shoot. He was such a great passer and floor general, especially at the fast pace his Phoenix Suns played, it was easy to forget about his shot. Don Nelson, the Warriors coach who groomed Nash while the two were in Dallas, used to chide Nash about not shooting more.

Nash's shooting was a reaction to defenses that wanted to force him to be a scorer. To prevent him from his playmaking mastery, which would allow multiple teammates to get going, teams would try to force Nash to score the bulk of the points by himself. The same plan was used on Magic Johnson, who could elevate the level of even average players.

Curry had the same skills as Nash, except his game unfolds the opposite way, outside in. The incredible athletes who dominate the game—Michael Jordan, Kobe Bryant, LeBron James—often worked on their outside shot as a rebuttal to defenses backing off them. The development of their outside shooting served as a Plan B for their ability to attack the rim on the strength of their physical prowess. Once they figured that out, it was curtains.

But for Curry, his outside shooting is what prompts fear in opposing teams and unlocks the diversity of his game. His ability to pass, his vision, ball-handling, and soft touch around the rim, are the Plan B to make defenses pay for being too devoted to stopping his shooting.

As a result, there is a spontaneity to Curry's style. He can dribble with the best of them, shoot on the move—from a pull-up 3-pointer or a high-arching floater in the lane—and anticipate the openings. It's a read-and-react game with more options. Rarely does the NBA see players who are just as good at creating for others as they are at scoring.

The result produces a significant part of the Curry appeal: flair. He uses his ball-handling to get open, and his mastery of shooting to finish. The combination can be sensational.

And the last few years, after being given the reins to the franchise and growing comfortable in his superstar skin, Curry has honed his attack mode.

He repeatedly talks about aggressiveness as the key to his game, which he says is not just looking for his shot but perennially putting pressure on the defense by hunting for shots, pushing the tempo in transition, and finding ways to penetrate the defense.

There were glimpses of what Curry would become during his rookie season. With the Warriors out of contention by the all-star break in the 2009–10 season, Nelson turned the team over to his rookie point guard. Armed with a bunch of journeymen veterans, undrafted players, and NBA Development League call-ups, Curry went on a tear the second half of the season. Victory rested on his shoulders and it brought out an aggressiveness.

After the all-star break his rookie year, Curry averaged 22.1 points and 7.7 assists. Seven times over the last thirty games of his rookie season, Curry had at least 25 points and ten assists—one of those a 36-point, thirteen-assist, ten-rebound triple double. He capped the season with 42 points, eight assists, and nine rebounds at Portland.

The surge vaulted Curry to second in the Rookie of the Year voting. It also served as a prelude of how he would eventually thrive in the NBA, though it took him some time to get back to that.

After the Warriors traded Monta Ellis, Curry was back as the primary ball-handler. With David Lee as his cohort, Curry began to develop his pick-and-roll expertise.

When coach Steve Kerr came along, the game opened up for Curry. The offense—centered on movement, passing, and pick-and-roll—played into Curry's wheelhouse in a way Mark Jackson's post-up, isolation offense didn't.

Under Jackson, Curry honed his game-management skills, cut down his turnovers, and improved his decision making and defense. Then playing at a faster tempo under Kerr, and with the floor spread out, Curry was in an optimal environment. And it produced magic.

As *San Jose Mercury News* columnist Tim Kawakami wrote, Curry is a "night-by-night world-wide sports epiphany, witnessed by everybody great or small who can't resist tuning into the greatest show of our time."

In 2015–16, with an MVP in his pocket and a championship ring on his finger, Curry was even more aggressive looking for his shot. He set a career-high in field goal attempts. And the flash was in full force.

Often compared to Nash, Curry became like Jamal Crawford at his peak with a more pure outside shot. In his prime, Crawford was an electric combo guard. He's got a cult following from his cleverness with the ball, instinct and vision on the court, and elite shot-making ability. Some streetball players were able to button up their games and made it to the NBA. But Crawford, in his eighteenth season, was an NBA player who has a streetballer's flair. He hit the tough shots—fadeaways, floaters, pull-ups with a hand in his face, long-range—and usually preceded them with some slick crossover dribble.

Crawford's peers revere him because he has been a tough player to guard for so long. Players who can shoot, dribble, and drive are multipronged threats that leave good defenders scratching their heads. Add on the ability to pass and it also gives the help defenders fits. Crawford was one of those guys. Crawford presented problems for his defenders plus an added intangible—he could embarrass you.

A wiry six-foot-five and a good leaper, Crawford was known for throwing the ball off the backboard to himself and dunking it. But his main highlights weren't dunks. They were near-impossible shots with a defender in his face. They were ball-handling moves that left the player guarding him confused while he slipped by for a score. He brought the ooohs and aaahs below the rim, which made him a feared commodity among his peers.

He's never made an all-star game, but few players are as respected among other NBA players as Crawford. And he sees himself in Curry's game.

The only difference, though, is in their approach. Crawford's game centers on his drive and ball-handling. He was such an elite penetrator, tricky with the ball and slithery with his drives. His ability to get to the rim was such a weapon, defenders had to back off of him. Of course, that only meant he had to enhance his arsenal of tricks—the fake around-the-back, consecutive behind-the-back dribbles, through-the-legs and around-the-back—to really get the defense off balance and create driving lanes. He also developed his mid-range jumper as a counter, to punish opponents for giving him space and to provide a way of finishing his attacks. The threat of a quick jumper or an explosion to the basket rendered his defenders jumpy, making his hesitations and pump fakes crippling to them.

Curry's game, conversely, is built around his shooting. He is as deadly from the outside as Crawford was driving. His outside shot is such a dominant element of his game, defenders latch close to him to prevent him from shooting. He developed his ability to penetrate to make defenders pay for pressing up on him.

The crossovers, the around-the-back moves, the sudden changes of direction are all designed to deconstruct the defense's goal of taking away his shot. And because Curry can immortalize a defender on Vine, break him down with some dribble highlight, he becomes a triple threat, incredibly frustrating to guard. Like Crawford, Curry can embarrass you.

In 2015–16, Curry emerged as one of the best penetrators in the game, using his outside shot and ball-handling to get into the lane. And his mastery of shooting allowed him to finish as if he were a big explosive guard.

Curry has become the evolution of Crawford's game in how he blends blacktop entertainment value at the highest levels. Curry's unprecedented shot-making, often set up by crafty ball-handling, provides the kind of showmanship usually reserved for dunkers.

And Curry does his damage behind the arc, making the penalty even greater for the defense.

"He has the same mentality. He goes for the jugular," Crawford said. "He has complete freedom on the court, and people don't understand how rare that is. He can take any shot. He can try any move. He can pull out any trick, and he doesn't have to worry about getting yanked out of the game, because the offense is based on him being able to break down the defense. People think it's all about being flashy. And some of it is. That was part of it for me, and it looks like it is part of it for Steph. But the big part of it is creating the misdirection, getting the defense to bend to your will. Curry is the next generation of that. He carries on that legacy. And when you can shoot like that, the whole game opens up. Nothing is off limits when you can shoot and handle the rock."

Unlike Crawford, Curry has transcended cult status to become a mainstream icon, a hero for the every-kid. Even people who don't know anything about basketball or sports have now heard of Stephen Curry.

Splash Brothers

o   o   o

"They are the greatest shooting backcourt that's ever played this game. I don't think it's a debate. They are two incredible shooters. And we have not seen a tandem as deadly as those guys as far as shooting the basketball."

—Mark Jackson

CHAPTER 6

There are layers to NBA stardom. Level 1 is simply having the skills to light it up at all. The ability to score, say, 30 points in an NBA game is a club with plenty members, but there is still some exclusivity to it. Not everyone can, even in optimal settings, go and get 30 for his team. But some are good enough that if a poor defense is in front of them, or their shot is clicking and they have the green light, they could produce a big night.

Level 2 would be the caliber of player who could get 30 against a good defense, which is a degree of difficulty that shrinks the club significantly. Not many players can manufacture such high production against teams that don't make many mistakes on defense. The Level 3 players can get it done even when those good defenses are focused on stopping them specifically. An incredible amount of mastery is required to carry a team when the scouting report is designed to take away a player's strengths and prey on his weaknesses.

But then there is another level: players who produce at high levels in the biggest games, when the good defenses are especially focused and the expectation becomes another foe. Few players can thrive while under immense pressure, such as in the playoffs. The elite are those who can summon greatness when needed most.

The best teams in the NBA in the last fifteen or twenty years have had at least two players at the highest levels, often three. The Miami Heat had LeBron James, Dwayne Wade, and Chris Bosh. All at least Level 3 players. The Spurs had Tim Duncan, Tony Parker, and Manu Ginobili. The Lakers had Kobe Bryant and Shaquille O'Neal, then Bryant and Pau Gasol. The Celtics had Paul Pierce, Kevin Garnett, and Ray Allen.

The Cavaliers won a championship because Kyrie Irving grew into one of those type of players on the biggest stage. LeBron James needed help.

The Clippers have had two of those players for years and have been in need of a third, which is why they went after Kevin Durant when Paul Pierce proved he was no longer that guy. The Pacers have one in Paul George, and a budding one in Myles Turner.

And some, like John Wall in Washington and Anthony Davis in New Orleans, are wasting away as lone stars with little hope until management can get them a cohort or two. The departure of Durant means Russell Westbrook will join them unless center Steven Adams keeps progressing.

This is how the NBA works. Players are so good, schemes so sophisticated, that winning big requires a plurality of greatness.

Since the Warriors became a playoff team, after trading guard Monta Ellis in 2012 and turning the franchise over to their point guard, Curry had been the only Warrior with that kind of potential. He was the only player tasked with the burden of being great on command. David Lee, Curry's cohort from 2012 to 2014, was a two-time all-star, but he wasn't the kind of talent who could take over a game on his own. Peak David Lee thumped a ceiling somewhere between Levels 2 and 3. Most of his Warriors tenure he enjoyed the perennial privilege of playing next to a player who terrified opponents. A good defense focused on stopping him usually succeeded.

In 2014, Klay Thompson became Curry's sidekick as Draymond Green emerged to take Lee's spot in the rotation. Thompson was a shooter who, like Lee, basked in the comfort that comes with playing next to Curry. Thompson showed flashes of greatness but struggled with consistency, largely because his skill set needed development. In the 2015 NBA Playoffs, it became evident how alone Curry was as an elite. His struggles almost automatically meant Warriors defeat.

The Warriors played seventeen more games after sweeping through the first round of those playoffs, and in them Thompson was feast or famine. He scored 20 or more in seven of those games and failed to top 15 points in eight of them. He lit up Cleveland for 34 points in Game 2 of the NBA Finals then totaled 40 points over the next four games.

Thompson was the best costar Curry ever had, yet Curry still didn't have the luxury of turning over the reins to another player who could carry him. He just had to find a way—through off nights, double-teams, intentional physicality, injuries—to come through in order for the Warriors to win. Green, a defensive wizard whose offensive game was built on intangibles, eventually emerged as the Warriors No. 2. But Green didn't allow Curry to take a backseat. He simply brought tremendous value because of his ability to impact the game on both ends. His skills helped magnify Curry's, not replace them.

But one thing that has always been consistent about Thompson's game is that he improves from year to year. He comes back from the off season with a more well-rounded game, certain skills more polished. And through the 2015–16 season, he had many more moments where he was just as valuable on the court as Curry. It was no longer an option for defenses to take their eyes off him and double or triple Curry. There was a time when opponents would have to live with Thompson being the guy who beat them, banking on Thompson having an off night. But he was proving to be much more reliable with his shooting and also markedly better at the other elements of his game. Off-shooting nights didn't necessarily doom Thompson, who became productive driving to the basket and posting up.

Because of injury during the 2016 playoffs Curry found he had no choice but to rely on Thompson. This was certainly on display in Game 6 of the Western Conference Finals. To take the weight off his own shoulders and entrust it to his sidekick was a remarkable sign of how far the two had come.

Thompson started heating up toward the end of the second quarter. He closed the first half with three bombs over the final four minutes, all assisted by Curry, who was drawing the focus of the Thunder's defense. Curry hadn't been good in this series, partly because of the injuries he'd incurred in the first round against the Rockets. The Thunder's aggressive defense didn't need help. Curry didn't respond well to the physicality and length of OKC. He was solid in Game 1, but not down the stretch and not enough to prevent Oklahoma City from stealing the series opener. He got progressively worse over the next three games, and the Warriors found themselves on the brink of embarrassing failure. After winning a record seventy-three games in the regular season, it was understood they needed to win a championship. But to not even make the Finals, to get blasted by Oklahoma City in the Western Conference Finals, was the opposite of a dignified way to go out.

Curry roared back in Game 5 with a game-high 31 points, keeping the Warriors alive for another game. But winning at Oklahoma City seemed insurmountable. In Games 3 and 4, the Warriors were outscored by a combined 52 points. That's brow-raising for any team. But for a team that hardly ever lost, it was like the *Titanic* crashing into that iceberg. And now they faced a must-win game back in Oklahoma City. Game 6.

The 3s made by Thompson were critical for their symbolism as much as anything. His first, with 4:23 left in the second quarter, came with the Warriors down 13. His second, the next trip down the floor, cut the Warriors' deficit to 7. His third, at the 2:09 mark, had the Warriors within four.

But Thompson did more than shave points off Oklahoma City's lead. He reminded the Warriors of their greatness. He restored their confidence and put doubt into the minds of the Thunder. In both of their blowout losses at OKC, the Warriors came unglued in the second quarter. The home team would make a run, their raucous fans would roar, and the Warriors came tumbling down. This time, though, Thompson killed that plan. The Warriors went into halftime down 5 points but dripping with belief. They'd gotten their mojo back. They'd taken the Thunder's best shot and finally seemed ready to deliver their own.

Emboldened, the Warriors changed the starting lineup to open the second half. They noticed that Kevin Durant had taken nineteen shots in the first half. They wanted him to take more, keep shooting until his arms fell off. So they replaced Harrison Barnes in the starting lineup with Andre Iguodala, who they could comfortably leave one-on-one with Durant. The lack of help would hopefully bait Durant into hero ball, stunting the Thunder's offense.

The Warriors defense was clicking. The only question was whether the visitors would get enough offense.

Ten seconds into the second half, Thompson answered. He opened the third quarter with a 3-pointer from the left wing. The next time down, he curled off a screen and drilled another 3-pointer from the right corner. In thirty-seven seconds, the Warriors had the lead, and Oklahoma City was faced with the daunting task of winning a close game against the desperate champions.

Thompson cooled off, but Curry found a rhythm in the third quarter. The Thunder weren't giving him any looks from behind the arc, swarming up with taller defenders, so Curry did his damage penetrating. He scored 11 points in just over a two-minute stretch of the third quarter. He had to work hard for those points, and when the quarter ended, the Warriors were still down 8. It was clear they would be a tough out, but they were on the ropes nonetheless.

Curry had just grinded out 14 points in the third quarter, working against double-teams, his sore knee, and the general funk his game was in. And the result was still an 8-point deficit. Steve Kerr typically rests Curry to start the fourth quarter, and he needed it this game. But Curry also knew the Warriors were one Thunder run from seeing that lead balloon quickly put victory out of reach. The Warriors needed some magic, and Curry wasn't in a position to give it.

So in that dead space between quarters, after the huddle is broken but before television is ready for the game to start, Curry went to Thompson.

"This is your time," Curry told him privately. "This is your moment. Do what you do. Put on a show and have fun."

If anybody could deliver something spectacular with him on the bench, it was Thompson. And if anybody could tell when Thompson was in one of his zones, it was Curry. So in order to bait the improbable, Curry leaned on his cohort.

This was a benchmark in their relationship, a shift in how the Warriors operated. These moments were always Curry time. For the last four years, the Warriors had leaned almost exclusively on him. Sure, others produced, but it was more found money than an expectation. Leaning on anyone else with such high stakes was risky.

While Curry sat, Thompson checked back into the game and opened the fourth quarter with another 3 from the right corner. A minute and a half later, he scored another 3, with Durant flying at him. Just over a minute later, Thompson took a handoff from Andrew Bogut, then hid behind the Warriors' seven-footer to get an open look at another 3-pointer. That made three in a row. Each of them keeping the Thunder within striking distance.

The shot that turned this from a hot night into a mind-blowing basketball experience came after Durant's fadeaway put the Thunder ahead by 7 with five minutes left. Thompson, on the ensuing possession, received the pass twenty-eight feet from the basket at the top of the key. Russell Westbrook crouched into a defensive position in front of Thompson, who was facing the right sidelines more than he was the basket. Without so much as a dribble, and in one motion, Thompson pulled up and faced the basket. It was the kind of shot where the coaches and fans scream "Noooooo" when they realized a shot was going up. But Thompson, already nine 3-pointers down, was on fire. He gave it one thought and fired.

He set an NBA record with his tenth 3-pointer in a playoff game. Sent the Warriors bench into a frenzy. Turned the once hostile arena into a nervous wreck. Left seasoned, professional NBA writers on media row rolling their eyes and looking at one another in disbelief. The Warriors were back down by 4 and the Thunder were in trouble. Thompson going insane had awakened the beast that had tormented the rest of the NBA all season.

And the Splash Brothers weren't done.

A minute later, Curry hit a 3-pointer, then another, tying the game at 99. He was awakened and in rhythm, too. It was tied at 101 when Iguodala stripped Westbrook and started the fast-break. Running ahead was Thompson. Iguodala took two dribbles and zipped it down the right sideline to him. In less time than a deep breath takes, Thompson had the shot sized up and launched right from where he caught it. With Durant in his grill.

The Warriors led 104–101 with 1:35 left. Curry put the finishing touches with a runner off the glass. They had staved off elimination again, reclaimed home court advantage, and shifted all the doubt and frustration over to Oklahoma City. And how it happened, in this Game 6, was a testament to how far the Warriors' star backcourt had come. It was years of growth coming to fruition, the fulfillment of a vision established nearly five years earlier.

Thompson made five 3s in the fourth quarter, racking up 19 of his 41 points over the final twelve minutes to save the Warriors' season. It was the moment that he and Curry cemented their on-court brotherhood.

"When the MVP has confidence in you, it means a lot," Thompson said. "It gives you a sense of urgency to go out there and play your game and just have fun. It's easy playing with Steph, because the air of confidence he has about him trickles down to everyone on this team."

It was even more surreal for the Game 6 hero as he entered the locker room. There on one knee to greet him was Joe Lacob, the brash franchise owner, self-made one-percenter, and Silicon

Valley venture capitalist who spearheaded the building of the Warriors from ashes into a juggernaut and who had been making bold predictions since he bought the team in 2010.

With his black blazer in his left hand, Lacob grinned like a schoolkid as he stretched his arms out in prostration while Thompson walked toward him. He bowed twice, quickly, before getting up and hugging his shooting guard.

"That was interesting," Thompson said from his locker while scrolling through messages on his phone. "The owner bowing? You don't see that every day. Gotta love Joe."

This new and improved Thompson didn't come out of nowhere. He set career highs in points, field goal percentage, and 3-pointers made in 2015–16. And throughout the playoffs, he assumed the position of carrying the Warriors while Curry missed games with injuries.

Thompson put up 34 in a win at Houston in the first play-off game Curry had ever missed. With Curry on the shelf after spraining his knee, Thompson ran off eight straight games with at least 20 points, including 37 in the second-round opener against Portland and 33 in the Game 5 clincher to eliminate the Blazers. Known for years to frustrate Warriors fans by disappearing, Thompson proved over and again that he was at least on the precipice of eliteness, as he was the one the Warriors had to lean on.

Curry would never say it, but it's a safe bet he has longed for a sidekick good enough to relegate him to a costar even if only on occasion. The burden of the lone superstar made the Celtics look so appealing to Kevin Garnett, prompted Chris Paul to ask for a trade from New Orleans, drove LeBron James to bolt for Miami. Curry played with the same weight. Part of him embraced it. His ability to handle the pressure was proof he belongs among the elite. But some part of Curry undoubtedly wished he had a partner to share the burden with, somebody who could alleviate the penalty of his poor games, siphon some of the focus of the defense. And now he has Thompson *and* Durant.

Thompson continued developing his game, becoming more than just a shooter. Over the years, he improved at working off the dribble, added a post-up game, and grew smarter with his shot selection. He became increasingly more aggressive, his confidence bolstered by his success at attacking.

Thompson has had big games next to Curry, even dominated enough to negate some poor outings by Curry. But the next step for Thompson was being able to carry the Warriors on call. In spots during the season the signs had been there that he was ready to be that guy.

The Warriors closed the 2015 calendar year in Houston. Curry was sidelined for his second consecutive game with a bruised calf. The previous night, the Mavericks had torched the Warriors in only the second loss of the season. Thompson had just 10 points on fifteen shots and looked like he wasn't ready to fill in for Curry. But in Houston, Thompson looked much more like a capable top-tier player. He put up 17 points in the first quarter while Curry went crazy in a blazer on the sidelines. Thompson then put up another 14 in the third quarter. Then he scored 7 points midway through the fourth quarter in the run that put the host Rockets away. Thompson finished with 38, showing he could carry the Warriors in relief. For this one, he was the focus of the defense and still got it done.

So when Curry went down in the playoffs, it didn't automatically doom the Warriors. Thompson showed he was ready for a larger load.

And Curry recognized the jump in Thompson's game. He seemed to sincerely appreciate Thompson's growth when, at the end of his press conference following the clinching win in the series against Portland, he made sure to praise his backcourt mate.

"I have to say one thing, though," Curry spontaneously uttered after answering the final question from the media. "You gotta talk about Klay . . . that dude had the best series I think I've ever seen him play on both ends of the floor. Defending Dame [Lillard] and exhausting all his energy to make it uncomfortable for him, and what he's able to do offensively. Hopefully that doesn't get lost in our series and the way that we played as a team. Because you look down, that dude had 33 points and chased Dame around for all thirty-four minutes he was on the court. So shout out to him for elevating his game on both ends of the floor."

Curry and Thompson have avoided issues largely because of their upbringing and personalities. Both grew up around the NBA, as children of NBA players. Thompson's dad Mychal was a No. 1 overall pick and won two championships with Magic Johnson's Showtime Lakers. Curry and Thompson were raised with means in two-parent households rooted by strong mothers, and the benefits of a stable home are present in the way they carry themselves.

They both are comfortable in the spotlight but don't clamor for it. They aren't enamored of the glitz of the NBA. Instead, they've seen the NBA from a different viewpoint: behind the scenes. They got to see practice and private gatherings and noncompetitive environments. They got to see the friendly side of the NBA, where the hierarchy was loosened and players were all just members of this exclusive fraternity. Neither of them come off as impressed by the money and fame, but rather by the competitiveness and the camaraderie.

Curry is a franchise player without the alpha male personality. He goes out of his way to be seen by his teammates as just one of the guys. He shuns several of the ceremonial perks of superstardom, almost to a fault.

Curry has occupied the same locker for years, third from the wall on the left side, right next to the entrance. To the right is Thompson's locker. As the Warriors improved and became a playoff team, the media increased, and in-demand players would get interviewed in the middle of the locker room in front of a banner. Curry had refused to be interviewed in that spot, opting to do postgame sessions at his locker as he always has. His teammates, instead, got the pedestal. That changes in the playoffs, when the NBA uses a podium for interviews. The Warriors have adopted that setup since acquiring Durant, ending Curry's locker interviews.

If there is one word his teammates use most to describe Curry it's "humble." They've seen his star rise and his ego remain grounded. That disposition not only allowed Thompson to grow as a player, but encouraged it. Even as Thompson chucked away, even when Warriors diehards were noticing and laughing about how Thompson seemed to never pass to his backcourt mate, Curry was unfazed.

And Thompson was clearly born without the gene that lusts after fame. He has to be prodded by his managers to seize the limelight and its advantages. Thompson is largely unconcerned with credit and public persona. His shoe deal with the Chinese shoe company Anta—taking the money over the credibility of a deal with a major American shoe company—shows how low that kind of attention falls on Thompson's priorities.

Thompson is usually trying to be the first one out of the locker room, whether he scores 30 or 12, unless he is stopped by reporters. He always answers questions but never seeks out a recorder. He's only recently embraced the idea of building his brand, a product of years of work from his representation. A strong case could be made that Thompson's lack of ego has played a big role in the Warriors' rise, because with Curry and Draymond Green ahead of him in status, it would be normal if Thompson harbored a resentment that affected their chemistry.

But Thompson is a different breed in that way. He just doesn't care about status. He is certainly an outgoing single guy who enjoys clubbing and having friends around him, but he just doesn't seem to get hung up about not being the star attraction. In some ways he likely feels it makes his life more free. As a result, Curry's meteoric rise didn't adversely impact Thompson. It didn't create any tension between the two. For that matter, neither did Green's sudden stardom, rendering Thompson a third wheel on the Warriors, seem to bother him.

A deft scorer in his own right, Thompson has fully bought into the defensive scheme where he does the thankless task of defending Curry's man. At six-foot-seven, 205 pounds, Thompson has proven to be a much tougher matchup for opposing point guards. The better ones have an athleticism advantage and can shoot over Curry, who is six-foot-three, 180 pounds. Plus Mark Jackson wanted to save the energy of Curry, who was carrying the offense. Thompson accepted the assignment without complaint, working to steadily improve at defending the hardest position in the NBA. Eventually, he became an exceptional defender, good enough to frustrate the best point guards in the league. Sometimes, his defense is his primary contribution. Many locker rooms have been disrupted for less. But Thompson embraces the dirty work.

All three Warriors made the 2016 All-Star Game in Toronto. Curry had an entourage of security, Warriors representatives, and agency reps as he made the rounds on his media tour, trailed by a handful of media. Ditto for Draymond Green. Thompson? His entourage was two deep: both forced upon him by protocol. He had plenty of time to sit and chat as one media member followed him around. And he loved the low-key setting.

"Shouldn't you be following Steph around?" Thompson said to the one reporter on his trail.

The growth of the Curry-Thompson relationship, from friendly teammates to a bonded tandem, took a boost when they were both selected to the Team USA roster for the FIBA Basketball World Cup. They had already played three seasons together with the Warriors. But when they arrived in Las Vegas for training camp in the summer of 2014, they were barely more than amiable teammates. Forever connected because of their ridiculous shooting ability, they were so different because their lives had little overlap besides their upbringing.

Curry, who entered the NBA two years before Thompson, was battling an ankle injury during Thompson's rookie year. They had one start together, in the fourth game of the 2011–12 season, as

Thompson filled in for Monta Ellis, before Curry went down with his injury. The Warriors traded Ellis and made Thompson the full-time starter in March 2012, but Curry was already shelved with the sprain.

Curry returned focused to disprove his critics. After off-season surgery, he spent the summer working out at Davidson and returned to the Warriors seeking to get his career back on track. Thompson, entering his second season, was still trying to get his bearings in the NBA, on and off the court.

Quiet, with an aloofness about him that left coaches and fans shaking their heads at times, Thompson was working on developing his game. He was becoming a defender, learning about shot selection and how to put the ball on the floor. Bonding with Curry wasn't yet a priority. He and Curry were the starting guards for the outset in 2012–13, as the Warriors had planned. But Thompson was much more of a role player on Curry and David Lee's team.

Thompson continued improving his game in 2013–14, and by the end of the year he was challenging Lee to be Curry's sidekick. But the playoffs revealed how much Curry was actually alone. The Los Angeles Clippers threw the kitchen sink at him and dared the other Warriors to beat them. Thompson was either hot or cold, and Lee had his hands full playing center since Andrew Bogut and Festus Ezeli had been injured. The Warriors pushed the Clippers to Game 7, where Curry and Green kept them in the game while Thompson and Lee struggled.

It is with this history that Curry and Thompson went into their Team USA experience together. Something was brewing with the Warriors, but neither had so much as hung out with the other. Their relationship off the court only existed at team functions, which made sense as Curry was married with a family while Thompson was single and a gym rat. But as they spent more than a month together with Team USA, which went on to win gold in Spain, they had a chance to build their chemistry as a backcourt.

They were first dubbed Splash Brothers on December 21, 2012. After making a combined seven 3s in the first half at Charlotte, warriors.com writer Brian Witt tweeted out the hashtag #Splash Brothers. Nineteen months later, they were becoming real brothers.

They went to lunch together. Hung out on the beach together. They played golf. Thompson wasn't so good with his drive, but because of the shorter course at the Canary Islands he only needed his irons, with which he is solid. He was able to put up a decent fight before respectably losing to Curry.

Curry even hit the club with Thompson one night. Curry scarcely makes his way into the nightlife scene, especially without his wife. He made an exception with Thompson, who is no stranger to a VIP lounge.

They went from teammates with similar childhoods to friends with a unique responsibility to each other. They already had a reputation as the best-shooting backcourt in the game, a claim first made by Mark Jackson in the 2013 playoffs and eventually proved right. But now they also had a rapport. They had a layered connection that translated onto the court.

Five months after their chemistry session on Team USA, Thompson pulled off one of the greatest feats in NBA history. He scored a record 37 points in a quarter in one of the most insane displays ever, finishing with 52 points. He made all thirteen of his shots that quarter, including nine 3s. He was in such a zone, anything he threw up went in—including one 3-point heave that came after the whistle and didn't count. And his biggest cheerleader was Curry. Nine of Thompson's baskets were assisted, six by Curry, who led the charge of feeding Thompson the ball.

A month after that, they were all-star starters together in New York. Thompson dubs that one of the best moments in his career, starting with Curry in Madison Square Garden. His admiration for Curry made that moment significant. After years of looking up to him, he was now side by side with Curry on one of the NBA's grandest stages.

They were all-stars together again in 2016. But before that, they got to share a moment in the Three-Point Shootout. Thompson was determined to take down Curry, the defending champion. When you're known for 3-point shooting, it is required to have a shootout win on your résumé, at least as Thompson believes. On top of that, Thompson has been in awe of Curry's shooting ability since they started playing together. Sometimes, Thompson is left to do nothing but shake his head at Curry's stroke. Thompson often talks about how weird it is to have such a shooter on the same team, even in the same ballpark, with him. It's still unfamiliar territory for Thompson to see another player shoot and be in awe.

Study the two closely and it's easy to deem Thompson the better shooter. Curry has an array of shots. Off the dribble, spotting up, going left, going right, defender in his face, wide open, mid-range or deep, he's just deadly. His combination of quick release and ball-handling turns his shooting skills into a Swiss Army Knife. But as far as sheer beauty, Thompson takes the cake. His form is textbook, and effortless. When his feet are set, he's probably even more reliable than Curry, even though he can't shoot from such a range of positions.

The friendly battles they have, mostly in practice drills, extended to the shootout. The 2015 edition, Thompson flamed out disappointedly in the final round, while Curry caught fire. In 2016, Thompson was so eager for revenge he was nervous. He needed one hot round to beat Curry, and when Thompson heated up, Curry became his biggest cheerleader. Even stood up when he sensed, before everyone else, that Thompson was feeling it.

Curry was excited for the same reason Thompson was nervous: they both now have a shootout championship, legitimizing their title as Splash Brothers and as the unofficial best-shooting backcourt of all time.

Three months later, when Curry was pulling off one of his feats in Portland, it was Thompson playing the role of hype man. Curry, in his first game back from injury, lit up the Blazers for

17 points in overtime. After one of his dagger 3-pointers, he famously turned to the Portland crowd and yelled, "I'm back!" Thompson then turned to the same fans, pointed to Curry and yelled, "He's back!"

For years, the two had fed off each other as shooting partners, pushing each other to new feats. But it had been Curry setting the bar as the elder and better player. It was Curry's scoring bursts in the postseason that gave Thompson a standard to shoot for, the diversity of Curry's game that gave Thompson the blueprint for a more effective repertoire.

Eventually, Thompson improved enough to return the favor. His defense motivated Curry to pick up his own, even switching back to defending point guards during their 2014–15 championship run—Curry's best defensive season in the NBA. Thompson's reliability as a scorer, and not just a shooter, gave Curry the comfort to turn to Thompson when he was feeling it and get him going when he wasn't.

They may have contrasting interests off the court—with Thompson known for the postgame parties at his house, and Curry known for sneaking off to watch a G-rated film with Riley. But Thompson is intimately woven into the story of Curry's ascension to Hall of Fame level. And if Curry adds to his legacy, it will be in part because Thompson keeps adding to his.

The Next Grant Hill

o   o   o

"If you're going to invest in somebody and believe in somebody, he's the type of guy you want to do it with."

—Bob Myers

CHAPTER 7

Putting on a blazer felt so different. He had his clothes for the night laid out on his bed at the Nines hotel in Portland's Pioneer Square, the black outfit popping against the plush white comforter. This time Curry didn't see disappointment and frustration as he stood over his blazer.

Following his afternoon nap, his normal pregame routine, Curry had woken up with new feelings rumbling in his gut. The nervous energy was normal. He always felt that. But the excitement, the hyper-ness of knowing it was a game day had some competition that day, May 9, 2016. Curry was struck by a spell of graciousness that changed the process of packing and getting dressed. This is normally a monotonous part of an NBA road trip. Re-collecting toiletries, folding clothes, and paying for incidentals before filing onto the team bus.

But Curry wasn't going through the motions; instead he was giving in to his emotions. Letting himself feel the appreciation, allowing the gratitude to course through his soul. It was Game 4 of the 2016 Western Conference Semifinals at Portland, and finally he was going to play.

On the previous road trip, Curry had refused to bring a blazer. It was an unacceptable concession that his optimism wouldn't allow. He had plans on playing Games 3 and 4 in the first-round series against Houston, after missing most of Game 1 and all of Game 2 with a foot injury. Bringing a blazer—which injured players are required to wear on the bench—would be leaving room for the possibility he wouldn't play.

This time, Curry was wearing a blazer because he wanted to, not to comply with the NBA's dress code. His grueling wait was over.

He had thought his season was over three weeks earlier. The last time Curry was playing—April 24, 2016, in Game 4 at Houston—he was reminded of the fragility of an NBA career. He had missed four games with a sprained right MCL. He wasn't 100 percent, but he was getting back on the court. If you know Curry, you know that matters to him tremendously. Feeling the leather ball in his hands. Hearing the buzz of the crowd. Solving a defense. Laughing with his teammates about the funny mistakes they all made. Curry loves this stuff.

Many NBA players don't love the game. They lost the joy as teens, when their potential transitioned basketball from a game to a career. They endure the process in exchange for the bounty. They labor through practice, grind through the schedule, struggle to put in the extra work necessary, because that's how the checks keep coming.

But Curry is a different breed. He finds practice fun. Off-season workouts are a welcome escape from the bustle of stardom. And games, he lives for those.

Knowing he was getting ready to play in one again—back with the guys, bouncing in the pregame huddle, chewing his mouthpiece—humbled him.

Knowing the Warriors needed him made it even sweeter. He had to watch from the bench, in a blazer, as Damian Lillard led a shooting barrage that overwhelmed the Warriors in Game 3. This was Curry's chance to save the day, stomp out the hope Portland had cultivated.

But all he could think about was the privilege of even getting to play. It was enough to bow Curry's head. He took a moment to acknowledge the absence of gnawing uncertainty, to feel the peace and relief. The guy who had everything was getting what he wanted most—to play. And that was worthy of a prayer.

He didn't call his wife, Ayesha, for this one. Or even his friend Bryant Barr, a go-to prayer partner. This was a moment he spent alone, swathed in humility and hope.

"As I walked out that door knowing I was going to play, I was just thankful," Curry said. "Given the things that I've been through with my injuries over the years, I was just happy to be playing."

Those who have followed Curry's career from the beginning understand why this was a sensitive and profound moment for him. They can imagine the memories his knee injury invoked, the old wounds at which it picked.

Many of the Warriors' new fans, and the legions of young kids who started wearing Steph Curry's jersey after his introduction to the worldwide stage in 2014, haven't seen him struggle like this. His injury-plagued 2016 playoffs may have been the first time they had seen their beloved star brought to his knees.

But before he became Stephen Curry the legend, there were legitimate questions as to whether he would ever have a prolonged career. In his third and fourth seasons, and even his first playoff campaign, Curry was most known for two things: his stellar shooting and his fragile ankles.

Even once it became clear Curry was an NBA-level talent and star in the making, the fear was whether he was too injury prone to manifest his potential. It was reminiscent of another great flame snuffed out by ankle injuries.

"Everywhere I turned," Curry said, "I had people telling me I was going to be the next Grant Hill story."

Hill was a star at every level. He was an all-American who won two national championships at Duke. He was drafted No. 3 overall by the Detroit Pistons and shared Rookie of the Year honors with Jason Kidd in 1995. He made the all-star game each of his first four seasons in the league, and was first-team All-NBA—in essence naming him a top 5 player in the league—in his third season.

In the strike-shortened 1999 season, Hill joined Wilt Chamberlain and Elgin Baylor as the only players in NBA history to lead their teams in scoring, rebounds, and assists more than once.

In his first six seasons, Hill totaled more than 9,300 points, more than 3,400 rebounds, and more than 2,700 assists. Three other players have reached those levels in six seasons: Oscar Robertson, Larry Bird, and LeBron James. Hill was on his way to the Hall of Fame.

He sprained his left ankle a week before the 2000 NBA Playoffs. He kept playing and was knocked out of the first-round series in Game 2. Hill then signed as a free agent with the Orlando Magic, who had no idea they were buying damaged goods. He played just four games in his first season with Orlando. Just fourteen in his second season with the team. He played twenty-nine the next season. His persistent ankle injuries prompted Hill to undergo a major surgery to try to save his career. Doctors re-fractured his ankle so they could reset it properly. He missed the entire 2003–4 season.

He eventually returned, but not nearly as the athlete he once was. He was still really good, even making the 2005 all-star team after his surgery, but no longer transcendent. He wound up playing eighteen seasons, including five with Phoenix in which he was a key player on a contending team. But Hill had been on the path to being an all-time great. His incredible skill coupled with his size, intelligence, and athleticism made him the total package, which it seemed would make him a legendary figure in NBA history.

But persistent ankle injuries robbed him of that highest level. He was left to thrive on skill and basketball IQ, deprived of his quickness and leaping ability.

This seemed to be the road Curry was headed on, the cloud of uncertainty hanging over his career.

Curry's ankle troubles appear to have begun in 2010 in Madrid, Spain. There wasn't any history of ankle injuries before then. He missed one game in three years at Davidson, spraining his left ankle, and made it through his entire rookie season without noticeable issues. But the one in Madrid seemed to start a troubling pattern.

Curry had nearly stolen NBA Rookie of the Year with an amazing second half of the season for an awful Warriors team. It was enough to earn him a spot in the national team tryouts. And, in part because several of the top players wanted to wait for the Summer Olympics, Curry made the team.

During a practice at La Caja Mágica on August 18, 2010, he landed on a teammate's foot and sprained his left ankle. It rolled severely enough to put a scare into Curry and Team USA coaches. He recovered nicely from the sprain, though, and was back on the court three days later for a friendly against Lithuania.

It was the third time Curry had sprained his left ankle in just over eighteen months: once in February 2009 while playing at Davidson, then again in March 2010, his rookie season with the Warriors. Then again in Spain.

Two months after the sprain in Madrid, Curry sprained his other ankle in a preseason game against the Lakers in San Diego. It was his first time spraining the right ankle and trainers at the time thought it was a product of compensating for a not fully healed left ankle. It was first in a series of right ankle sprains, even though Curry missed the rest of training camp and preseason resting the injured ankle.

He re-sprained his right ankle in the opener of the 2010–11 season. Two days later, trying to maneuver a Blake Griffin screen, Curry had the first of what he called "phantom sprains"—when it rolled without any contact. That one cost him the next two games.

He managed to make it until December before tweaking it again, another phantom sprain on a simple inside-out dribble in San Antonio. That knocked him out until Christmas. Curry wouldn't miss another game the rest of the season, but he wasn't done with ankle sprains. He tweaked it again in practice in January. And ended up having surgery in the off season.

When he left OrthoCarolina in Charlotte, where foot and ankle specialist Dr. Bob Anderson repaired two ligament tears, Curry was relieved. He felt optimistic that his ankle troubles could finally be solved. He spent the off season rehabbing and was cleared for full contact in mid-September.

The 2011 NBA lockout gave him more time to heal up and get his conditioning together. Curry got back into game shape playing at Davidson College. When the NBA training camp did get going in December, Curry looked really good, torching young guards Ish Smith and Charles Jenkins. But in the final preseason game, Curry sprained his right ankle again. Guarding Sacramento Kings guard Jimmer Fredette, he rolled it as he planted his right foot and reached for the steal. He tried to keep going but ended up limping off to the side before needing to be helped off.

Curry made it back in time for the season opener on Christmas Day. But on December 26, the second game of the season, he landed on the foot of Kyle Korver after a fast-break layup against Chicago. Curry left that game and missed the next.

While he was out, he took a trip to the Nike headquarters in Beaverton, Oregon. They ran some tests in hopes of designing a shoe that would support Curry's unstable ankle.

He returned to action on New Year's Eve. But four days later, another phantom sprain occurred. In San Antonio on January 4, 2012, he was trying to start a fast-break, but his ankle rolled over when he planted. Once again, the all too familiar sight of Curry limping on the court, his stubbornness trying to keep him upright while the pain was telling him to go down. "Not again" crossed everyone's mind as Curry needed help off the court. Even his teammates afterward declared it was time for Curry to sit out and get his ankle right. He missed eight games.

He returned to action on January 20, after fifteen days of rest and rehab. It was the longest stretch he'd ever sat out. Then coach Mark Jackson was extra conservative, holding Curry out even after he felt he was ready to go. Seven weeks later, in a home game against Dallas, Curry dribbled to his right on the perimeter. He stubbed his toe and sprained his ankle again and had to leave the game. It was his fourth sprain since the off-season surgery that was supposed to have cured his ankle troubles.

Curry played the next night but was clearly limited. Three minutes into the second half, Jackson pulled Curry for good. Those nine minutes, thirteen seconds he totaled against the Clippers would be the last he played all season. He worked to get back into action before the final game. But two days later, the Warriors pulled off a blockbuster trade—getting center Andrew Bogut for Ellis and backup big men Ekpe Udoh and Kwame Brown.

The trade decimated the Warriors' roster, as it shipped out three players and got one unhealthy one in return. Bogut was already out for the season with a fractured left ankle. In executing the trade, the Warriors all but stuck a fork in the strike-shortened 2011–12 season, robbing the incentive for Curry to return.

That didn't stop him from trying. He was still rehabbing, still lobbying, still trying to convince the team to put him back on the court. The Warriors weren't sniffing the postseason, and the roster was filled out with NBA Development League call-ups. This was the time for most veterans to shut it down, embellish their late-season aches to start their vacation early.

It wasn't until April 18, after their sixth straight loss, that Curry finally gave up the battle. Five games remained in the season, but Curry wasn't healed enough to take the three-game road trip. He was hoping to make that trip, a last-ditch effort to put his ankle issues behind him. Because if he could play, it would prove that he would be back to himself eventually. He needed at least *that* victory.

But when he wasn't cleared, that left him just the final two meaningless home games. Even he couldn't argue the decision to shut him down.

"I wanted to go out and get some minutes, test it out and feel confident going into next season that the ankle's going to hold up," Curry said.

A week after Curry learned he was done for the year, he was holed up in a sterile room with French vanilla walls in Van Nuys, California, praying with his father and his agent, Jeff Austin.

Getting examined by Dr. Richard Ferkel, and knowing they had done everything—rest, building up other muscles to take the pressure off his ankle, different wrapping techniques, custom shoes—led to fears Curry would need ankle reconstruction. If so, that was career-threatening.

Replacing damaged ligaments with new ones is risky for a player that thrives on change of direction and sudden bursts. Not only would he have been out at least six months, but there was no guarantee he would get back his same range and explosiveness after such a major surgery.

Ferkel couldn't have known without cutting the ankle open. So Curry went into surgery not knowing if he was done with basketball. Or if he would be facing soul-challenging rehabilitation to try to salvage his career on a reconstructed ankle. Complications are always a possibility. Many potentially Hall of Fame–bound players, from Grant Hill to Penny Hardaway, are proof.

But when Curry returned to consciousness, he got the best news possible. All Ferkel had had to do was clean out debris. This was a relatively minor procedure and an incredible outcome. Curry just needed time to heal, more rehabilitation, and he would be ready for training camp. And his motivation was at an all-time high.

Curry's ego had been thoroughly bruised by how easily he was written off. Yeah, he was talented. But he was deemed fragile, injury prone. His repeated ankle issues had put him in a space he so vehemently despised: being seen as weak. You tell Curry he can't do it, that the road is too tough, and it only incites him to go harder.

Curry recovered from surgery in time for training camp. But Jackson brought him along slowly, holding him out of the first preseason game and playing him sparingly in the second. He'd finally gotten up to his normal minutes when a freak accident led to another sprained ankle.

He was waiting for an inbounds pass when Wesley Matthews crept up from behind to steal the ball. In the process, he kicked Curry's right heel while the Warriors' guard's toe was planted, spraining his ankle again.

Curry hobbled off the court once more. But he and the trainers were encouraged. It had taken a significant kick to sprain it; this was not a phantom sprain. And it held up pretty well despite how severe it looked. Curry even tried to get back in the game, though Jackson shut that down.

Two days later, several Warriors accepted Jackson's invitation to attend his congregation. Jackson was the co-pastor of True Love Worship Center International in Van Nuys.

A part of the tradition at Jackson's church was a spirited service including worshippers jogging along the walls of the congregation in praise. Curry, two days removed from his latest sprain, found himself taking laps with Jackson and the other members filled with the spirit. Then after Jackson's sermon, his wife and co-pastor, Desiree, continued the worship with an impromptu sermon and benediction. She also called Curry to the altar.

They took off his shoes and socks, anointed his ankle with oil and prayed for healing. The parishioners lifted their voices in chants and amens, calling on God to bless one of His Christian ambassadors. Service at Jackson's church was much more passionate and engaging than Curry was used to back in Charlotte. But he humbly accepted the blessing that was being offered and returned to his seat with a smile on his face.

"Where you going?" Desiree asked the star point guard in front of the congregation. Curry responded with his go-to look of bewilderment, a half smile and widened eyes. He thought he was supposed to return back among the flock when she was done.

"You don't get a blessing from the Lord and just walk off!" she shouted. "Show us you believe in the power of God."

It took Curry a second to understand what she meant. Then the old Bible stories rushed to his mind. Like when Jesus healed the lame man at the Pool of Bethesda, that man had to pick up his mat and walk. If he believed he was healed, he needed to show it.

So Curry started shimmying and hopping on his right foot, much to the delight of the congregation.

"I didn't know what else to do," Curry said.

Returning from surgery wasn't just a pride thing, either. Curry was due for an extension on his rookie contract, and his ankle issues ended up costing him, in essence, more than $29 million of NBA salary.

This is why Curry was the MVP and yet only the fifth highest paid player on the team in 2014–15. The $12.1 million he earned for the 2016–17 season is a career high, yet it is only the fourth highest on the team. His contract proved to be a deal for management as Curry outperformed it by a mile. The savings on Curry is how the Warriors were able to sign Andre Iguodala, and to re-sign Klay Thompson and Draymond Green to contract extensions, and get Kevin Durant. All of these could happen because Curry's contract turned out to be such a bargain. He isn't due for a new one until the summer of 2017. It will be massive, and four years late.

He signed a four-year, $44 million contract on Halloween of 2012. It was $4 million less than was given to then Denver guard Ty Lawson, who had been drafted eleven slots after Curry in 2009.

The prize of the draft that year, Blake Griffin, was the only player to get a maximum extension. He signed a five-year deal. Over the same four years Curry made $44 million, Griffin made more than $73 million.

Curry wasn't yet producing like a max player, but there was no question he had that kind of potential. Plus his hometown team, then the Charlotte Bobcats, would have definitely given Curry a max contract for the publicity alone. Curry is a beloved son in Charlotte. The assumption is the franchise would have paid top dollar to get him.

That reality, that Curry could be a high-level point guard and that at least one team would have done anything to get him, made letting Curry become a free agent a risk for the Warriors. Still, he was fresh off his second ankle surgery, and the team wasn't going to give him a huge deal without knowing if his ankle would hold up.

The Warriors were taking a risk by offering Curry a four-year deal. If his ankle issues weren't solved, he would be the latest in a line of bad contracts the team had doled out over the years, the very kind of contracts new general manager Bob Myers was trying to avoid.

Curry's choice: take the four years of security or test the market—and his ankle—in a year. If he didn't sign the extension, he would have been a restricted free agent at the end of the season. Charlotte or any other team would have had the chance to jump on him. But that came with risk. If Curry got hurt again during the 2012–13 season, if his season was marred by sprains and ended with him on the bench, he could do more damage to his value.

Curry had made it to this point by betting on himself. But this time, he took the guarantee. Knowing he could end up worth much more than $44 million on the market, he opted for four years of salary security. Not even he was certain of what to make of his right ankle.

But in another sense, he had already won. Getting the Warriors to offer him a four-year deal paying $11 million per year proved he had overcome. Six months earlier, he was in a hospital gown with his career up in the air, yet he still managed to land a long-term contract.

Curry still wasn't done with his ankle issues. But he had even more reason to not be conquered by them. His desire to play wasn't extinguished by the money. Instead, the thirst to prove his worth was only intensified. On top of the normal chip on his shoulder was motivation to reward the Warriors for their loyalty.

Curry made it three months without another sprain. Then, on January 15, 2013, at a shootaround, he went for a rebound and landed on the foot of Warriors center Festus Ezeli, which cost him two games. Then, on the 28th, in Toronto, he landed on the foot of Ed Davis to re-aggravate the injury. Curry was again in that place, limping, trying to will his way back onto the court. But Jackson refused. Curry missed two more games.

The real adversity came in the Warriors' first postseason appearance. In Game 2 in the first round of the series against Denver in the 2013 NBA Playoffs, Curry came to a sudden stop at a double-team and sprained his left ankle. It wasn't the surgically repaired ankle, but the sight of Curry limping on the court, trying to work away the pain, was enough to terrify the fan base.

Curry had rolled it pretty good, too. It needed rest. But the Warriors had just upset the Nuggets to take control of the series. They were returning home for their first playoff game at Oracle in six years. He refused to miss it. He was going to do whatever it took, and the stakes were high enough that Jackson was allowing it this time.

Around-the-clock treatment, cortisone shots to numb the pain, easy defensive assignments. Whatever it took. The Warriors won the series, pulling off the upset and advancing to the next round.

Curry tweaked his left ankle again in the second round against San Antonio. He played ten more games after the first sprain, and became increasingly less himself with each game.

But he was on the court. That's what mattered to him most. He couldn't stand not being on the court.

Curry played at least seventy-eight games in four seasons straight. He played eighty in 2014–15. He was shooting to play in all eighty-two, a personal milestone to eradicate all doubts about his durability. Fully healthy, he had the best season of his career and led the Warriors to a championship, the franchise's first since 1975. The ankle issues seemed fully behind him.

But the 2016 playoffs saw a return to the injury-prone Curry. Injuries are included in the grind of winning a championship. Part of the challenge of the grueling NBA season is staying healthy.

The Warriors caught injury breaks throughout their 2015 run to the title. The opposing starting point guard in each round was either knocked out with an injury or still hobbled from a recent injury. The Cavaliers were without Kyrie Irving and Kevin Love, both starters, leaving LeBron James with a limited supporting cast in the 2015 Finals.

The scales balanced in 2016. And the injury bug hit the Warriors' most important player. He sustained two injuries in this postseason and was never himself even when he came back. Eventually, it caught up with the Warriors and they lost the championship.

Curry's injury in the first round was relatively minor. He took a fadeaway jumper and landed awkwardly, tweaking his right foot. He was pulled in the second half and was held out of Game 2. Curry was expecting to play Game 3 in Houston. But Steve Kerr was playing it safe and sat Curry so he could get more practice time in first.

The Warriors lost Game 3 without Curry. He returned for Game 4, in time to prevent the Rockets from turning the series into a nail-biter. But just before the end of the first half, the whole season suddenly looked in jeopardy.

In the final seconds of the second quarter, Rockets guard Trevor Ariza was angling up the court looking for a last-second shot. Curry was covering James Harden until he saw Ariza dribbling uncontested, so Curry switched over to pick up Ariza. Rockets big man Donatas Motiejūnas was running up the court and tripped, sliding from near half-court all the way to the free throw line. He left a trail of sweat.

Following Ariza led Curry right into Motiejūnas's slime. Curry, scrambling to prevent an open 3, had his left foot slip from under him. His legs split apart. He lost his balance. His right knee bent inward and banged on the hardwood. Right above the 3-point line, Curry rolled over holding his right knee, in obvious pain. The MVP was down and it didn't look good.

Curry asked Brandon Rush to help him to his feet. The Warriors' title hopes limped straight to the locker room.

He'd never had a knee injury before, but he knew this kind of pain wasn't a good sign. He knew how fast and large it had swollen meant that something serious happened beneath the surface. The trainers immediately ruled out a torn ACL with their preliminary test. Their initial prognosis was a sprained right MCL, but they couldn't know for sure without an MRI. Curry's heart couldn't handle that news. His psyche wasn't ready for this kind of disappointment.

He had fought so hard to get back on the court. Now he was out again.

The Warriors were so superior to the Houston Rockets, they didn't need Curry to beat them. But it looked as if the Blazers— who advanced to the second round thanks to injuries to two Clippers stars—had a shot to upset the Warriors without Curry, who sat and watched the first three games of the series.

This stint sitting out conjured bad memories of darker times.

He returned to action in Game 4 against Portland, coming off the bench for the first time in four years. His rustiness and limitations showed. Through three quarters, Curry played twenty-two minutes. He missed two-thirds of his eighteen shots, including all nine of his 3-point attempts.

Curry is what Kerr calls a rhythm player. He lives on feel and energy, reading and reacting. It's why being physical with him is an effective defense because it robs him of his normal flow. But this time, his rhythm was being interrupted from within. He'd missed six of the first eight playoff games and totaled just over thirty-eight minutes in the two games he did play. The medial collateral ligament in his right knee was stable but not all the way recovered. But Curry would have to make up for it with his will.

Late in the fourth quarter, Curry found his rhythm. He had to. Backup point guard Shaun Livingston was ejected late in the second quarter after picking up back-to-back technical fouls. Something that is almost unheard of for the laid-back Livingston. Curry's minutes limit was out the window and Damian Lillard, one of a few NBA guards able to match Curry basket for basket, surged his Blazers into the lead. This series was in real danger of shifting to an all-out nail-biter. A third straight loss in Portland, dating back to the regular season, would have put all the pressure on the top-seeded Warriors.

But with two minutes left in the fourth quarter, Curry curled off a Draymond Green screen and leaned into a pull-up 3-pointer. After a Lillard jumper, it was clear Curry had found his groove. Curry strung together six crossover dribbles, eluding several swipes from Blazers shooting guard C. J. McCollum in front of him, then zipped a left-handed pass to Green for a tomahawk dunk. It was the first time he had looked like himself since before his first injury in Game 1. The adrenaline of being back, of being in a tightly contested game, of yet another back-and-forth showdown with Lillard, helped Curry overcome the rust and mobility issues. It propelled him to one of the signature moments of his career.

The game went into overtime when Curry's floater off the glass missed the mark as the buzzer sounded. He clapped his hands under the basket from the blown opportunity. But Curry was just getting started.

He began overtime with a forceful drive left and a sudden pull-up, banking it in with one hand from just outside the paint. It was as bouncy as he'd looked all night. After Portland ran off 5 straight points to take a 3-point lead, Curry looked for his shot again. He pump-faked a 3-pointer, getting his defender in the air, then passed it to Festus Ezeli—who handed it off right back, and

Curry stuck the open look and tied the game. He was clearly in takeover mode.

The next time down, Curry snuck behind the defense to snag an offensive rebound from Portland big man Mason Plumlee, dropping it back in for 2 more points and flexing his biceps as he ran back on defense. A steal by Green led to a breakaway layup for Curry, who outraced everybody for the easy finger roll.

After a Portland miss, Curry came back down, veered left off a screen from Green. He was wide open, thanks to a lapse from Blazers forward Al-Farouq Aminu, and Curry stuck the 3-pointer. It was the fourth straight possession Curry had scored, 10 points in a minute and thirty seconds. With the Moda Center crowd gasping in awe, Curry walked away like a hero in an action movie.

"I'm here," he shouted after an abbreviated shimmy.

Followed by: "I'm back," pointing emphatically to the hardwood beneath him with each syllable. "I'm back."

And he wasn't done. With the Warriors up 5 and just over a minute left, Curry put the Blazers to bed in dramatic fashion. Another pick-and-roll with Green had Aminu back on him. Curry dribbled left then got free with an around-the-back dribble to his right. He stepped back into a twenty-five-footer and drilled it. Another collective gasp consumed the arena.

It was a jaw-dropping performance even for a player who regularly dropped jaws. Curry has scored 20 points in a quarter before in the playoffs. He's scored 40 in a playoff game before. But this was different. He scored 17 points in overtime, the most ever in any NBA game. While coming back from an injury, in a hostile environment where the Warriors had struggled, against a competent rival in Lillard. This was a moment, the kind that becomes part of NBA lore.

"Can you believe this?" Curry said as he walked to the locker room. "No words."

In many ways, though, this performance wound up working against him. The truth is, Curry's knee had progressed enough to get him back on the court. But he wasn't fully back. With adrenaline and a relatively soft Blazers' defense, however, the bar had been set.

Eventually, the limitations of his right knee became obvious. As the playoffs grew on, and the defenses got tougher, Curry's tendencies revealed that he wasn't 100 percent.

The Thunder turned up the aggressiveness. Stocked with athletes, they made him feel the pressure on the perimeter. And it was clear Curry didn't have his full arsenal. Oklahoma City blitzed him on pick-and-rolls—forcing him to pass the ball—and, far too much for Kerr's liking, deflected his passes. The Warriors invite the double-team because it left Green with a four-on-three as he attacked the defense.

If the scheme worked well, Curry ended up with an opposing big man switched onto him. Normally, that is a favorable matchup for Curry. Most big men aren't used to chasing guards on the perimeter.

Curry's fancy dribbling, sudden jerks, and quick release leave larger defenders struggling to predict what's going to happen. If they press up, a good crossover with a direction shift usually gets him past. If they stay back, a step-back 3-pointer is usually on the menu. And if he does give up the ball, he'll run the big men through a series of screens and get it back.

But the zip in Curry's crossovers was gone. The legs needed for deep 3s weren't there like normal. On top of that, the Thunder had some superior athletes up to the task. Serge Ibaka, a six-foot-nine power forward, with his long arms and quickness was able to keep Curry in front of him. Steve Adams, a seven-foot center, was able to smother the Warriors' guard, and he didn't have the burst to get away. And whenever Curry played off the ball, six-foot-seven defensive specialist Andre Roberson's mission in life was to affix himself to Curry's jersey.

With all of that comes grabbing, holding, and bumping away from the attention of the refs. Curry is trapped and blitzed and handled more than any guard in the league. The Western Conference Finals underscored just the amount of movement and misdirection Curry uses, largely because it was absent.

Cleveland ramped up the pressure even more. They played a smaller lineup so they could switch on every screen. Tristan Thompson and LeBron James were even better at tracking Curry on the perimeter.

Another element both the Thunder and the Cavaliers employed: going at Curry's defense. The Warriors' point guard is great in the team defense setting and has some skills that serve him well on that end—quick hands, underrated toughness, good instincts. But though he is better than most think, he still can be exploited for his lack of size. And even though he held his own more than not, the weight of being under attack either got him in foul trouble or sapped some of his energy.

A perfect storm of factors had rendered him ineffective: aggressive swarming defense from the opponents, the physicality allowed by the refs, an offensive scheme that never adjusted, and a right knee that had him noticeably less than 100 percent.

As the playoffs progressed, Curry became more of a specialist than the dynamic offensive player who dominated the NBA. His interior scoring diminished considerably, and he spent most of his possessions heaving 3-pointers. It was painfully obvious for Warriors fans watching him play that he just wasn't anywhere near his normal self.

While he is most recognized as the best shooter in league history, that has never been what made Curry dominant. It's always been the variety of ways he can hurt a defense. His shooting is but the anchor of a multifaceted arsenal that makes him such a dangerous offensive weapon. His 3-pointers force teams to press up on him, and his ball-handling and shiftiness counters by getting into the lane. Inside the paint, Curry's shooting genius makes him one of the best finishing guards in the league despite his lack of vertical explosiveness. He also has great vision and passing ability, so he can find his teammates from within the teeth of the defense.

This had become the model for his success: either raining bombs on opposing defenses or dicing them up inside as they tried to take away the defense. But that Curry was missing. There was no dicing, no zipping between double-teams, no wrong-footed floaters. He became one-dimensional and much more defendable.

In the last two rounds of the playoffs, Curry lived and died by the 3. Of his shots in those fourteen games, 59.5 percent were from behind the arc. On top of that, only 12.5 percent of his attempts were from inside five feet, way down from the regular season, when it was 29.7 percent.

After each game, he'd sit at his locker, taking his time getting dressed, and unpackaging his right knee. The tape was heavily layered, like his fragile knee was being shipped overseas. The gauze created a pentagon around his bare kneecap, exposing the redness and puffiness that didn't match his left knee.

Through it all, Curry refused to take the out his injury was giving him. Pride and gratitude shut down dialogue about his knee. Curry is usually willing to break down an injury, explain what's happening. He likes that inside-the-game type of conversation. He could tell you about every ligament in his ankle, the meaning behind the different types of pain, and in what ways he'll be limited. But about this injury, all he would say is "I'm fine" and "I need to play better."

His pride wouldn't let him even sound like he was making an excuse for his poor play. Curry grew up on the NBA. He knows how this works. For the great ones, injuries aren't impediments but context in the case for their greatness. Michael Jordan carried his team despite food poisoning. Kobe Bryant treated broken fingers like paper cuts. Allen Iverson should have been in a body cast and yet he was still driving the lane. That's just what greats do.

And Curry wasn't about to provide fodder for naysayers to call him weak. He's been fighting the soft label his whole career, and that battle was still being fought every time he was asked about his knee.

Also his gratitude wouldn't let him complain. This was what he wanted, to be in the action. Focusing on what he couldn't do on the court, giving credence to his suboptimal knee, would have been akin to scoffing at his blessing. Because when he was shedding tears in front of the bench, he wasn't hoping for 100 percent. When he was praying before his MRI results, it wasn't for his knee to be perfect.

He just wanted to play.

The knee injury not being recovered eventually took its toll. Curry was able to play because he couldn't do further damage. He just had to tolerate the pain. But his mobility was increasingly an issue.

He couldn't make the sharp cuts that are so critical to his game. He couldn't change direction on a dime, his method for getting free of defenders. But he could run. And he could shoot. And that was enough.

Because when you've been through what he has, being on the court is the gift.

Curry Hate

o   o   o

"For him to be that first player to get that unanimously, I think it tells you how watered-down our league is."

—Tracy McGrady

CHAPTER 8

Kevin Durant, after a pair of free throws, drilled a 3-pointer from a few shades right of the top of the key. A wave of nervousness swooshed through Oracle Arena. The Warriors' 13-point lead was cut to 5 in just over a minute's span. Worse, Durant had that look in his eye, the bounce in his step of an all-time great ready to put on his cape. Down three games to one in the 2016 Western Conference Finals, the Warriors' season had never looked more on the brink. And few things terrified Warriors fans more than Durant in rhythm. He had burned their beloved many times before. Two more free throws gave him 9 points in the fourth quarter, 35 for the game, with four minutes remaining in the Warriors' season.

But a series of unexpected events stubbed Durant's wave of momentum.

First, Curry hustled to get a hand up on Durant's 3-pointer from the top of the key, robbing him of an open look. Durant missed badly off the right side of the rim. The Thunder got the rebound and the ball made its way to Durant again, and Curry ended up back in front of the six-foot-eleven former MVP. This time, Durant drove the lane and tried a floater over his smaller defender. But Curry stripped him on the way up, his quick hands striking before Durant could take advantage of those everlasting arms. Andrew Bogut then swatted the ball away from Durant and Curry scooped up the loose ball. Defensive stop complete.

Oklahoma City, down 8 with a minute and a half remaining, had one last-ditch effort to threaten the Warriors. Durant came off a down-screen and popped back toward the top of the key. Curry switched onto him again. Determined, Durant put his head down and dribbled forcefully toward the rim, dipping his left shoulder into Curry's chest. But Curry timed Durant's dribbles and, with another quick swipe, knocked the ball away. Curry scooped up the ball and pushed it the other way. He crossed half-court and slowed it down, eating up the clock and letting the Oracle crowd's cheers serenade the Warriors.

Curry, caught up in the intensity of the moment, pounded his chest twice while screaming to himself and dribbling away the seconds. He capped the highlight play by driving around Thunder center Steven Adams and scooping in a reverse layup. The dagger.

Curry ran down the sidelines as the building erupted and the Thunder called a timeout. He stopped near half-court and screamed into the sea of yellow.

"We ain't going home! We ain't going home!"

Curry scored 9 straight points for the Warriors. But that wasn't what made this ending unique. Nor was it that the Warriors stayed alive with a Game 5 win. The surprise of this ending was the three possessions in crunch time that Curry stopped Durant. It was the diminutive guard known as a poor defender who thrice thwarted one of the game's most elite scorers.

It was enough for one of the postgame questions to include the subject of Curry's defense. Durant and Thunder guard Russell Westbrook, on the interview podium together as usual, were asked if Curry was an underrated defender.

Westbrook laughed.

Actually, it was more of a snicker that burped out spontaneously, and lingered. He buried his face behind his hand, eventually revealing his grin as he scratched his jaw. This wasn't a knee-slapping laugh as if he'd just heard a joke. This was an "Are you kidding me?" laugh. Westbrook didn't hear anything funny. He heard something ridiculous. The audacity of the question prompted his chuckle.

Durant answered with words, finding the most respectful way he could to disagree with the premise of the question.

Durant had been friendly with Curry over the years, and he did what you expect competitors to do. Some are willing to offer up admiration in the heat of battle, and maybe Durant would have, had Westbrook's laughter not preempted him. But the former MVP was certainly going to back up his teammate. Durant walked the fine line between not praising his opponent while also not disrespecting him.

"I mean, getting steals . . . that's a part of playing defense," Durant said with Westbrook on the podium next to him. "But he's pretty good. But he doesn't guard the best point guards. I think they do a good job of putting a couple of guys on Russell from Thompson to Iguodala, and Steph, they throw him in there sometimes. He moves his feet pretty well. He's good with his hands. But, you know, I like our matchup with him guarding Russ."

Westbrook, on the other hand, mocked Curry. He didn't offer his foe the courtesy afforded in the NBA brotherhood. He dismissed Curry.

Part of that, most of it, was likely Westbrook's fiery approach to basketball. He is an angry competitor who throws etiquette out the door in pursuit of winning. Curry and Westbrook have been going at it for years, too. They are rivals playing the same position and their teams were in a classic showdown. So Westbrook not heaping praise on Curry wasn't a problem, nor was it alarming.

But he laughed. That's what angered the Warriors locker room behind the scenes. That's what prodded Curry. Nobody was upset that Durant basically said Curry wasn't a good defender. The question making its rounds in the bowels of Oracle after the game was "Did you see Westbrook laugh at Curry?"

Westbrook and Curry didn't seem to have any personal beef from off the court. But this was another moment where some of the growing resentment of Curry in NBA circles bubbled to the surface.

A reporter was trying to get Westbrook to give Curry credit for something, and Westbrook didn't think Curry deserved it. He thought the idea was laughable, and he had zero reservations about conveying his feelings about it.

Yes, Westbrook is a rough-around-the-edges kind of person who isn't interested in hiding his standoffish tendencies, especially not in the heat of a series. But this wasn't the first or last time he took a shot at Curry.

A commercial for the Jordan brand attempted to introduce Westbrook as a superstar, "the new big bang." The monologue included a thinly veiled shot at the Warriors' point guard.

"Clear the area. Clear the lane. He ain't playing games. He got zero time for your hugs and your dap. What y'all expect? Another choirboy running point?"

That was a harmless, clever marketing ploy. But Westbrook's progression from a playful jab about him coming for the MVP to laughing at him on a nationally televised podium paralleled the rise in Curry's disapproval ratings.

Westbrook is representative of a contingent of NBA insiders and fans who rebel against the rampant Curry love. He is blatant enough to let it show, but Westbrook is not alone. And the final straw, the moment that made vocalizing this resentment trendy, came on May 10, 2016.

The day after his epic performance at Portland in Game 4, the NBA announced that Curry was the MVP for the second consecutive season, joining an elite group of NBA legends. But that wasn't the only history Curry made. He was also the first ever to win the award with a unanimous vote. Each of the 131 media members who voted for the award had Curry as their top choice, the first time in sixty-one years of balloting that all of the voters agreed on the MVP.

The reasons were legitimate. The Warriors won seventy-three

games, eclipsing the regular season wins record set by the 1995–96 Chicago Bulls. On top of that, Curry put together a season like the NBA hadn't seen before, jumping his average from 23.8 to 30.1 points per game by shooting a higher percentage.

Also, the NBA started revealing the ballot results, including names of voters, in 2014. That along with the popularity of social media has put a consequence on unpopular votes, no doubt pressuring voters into making a safe pick. In 2013, LeBron James came one vote shy of a unanimous MVP, and that voter was heavily criticized for not falling in line with the obvious consensus of James being MVP.

Still, the reasons didn't matter. What mattered was that Curry became the first in the modern era to receive such an honor. Not Larry Bird. Not Shaquille O'Neal. Not LeBron James. All of them had come close. Both O'Neal and James had been one vote shy.

And the real kicker: Michael Jordan was never a unanimous MVP. Curry getting honors not bestowed upon the unofficial greatest of all time was just too much for many to take. He already, for two years prior, had gotten more hype than any athlete in the NBA. Curry became the poster child of the league, the golden boy of a global brand.

His face was plastered everywhere. His game was revered by experts and casual fans. Even his shoe sales were beating out the industry elites. A Morgan Stanley analyst said Curry's shoes were outselling everyone but Michael Jordan and Curry was worth $14 billion to Under Armour. Everything he touched turned to gold. In December 2015, Google announced that Curry was the number one trending player in the NBA for 2015 and the Warriors were the top trending team. In January 2016, the NBA announced that Curry had the highest-selling jersey in the league again. The next month, a BuzzFeed report cited YouTube data in dubbing Curry the most popular athlete on YouTube, with over 140 million views in six months.

In April 2016, the website FiveThirtyEight.com detailed how

the Warriors drew more than three times the traffic that any other team did on ESPN's online NBA hub. In May, *SportsPro* magazine named Curry the most marketable athlete in the world.

But many of his peers, who represent a sizeable segment of fans, don't believe he deserved all that.

"I'm not in the business of ranking or debating who is what," Curry barked from the podium when a question pitted him against LeBron. "At the end of the day it's about winning and the fact that we won a championship last year and were the last team standing. It's really annoying for me to be—that's not what I'm playing for, to be the face of the NBA or to be this or that or to take LeBron's throne or whatever. I'm trying to chase rings, and that's all I'm about."

The irritation with Curry's rampant popularity is due to a multitude of factors but can be encompassed in this one umbrella reality over them all: Curry was never supposed to be here.

The lofty perch on which he sits, as one of the game's elite players and bound for the Hall of Fame, is a violation of the usual protocol on several levels. It attacks the standards already established in most basketball minds. It also illustrates some of the social issues still evident in society. And it all happened so fast, most haven't had a chance to process their cringing reactions.

Many certainly haven't processed this fact: none of the hype is Curry's doing.

Curry was reared in NBA practices. He was big brothered by NBA players since he could make a basket. He is an heir to the exclusive fraternity, and that position is among the most sacred values to Curry. He is meticulous about not violating the codes that have been ingrained in him through affiliation. That's why he refuses to take shots at his fellow players or air behind-the-scenes grievances.

When he was a rookie, star guard Monta Ellis declared on the first day of the 2009–10 training camp that the Warriors couldn't win with Curry and Ellis. He hadn't played a game yet and a teammate was throwing shade his way. As the season began, Curry and Ellis had a chilly relationship. The Warriors told Ellis they wouldn't draft a point guard, that he was their guy. Then Curry fell to the Warriors at No. 7 and all that changed. Ellis, bitter at the organization, took it out on the rookie.

Whenever Curry—the giddy new rookie from a mid-major college dripping with the sappiness of team unity and camaraderie—checked into the game and replaced Ellis, he would stick his hand out to slap a five with his veteran teammate. It's a common practice for the players swapping places to encourage each other with high five or a pat. But whenever Curry reached, he was met with air. Ellis wouldn't reciprocate. This went on for some time.

When asked about it privately, Curry—surprised that someone had noticed—made a friendly wager that he would get his high five. What most would see as a sign of disrespect, Curry saw as a chance to prove himself. He set out to win over Ellis, and the high five would be the symbol that he'd succeeded. He embraced the challenge because that was what rookies were supposed to do—take crap from veterans and overcome. It was a rite of passage into his father's league. And when he got the high five from Ellis, he playfully celebrated on the low before play resumed.

Curry's allegiance to the fraternity is most present in his overt appreciation for being grouped with the other stars. He cherishes any of those moments where he is one of the boys, rubbing shoulders as one of the game's elite. That's how he saw it play out as a kid behind the curtain, the appreciation fellow stars had for one another, the relationships that transcended the battles on the court.

After the Warriors eliminated the Thunder, Durant remained on the court and shared a hug and some words with the Warriors' stars he'd battled against for seven games. He and Curry found each other near center court.

Curry was looking for Westbrook so they could have that moment, too, but Westbrook was a quick departure.

"This is what it's all about," Curry said he whispered to Durant. "This is what we play for. Those battles, those moments people will remember for a long time."

He lives for those moments. It's why he loved his Team USA experiences and was crushed to be left off the 2012 Olympic team, and disappointed his knee injury forced him to skip the 2016 Olympics. That's why, though the players had voted against him as MVP eight months earlier, Curry was the most hyped guy on the sidelines at the 2016 All-Star Game in Toronto. He ran and jumped around and celebrated his fellow stars like they were his Warriors teammates.

Even now, while the NBA has made it a blueprint to rough him up, Curry refuses to fully embrace flopping. It's a rampant part of the league, embellishing contact to draw fouls. If Curry did it, he would get to the free throw line much more, racking up even more points and making it a risky endeavor for opponents to rough him up. But Curry bucks against it. He's begun trying to draw fouls on 3-pointers, and he complains to the referees like every other NBA player. But with the contact he receives, he could go full James Harden. But that would violate the unwritten rules of nineties basketball on which he was weaned. It would be an attack on how he was groomed to play, and it would give cause to further questioning of his membership.

Curry is stubborn enough to prefer fighting through it, proving his toughness and collecting bonus points for enduring. He began the 2016–17 season determined to attack the basket.

This is a lot about acceptance, about Curry wanting it and about factions in the fraternity and the fan base not granting it. That's the irony of the backlash against Curry. He got to this level of greatness because of his relentless pursuit of acceptance into this elite company, to have his birthright validated. And his pursuit worked so well that it's causing the rejection he worked to avoid.

In some respects, it's not possible to get as popular as Curry without detractors, no matter the reason for the detraction. What Curry faces is no different than what every other elite player has faced. That's another reason he is particular about not complaining. The hate, too, is a rite of passage. Handling the criticism and the naysayers according to the code is how he solidifies his acceptance.

That's why he refused to take the out his injured knee gave him late in the playoffs. That's why when asked about the verbal exchange between him and Westbrook in the Western Conference Finals, and he and LeBron James in the Finals, Curry declined to reveal what was said and wrote it off publicly as the typical heat of competition. He is just not going to do anything to betray his place in the fraternity of greats.

Curry's embrace could come in due time. It may take longevity to fully appreciate him. The unspoken sentiment behind all of the Curry criticism from current and former players is "Let's hold off on anointing Curry the G.O.A.T." Maybe if he proves he is not a flash in the pan, as he gets to the other side of his prime having weathered it all, he will be appreciated by the fraternity. The same collective has heaped more praise on less deserving players. They've always loved players like Chris Paul and Carmelo Anthony, who have played much longer but still haven't accomplished what Curry has by winning MVP, winning a championship, and expanding the game commercially. But perhaps over time, when the documentaries are done, Curry will be revered as one of the greats en masse by the society of NBA players.

He is not there yet. For the better part of two years, it was clear he wasn't overwhelmingly welcomed. Eventually, many were forced to finally concede he was the greatest shooter they'd seen—a major concession considering, to let nineties players tell it, the likes of Reggie Miller and Larry Bird never missed. Even that title comes with a "but" and serves as a glass ceiling on Curry.

When he won his first MVP, it was discounted by many because his team was loaded, then his colleagues went out and voted

James Harden their MVP. Curry came back with a vengeance, played even better to prove himself. When he won his second MVP, he was chided because he won it unanimously. And then in the Finals, when he played poorly and was upstaged by LeBron James, his failure was proof for his detractors.

Curry isn't the first star to fail on the biggest stage of the Finals. But perhaps no other MVP's failures were met with such glee. Of course, no MVP has played as poorly as Curry did in a decisive Game 7. Still, his struggles were received by many like the fall of a villain.

To understand the hesitancy to embrace Curry as one of the all-time elite, even in NBA circles, requires comprehending a bunch of factors. Many of them Curry has been dealing with for years. His fight for acceptance began as soon as it became clear he was good at hoop.

"He's been dealing with it all his life," Seth Curry said. "We both have. We've always had to prove ourselves. Whatever the reasons, my dad played in the NBA or our looks or whatever, people thought it was going to go a certain way against us. And every time we'd have to show them it wasn't."

Strike one against Curry: being the son of an NBA player.

On the surface, it would seem that having a professional basketball player as a father would give a player a certain credibility. But having that on the résumé doesn't scream pedigree as much as it screams privilege.

Basketball, started by a Canadian with a peach basket, has long since been an inner city pastime. That isn't to say it is exclusive to those parts. No doubt, the game is enjoyed by and belongs to the rural, the urban, the suburban, and the wealthy. But for decades now, basketball has been to the inner city what baseball is to America. It doesn't require money to play, just a rim and a ball. It can be played with two players or twenty. One can even engage alone. It's the perfect sport for the have-nots. And since the days of Jordan, it has been adopted religiously by the hip-hop community.

Many of today's players, and those of yesteryear, were born under this basketball paradigm. They were raised in urban blights. They forged themselves from nothing. A high level of respect is automatically granted to those cut from that cloth.

Curry, though, represents privilege. He was the kid crossing the tracks into the inner city for the good competition. The rich kid from the traditional family is going to always be met with skepticism in that urban world. Curry exemplifies that.

He embodies the players who learned the game in air-conditioned gyms, on manicured courts—he isn't supposed to be able to hang on the blacktop. He doesn't get the inherent credibility of those who cut their teeth playing against neighborhood bullies and ex-cons, against cats in denim jeans and work boots with no shirt, sweating out the heat of the summer. Curry's game is pretty. He isn't supposed to have the grit required to thrive in settings where the game is bruising and not beautiful. Curry represents those who had the smooth ride, who never had to play with busted shoes, who could afford fancy camps and travel tournaments. The automatic assumption is that he got access and attention because of money, because of his NBA father, and not because of his game.

Even how Curry presents himself is a picture of someone already familiar with big money. You don't see him in gaudy jewelry, blanketed in name-brand apparel. He doesn't have seven cars. You don't see him spending thousands in the VIP section of clubs. Splurging is normal behavior for those who come into large sums of money. It is a natural response to enjoy nice things when you come from nothing, to fortify your life in luxury when you've been swallowed up by poverty for so long.

That is not to say Curry doesn't enjoy luxury. He splurges like most rich people. He isn't driving around in a Camry. He has a private stylist and a millions-of-dollars California mansion. Many saw his daughter Riley's fancy new digs on an episode of TLC's *Playhouse Masters*. But Curry doesn't give off that new money vibe. It underscores the difference in background between him and his peers. Compounding matters: that difference leads to him being embraced by mainstream and corporate America, which fuels the resentment.

Curry has been attacking these perceptions for decades. And now, at the height of his career, they are still there. He is still a child of privilege in a sport dominated by the underprivileged, which means he will perpetually be met with a healthy dose of skepticism that he must first tear down.

For the most part, Curry does. He and his brother have been earning respect since they used to light up the YMCA in Charlotte. Still, they won't be revered by those who were raised impoverished.

Strike two against Curry: he's light-skinned.

It may seem silly on the surface, but skin tone is a deep-seated issue in African-American life. And many of the dignitaries, players, and fans who dissent from the popular opinion that Curry is amazing use the kind of coded language born of this intracultural phenomenon.

The intricacies of complexion in the African-American community are centuries old and layered in nuance. With apologies to the complex history of this topic, the best way to explain it is that those with lighter skin aren't always as readily embraced by those of darker skin due to perceptions developed through the generations. Curry falls into a group often deemed more attractive, more acceptable to the mainstream, and as a result more privileged.

As Michael Eric Dyson wrote about Curry for ESPN's *The Undefeated*, "Suspicion surrounds him because of his light skin, and because he's been lauded by both the NBA and media establishments. The subliminal message has become explicit: Curry is a brother we may not be able to embrace because the powers that be embrace him, too."

Another assumption that comes with brighter skin is weakness, founded on the idea that privilege has disconnected the light-skinned from the kind of struggles and disadvantages that toughen and harden.

And Curry is especially light, enough to distract from the kinky hair that illustrates his blackness.

In August 2014, in a promotional interview for the NBA 2K video game, Durant told a story from when he was ten years old. His AAU team had driven from the Washington, D.C., area to play in Charlotte. Durant entered the gym and saw a kid take a shot from near half-court. "He's not making that," Durant said he thought. Splash. The kid took another one. Splash.

The kid raining 3-point bombs was Stephen Curry.

"I thought he was white, but he was this yellow kid," Durant said as Curry and James Harden broke into laughter on the panel discussion. "I'm just being real now. Where I come from, we don't see the light-skinned guys where I come from. It's all guys like me."

Durant's tale was lighthearted and void of malice. But it does underscore how Curry's image immediately puts his blackness in question, which from the urban perspective that shapes many of the NBA minds, also puts his toughness into question.

On January 3, 2016, Los Angeles Lakers guard Jordan Clarkson posterized Phoenix center Alex Len. Clarkson drove the lane and, bouncing off two feet, dunked home a powerful tomahawk, cocking it back and slamming it forcefully past the swipe of the Suns' seven-footer. One clip of the highlight dunk has been looped nearly two million times.

When asked about the dunk, Clarkson—who is a shade darker than Curry—revealed the advice he'd gotten from Kobe Bryant.

"All I remember was Kobe telling me that I've been going to the hole like a light-skinned dude," Clarkson told reporters after the game. "So I've got to start doing it like a dark-skinned [dude]. So when I seen the lane opened up, that's all I remember."

Certain characteristics aren't automatically attributed to

African-Americans with lighter skin. That kind of credibility has to be earned, often by obliterating stereotypes. Westbrook sits perfectly in the middle of this war. But he eliminates any potential to be slighted with his overt aggression and demonstrative demeanor. Westbrook grimaces and flexes away whatever doubt there might be connected to his light-brown tone.

Curry, however, practically feeds his stereotypes. His dangling mouthpiece, comical celebrations, and pervasive smile on the court obscure the evidence that contradicts his soft label.

Many players are derided for being injury prone and not being able to play through injuries. But Curry has fought back from career-threatening ankle injuries, thrives as a smaller figure in a league of sizable players, and has yet to back down from a challenge. Yet he can't fully shake the reputation that he is soft. He plays defense better than many of the revered guards in the NBA. Shy of elite speed, Curry leans on his will and an underrated toughness. Yet he's deemed a poor defender, even though analytics suggest he's at least pretty good on that end.

Well trained in bucking perceptions, Curry is diligent about debunking stereotypes. Ball-hawking point guard Chris Paul gets really physical when he turns up the pressure on defense. He would overwhelm Curry, smothering him into turnovers, unless the referees called a foul. It was enough to force then coach Mark Jackson to take Curry off the ball late in games against the Clippers, letting Jarrett Jack run the point and running Paul off a series of screens to get Curry free.

Curry responded by working on his physique, chiseling his body and strengthening his core. He got a Muscle Milk endorsement out of the deal and can also deadlift more than twice his weight. Paul can't overwhelm Curry physically anymore.

Draymond Green, who is bona fide hardcore, loves Curry in part because he has what NBA players call "dog" in him. Since his rookie year, Green has been going at his teammates in practice and mixing it up with the game's toughest players. When he was a rookie, Green denounced his veteran mentor because he felt the second-year big man was too soft. If he spots a player going against him who doesn't welcome his aggressiveness and physicality, Green gets excited and turns it up a notch.

Green is every bit as tough as his dark skin would stereotype him to be. And he will tell anyone who will listen about Curry's toughness.

"He is way tougher than people think," Green said. "Way, way tougher. I know people look at him and think a certain thing, he's soft or whatever. I hope people keep underestimating his toughness because he's going to keep proving them wrong."

Oscar Robertson, a Hall of Famer and certified legend, made waves when he said Curry thrives because the modern NBA defense is soft. Like all the former players who try to explain Curry's dominance of the NBA, Robertson suggested it was a matter of physicality. In their day, they would have pressed up on Curry, handled him. The implication was that Curry wouldn't have been able to handle it. The hand checks and elbows, the hard fouls and bumps in the lane, would have been an impediment for Curry's pretty style of play. The code in the explanation is Curry wouldn't have weathered the beatings, he wouldn't have braved the contact, wouldn't have had the mental toughness to figure out how to conquer the brute.

The fact is, Curry is the most trapped, blitzed, grabbed and held, roughed-up guard in the NBA. Indeed, the rules are different now. The current era emphasizes freedom of movement and favors the offensive part of the game. The seventies, eighties, and nineties allowed more force.

Even though 20 of the top 30 players with the most free throw attempts in NBA history spent their prime in the nineties or earlier—which shows they actually did call fouls before this "soft era"—old-school basketball was much too grueling, as is retold.

Oddly enough, Curry spends many of his court minutes playing shooting guard as the Warriors seek to take advantage of his shooting. He switches from a Steve Nash type to doing his best impression of Reggie Miller, juking around screens trying to lose defenders to get free for a shot. And since the ball isn't with Curry, neither is the keen attention of the officials, which means an incredible amount of holding and grabbing Curry has to fight through—just like Miller in the nineties.

And while some critics think Curry spends too much time off the ball, where he becomes a one-dimensional player who the defense is allowed to wear down with physicality, Curry has never complained to his coach about putting the ball back in his hands. Bigger players have publicly talked about not wanting to play center, but the diminutive guard shuts his mouth and runs his routes. He's likely very proud that he's never been fined for criticizing officials for the lack of fouls called on him away from the ball.

Yet that display of toughness doesn't warrant him credit among his predecessors. It doesn't stop a contingent of fans from deeming him weak.

To be sure, Curry being overpowered is certainly possible. In the end, he is six-foot-three, 180 pounds. Any talk of his strength comes with a "for his size" qualification. But if being overpowered by a bigger and stronger player is a knock, just about everybody who faced off with Shaquille O'Neal is soft. Curry, like others, isn't granted credit for being willing to mix it up, for continuously coming back at his foes. And his looks have something to do with it.

The color issue played out in unique fashion during the NBA Finals. Curry released a low-top version of his Curry Two signature shoes. They were absolutely destroyed on social media. They became a punch line. The running joke on Twitter and Instagram was to connect them to anything old, white, or style-challenged. A popular meme had Curry's shoes Photoshopped onto the feet of an elderly woman who had fallen and couldn't get up.

"I think it started out as just something easy to make fun of,"

Russ Bengtson, a sneaker aficionado and veteran NBA scribe, said. "There wasn't much else about Curry himself or the Warriors to ridicule. And then it just got out of hand. From my perspective, it was basically cyberbullying, only the 'victim' was a shoe. I definitely think people enjoyed it because it was Curry. He'd been more or less untouchable to that point."

Plenty of athletes release ugly shoes. Even the Jordan Brand, the shoe house of Michael Jordan, emperor of the sneaker community, has its fair share of misses. But the trouncing of Curry's shoe felt like something more, like an indictment of Curry. It was as if the shoes justified the skepticism about embracing him, as if they revealed that Curry was indeed an outsider appropriating inner city culture.

In the real world, the social media contingent ridiculing Curry's shoes is but a fraction of his audience. And these mediums—which allow for anonymity and not for accountability—are incubators for bullying, cruelty, and judgment.

Still, undoubtedly, an element of Curry hate was revealed. Like basketball, sneakers are a staple of urban life and hip-hop culture. The reaction to his shoe was but another way to reject Curry's membership.

Curry's addressing of the reaction to his shoe was right in line with his modus operandi: he responded in a way that might validate his membership. He didn't take a shot at the critics or dismiss their take. He didn't settle for the high road or dish out a company line.

Instead, Curry dished back in a way that let his critics know he was game for some back-and-forth. After the Warriors won Game 4 in Cleveland, taking a 3–1 series lead in the NBA Finals, he was asked about the criticism of his shoe. He doubled down. He said he wished he'd brought a pair with him on the road because he certainly would have worn them proudly. Curry stuck with his stance that he believed his shoes were hot and he wished he could show off, as he put it, "how fire they are."

It would have been easy to have hurt feelings, to respond from a place of insecurity and embarrassment. Instead, Curry embraced the banter and stood his ground. He even shared the joke about his shoes that he liked the best. Two days later, at practice in Oakland, he made sure to wear the shoes during media interviews. With a Sharpie, he wrote "Straight fire" on the top of his shoe and even hand-drew a red fire emoji.

That was Curry showing that he speaks the language, that he is willing to provide the validation for the acceptance he's denied. Just like he did with Monta Ellis. Of course, the spirit behind that humility leads to another factor for the MVPs' disapprovals.

Strike three against Curry: he has a wholesome image.

There is a reason they call him the Baby Faced Assassin. He needs a goatee to prove he has conquered adolescence. He is open about his Christianity and has a strong public presence with his family. There are two Instagram accounts—Team Curry Family and Curry Family Media—dedicated to posting pictures of the Currys. Combined, they have more than two thousand photos posted and more than 150,000 followers.

Privately, Curry doesn't like the Goody Two-shoes reputation. It's a setup, in his mind. The more "good" he is perceived to be, the more his demise will be anticipated, celebrated. And the slip-ups are inevitable because Curry's stance is that he's flawed like all humans. He isn't immune to struggles and weaknesses, a realization that has helped him avoid the common pitfalls of NBA players.

After a practice once, Curry was asked if it felt good to embarrass opponents. Because Curry is the quintessential nice guy off the court, the questioner wondered if he relishes the opportunity to be mean on the court. But Curry rejected the premise.

"That would imply that I'm never mean off the court," he said. "That's crazy. I have bad days, too."

His teammates have called him Golden Boy and monikers of that ilk. He accepts it, but he doesn't prefer it. Any situation that exalts him as holier than thou Curry tries to elude like it's a defender chasing him around the screen. Anyone who asks about his faith he will happily answer, but he avoids the grandiose proclamations and delights in the intimate actions away from the spotlight.

Curry was a sophomore in high school when Dwight Howard was drafted into the NBA straight out of his high school. He remembers Howard announcing his faith and how he'd evangelize the NBA. His nickname was "Choirboy" and he revealed dreams of the cross being part of the NBA logo. He spoke openly about his faith, his character, and his desire to change the lives of people.

That made Howard a target, and his spiritual declarations haven't panned out in the pros. Curry decided early that it wouldn't be his route. He delicately walks the line between being unashamed and unabashed. The problem for Curry, though, is that actions speak louder than words. His lifestyle makes him as much of a target as soapboxing would have.

There are no pictures of him in the club unless his wife is with him, no TMZ-worthy behaviors to his credit. His entourage is a close-knit and hard-to-crack inner circle that consists mostly of family, including his parents. And friends who are like family. And businesspeople who've been embraced into the family.

During NBA All-Star Weekend, Curry—like many players do—threw a party in Toronto. But his was much different than the norm. Most NBA players who were invited didn't show. Fabolous performed, and Drake, who's become a friend of the family over the last couple years, made an appearance. But the party was tame enough for the preteen son of Curry's middle school coach to indulge.

Curry's wholesomeness, though not self-professed, makes him beloved by many. Parents favor him because they prefer his example for their children. Corporations gravitate to him because, in seven years in the league, he's proved a safe endorser. The media loves him because he's perennially kind and his willingness to give interviews hasn't decreased with his growing fame.

In many ways, Curry has unwittingly fashioned himself as the anti-superstar, a contradiction to the caricature of NBA athletes that draws such disdain. He can't stand being pitted against his fellow players, but it happens. And because it does, he pays the price in the form of people hunting for his flaws. And this past season, it was open season.

In March of 2016, the North Carolina state legislature passed a new bill to prevent its municipalities from creating their own antidiscrimination laws. That was a big deal because it was in response to an ordinance passed by the city of Charlotte that allowed those who identify as transgender to use the restroom that corresponds with their gender identity.

The NBA staunchly opposed the new bill, which it viewed as discrimination against the LGBTQ community, and threatened to remove the 2017 All-Star Game from Charlotte. Naturally, Curry, a native of Charlotte, was sought for comment. It was just the kind of situation he sought to avoid—standing on a soapbox, having his Christianity on public trial.

Curry gave an answer that was intentionally not an answer.

"I know the NBA has a stance on equality and incorporating all the beliefs and people from all sorts of backgrounds," Curry said. "It's interesting how that intersection is with the state law and the NBA having an event there. Hopefully, the right things need to happen that the all-star game stays in Charlotte, because that would be huge for the city . . . just to show what Charlotte's all about, regardless of where you fall on that law. Hopefully they can figure it out and keep it there. I think it's really important for the city of Charlotte. I'm sure we can figure it out."

That statement was right in line with Curry's norm. Noncontroversial. Choreographed in a way where he doesn't upset his fellow Christians or insult the LGBTQ community. Curry likes to reside in these spaces, shielded from the expectations of others.

He is an expert at filling a tape recorder without saying much to prick ears. On such a polarizing topic especially, he was going to play it safe.

But his lack of a response didn't satisfy either side of the issue. And members of the LGBTQ community dug for dirt on Curry. They found disparaging comments about gays from the minister at his church in Charlotte and connected them to the reigning MVP. Next thing Curry knew, he was under attack. Even though the Warriors president Rick Welts, the first openly gay executive in professional sports, all but swears by Curry, he was suddenly being probed for bigotry.

It was enough to prompt Curry to speak again, clarifying his stance against discrimination of any form. It was also a sign of how big his name has gotten. His status was so high, he had to start bracing for a fall.

In the NBA Finals, during a timeout midway through the fourth quarter, the ABC cameras stuck on Curry walking to the bench. In the background, a voluptuous woman in yellow tights and a blue half top jumped off the screen. She appeared to be staring at Curry seductively, trying to get his attention. The image went viral with the woman being pegged as Curry's "side piece."

Never mind that Curry is happily married. Never mind that the woman has been coming to Warriors games for years and even traveled to road games during the playoffs—all with the same man. It spread across online gossip sites. In search of a potential Curry mistress, the identity of the woman was discovered: a model named Roni Rose. Her Instagram followers soared from the attention. It was almost as if many wanted Curry to have a mistress.

This is the blowback from being wholesome, especially when that reputation is born of religious origins. People who aren't buying it lock in on the cracks in his veneer.

"It's not that he is a Christian," said Walter Hoye, who has been a Warriors chaplain for years. "It's that he is trying to live it. That makes him a target. People don't understand the amount of pressure he is under. People are waiting for him to do wrong, and he is human so of course he will. It is a tremendous amount of pressure when people are waiting for you to make a mistake, hoping they find something wrong you are doing. He feels the pressure but he still fights to live it."

Game 6 of the NBA Finals proved to be a peak in the Curry hate. After two years of incomparable positivity, Curry detractors got an avalanche of material.

First, the Warriors were getting dominated, and Curry looked helpless to stop it. The Cavaliers jumped out to an 8–0 lead as The Q roared with a fury akin to an underground pit fight. Then, six minutes into the game, Curry picked up his second foul, delighting the fans and prompting coach Steve Kerr to bench him. This proved to be a costly decision.

The Warriors were down 8 at the time. By the end of the first quarter, they were down 31–11. The wheels had fallen off. The Warriors got down by as much as 24 in the third quarter, negating earlier efforts to get back in the game.

Thompson got hot in the third quarter to put a scare in the Cavaliers. He scored 15 points in the period, and the Warriors went into the fourth quarter with a fighting chance, down just 9 points. It was a 7-point game after back-to-back 3-pointers from Curry and Leandro Barbosa. But LeBron James took over. A driving layup. A laser pass to set up a J. R. Smith 3-pointer. Back-to-back lobs to Tristan Thompson. The Cavaliers' lead was 13.

Then, with 4:32 left and the game getting away from the Warriors, James provided the exclamation point. Curry drove the lane and tried to lose James by faking a reverse layup to the right side of the rim before going up on the left. It was one of Curry's favorite moves and it usually worked. But James didn't bite. Instead, when Curry did shoot, James spiked the ball out of bounds with his left hand.

He looked every bit of six-foot-eight, and Curry had never looked more like a six-foot-three guard. It was the kind of block a big brother would do on his little brother, to belittle more than to prevent a basket. And after the block, James did what he normally doesn't—he turned to Curry and talked trash.

And Curry haters across the nation erupted. James had become the anointed leader for the anti-Curry sect. Easily one of the most criticized and scrutinized NBA players ever, James's favor soared when pitted against Curry. Because he was the one validating all the doubts and irritations with Curry.

James was the slayer of the overhyped. He was the Philistine who would put David in his place. He was leading the charge to save the record books from the prisoners of the moment, who dared compare these Warriors to Michael Jordan's Bulls and Magic Johnson's Lakers and Larry Bird's Celtics. It wasn't just that LeBron was playing sensationally, but he was exposing the myth of Curry.

The block would have been enough, but ten seconds later, after a timeout, Curry haters got the cherry on top. Curry went for a steal and knocked the ball away from an unaware James. Curry lunged again for the loose ball, but James snatched it above his reach. While Curry began his retreat down the court to the defensive end, James landed on Curry, prompting a foul call *on Curry*. It was Curry's sixth, kicking him out of the game. And he lost it.

He took out his mouthpiece and fired it like he was trying to throw out a runner at the plate. Curry has been known to toss his mouthpiece in frustration. He did it in Game 2 after he finally made a 3-pointer, firing it at the face of the scorer's table after ending a streak of missed open 3-pointers.

But this time, Curry's mouthpiece went toward the crowd. It hit a fan sitting courtside right in the face as he cheered Curry's disqualification. The fan, Andrew Forbes, was the son of Cavaliers minority owner Nate Forbes. Curry then began cursing at the referee, prompting his immediate ejection.

It was a rare meltdown, but one that gave validation to his critics.

It was called a temper tantrum, an undertone that speaks to the privileged kid who can't handle things when it gets tough. The sight of an NBA player losing it with an official is hardly new. But this was Curry, the NBA's golden boy. Him losing control was evidence of his unworthiness.

It was a blight on his wholesome image, a moment that even had fellow Christians wagging their finger at Curry. And then after the game, in a rash moment, Ayesha tweeted that the NBA was rigged.

Though many Warriors fans agreed with Ayesha, who was frustrated with the amount of uncalled fouls her husband endured, she made herself sound unlikeable. She spoke for a legion of fans who were certain the NBA had ordered from on-high to get the series to Game 7 and get LeBron James his storybook ending. But to everyone else, she was the privileged crying about injustice. She was ripping the very league that made her famous. She was sounding the trumpet as a victim of an organization that for the better part of two years propped her husband up as an elite star, elevating his status globally.

Of course her tweet was a burst of passion and not a moment of analytical reasoning. Of course she was specifically, exclusively, talking about how the game was officiated and not concluding that the NBA system was holding Curry and the Warriors down. She later deleted the tweet and apologized.

But the damage was done. She'd given evidence for the perception that the Curry brand wasn't built on toughness, that his success was predicated on circumstance and not worthiness. The perfect family had given naysayers all the fodder they would need. In a dramatic plot twist, Curry was the villain receiving his comeuppance.

To be sure, the Curry hate was new and sudden and startling in its passion. It was almost as if it were compensation for the three years of fervent love Curry had received. In 2012 he emerged as a cult figure among hardcore NBA fans, and grew into a magnetic novelty people wanted to watch in 2013. By 2014, he was a star, celebrated for his uniqueness and propped up as an inspiration. By 2015, he was hogging the spotlight, peddled as the face of the NBA, an inescapable presence in the mainstream.

For years, Curry had only known adoration. And balance was restored in a matter of months. And yet Curry turned up the heat on himself by embracing, pursuing, Durant.

Developing a super-team, stocked with dynasty-level talent, was like pouring water on a grease fire. The Warriors, once lovable underdogs, instantly became the most hated team in the NBA, perhaps in this millennium. Adding Durant rendered every other team an underdog, shifting the populace against Golden State. It also gave Curry's critics more fire.

Curry welcoming a player who could challenge his throne, after losing to LeBron, was akin to confessing he was not all he claimed to be—for those who despised the thought of him sharing a mantle with Jordan. His meekness was seen as weakness.

Players are often criticized for being selfish and greedy. Yet Curry is derided by his peers for being humble and team oriented. Players are often criticized for caring more about personal success than winning. Yet NBA greats consider it a knock that he sacrificed his spotlight and embraced escalated pressure for the pursuit of more championships. That's how strong Curry hate has grown—he could have gotten more favor for buying into stereotypes NBA players have long embodied than he received for bucking them.

By inviting Durant, he opted against appeasing. He could have opposed the roster upgrade, accrued points for machismo by preferring to beat the other greats on his own. But Curry rejected the opportunity to restore his good name the easy way. He could have gained credibility by embracing his status as underdog, as Westbrook did by re-signing with Oklahoma City after Durant left, branding himself as loyal and tough.

Instead, Curry turned up the heat on himself.

Exceptionally Unathletic

o   o   o

"You have Brandon Jennings, who frankly has far more talent and upside . . . You have guys like Jeff Teague, Jonny Flynn, Ty Lawson . . . even Jrue Holiday at UCLA, are seen as guys with more upside. And then you have Steph who is a spectacular shooter but not a true point. He's going to measure out at just over 6-1, not at 6-3 that he is listed at, and there is just this sense that he is not the big-time athlete . . . But look, this is a guy that was unrecruited by the ACC and has made his way to being a potential lottery pick. It speaks volumes for hard work."

—Doug Gottlieb

CHAPTER 9

In the summer following the Warriors' epic NBA Finals collapse, coach and trainer Brandon Payne created a new drill for his top client. Designed to simulate the intensity of live NBA sequences, the drill is called quarters. The mere mention of it makes Curry roll his eyes.

"There are times I thought a normal, sane human being would just quit," said Payne, founder of Carolinas-based Accelerate Basketball Training. "Some things I have him do are just so difficult that I expect him to say, 'Hold on. That's too far.'"

Quarters, Payne thought, would be the drill that finally prompted Curry to press the pause button. Here is how it goes.

Curry is to run up the court to the offensive end, where he is tasked with executing three plays. What he is supposed to do is relayed through lights or numbers, which have already been assigned certain actions. He must process the signal and execute the corresponding task.

The assignments vary and come at Curry randomly. One possession might include making a 3-pointer off a certain dribble move, then curling off a screen for a catch and shoot, then reversing to the opposite side of the paint for a third and final action, such as a step-back 3.

All of this must happen within twenty seconds, simulating the shot clock, which means it all must happen at game speed.

When the offensive possession is completed, Curry is to run at full speed to the other end of the court, where three more actions await him for the defensive possession. To increase the degree of difficulty, Brandon Thomas is inserted into the drills.

Thomas, a former De La Salle High School star who played two years of ball at Whittier College, is a bull. He isn't especially big, but he is strong and powerful. He is one of those rock-solid guards who know how to drive with force, use their low center of gravity to deliver a blow. He mimics the physicality Curry must endure.

So a defensive possession might be to chase Thomas around a ball screen, then stop his drive and keep him out of the paint. And Thomas has license to bulldoze; that way Curry can learn to translate lateral quickness into leverage. Then after getting pounded by Thomas, Curry might have to end the possession by closing out aggressively on a 3-pointer.

All of that counts as one. A quarter is four of those consecutively, without stopping. And if he fails to execute any part—and Payne is watching closely—gets even one read wrong, the entire possession doesn't count toward the quarter. So it could take six trips up and down to complete the quarter.

The drill is complete when Curry successfully executes four quarters.

While he is exhausted, having spent nearly every ounce of his physical and mental energy, he immediately shifts to a stationary drill to test his decision making. Payne has a database of Curry results. He knows Curry is ready when he makes the same decisions while fully fatigued as he does when he is fresh.

"I keep waiting for him to complain," Payne said. "I keep waiting for him to tell me I'm crazy. And he never does. He's just ready to work. That's impressive. To watch him work through this stuff, it is impressive."

While Curry was rehabbing after ankle surgery in April of 2012, Gerald Henderson—who was also in the 2009 draft class after starring at Duke, selected No. 12 overall—told Curry about

Accelerate Basketball. Henderson called up Payne and asked if Curry could come work out.

The answer was an emphatic yes. Payne, a former head coach at Wingate University who started his own athlete training business in 2009, was working with several NBA players connected to the Carolinas: Kemba Walker, Tyrus Thomas, Antawn Jamison, Matt Carroll. Still, he jumped on the chance to work with Curry.

This was at the point in Curry's career when he was most written off. He had missed almost all of the lockout-shortened 2011–12 season with repeated ankle injuries, and the expectation was that injuries would doom his career. Curry was still rehabbing when Henderson brought him to the Accelerate facility—which was in South Carolina, some twenty miles below Charlotte, on the state border near Weddington, where Ayesha Curry grew up.

Payne sensed this was a game-changer, even though his small staff didn't. Behind the scenes, he lit into them for not giving Curry enough attention. He salivated at Curry's high skill level and was eager to work with the Warriors guard.

Payne describes himself as a mediocre player and limited athlete who had to search out advantages on the court. His vision is centered on maximizing a player's particular physical abilities and marrying them with the fundamentals and skills of basketball. His mad-scientist approach includes understanding the game, the body, and the brain, and finding ways to manipulate all three. His philosophy is undergirded in efficiency. A player's athleticism can be improved by getting stronger in the right ways and eliminating wasted motions.

Curry was the perfect project. Not just because he was skilled. Not just because he needed to get stronger and faster. But because he was willing to work. Curry matched Payne's insatiable appetite for improvement. In this hobbled guard, Payne found a hunger to reach his limits and push them. And this was while Curry couldn't even move.

Their first sessions were all stationary, as Curry's right ankle was still healing. But Payne knew he was onto something by the way Curry attacked those drills. On top of that, Curry was taking classes at Davidson toward his degree. The NBA was in a lockout and wouldn't resume until December. So Curry would get up early and work out with Payne, up until the last possible minute, then hustle to make it to his classes at Davidson.

Because Curry couldn't put stress on his ankle, Payne was tasked with coming up with ways to help him improve his game sans running and jumping.

"We had to be so creative," Payne said. "So that kind of started this whole ball rolling, him having the time and taking the time to learn everything about what we're doing. It forced us to kind of change how we did things. Forced us to research and come up with new ideas."

Payne came to learn what those who have been with Curry are typically impressed with: he loves to work. Many of the great ones tend to have an otherworldly work ethic, a drive that pushes them to push themselves. Curry's is equally as epic though his version is unique.

Curry's greatest perceived flaw is his lacking athleticism. He isn't blazing fast, like many point guards in the NBA. He can't jump out of the gym. He isn't endowed with bullying strength. In modern basketball, that equates to being unathletic.

This is both true and a misconception. His lack of athleticism is both Curry's biggest weakness and his greatest ally.

Curry does not have the explosive strength that is so rampant in the NBA. Yet he is an incredible athlete. Like the amplified hearing of a blind person, Curry's exceptionalism in other areas of athletic prowess compensates for his lack of explosion. Curry's best attributes lie in areas that go unnoticed to the untrained eye, traits that aren't as breathtaking as Aaron Gordon's skywalking or John Wall's speed.

At the same time, Curry's lack of typical athleticism underscores his need for skill, feeding a furious drive for development.

The foundation of all elites, those who rise to the top of their sport, are physical gifts the typical human doesn't possess. And they are enhanced with the kind of work ethic to which normal humans can't relate. Curry is no exception. He is both an incredible athlete and an insane worker. The combination of his talent and his drive has produced a sort of bionic athlete.

He still looks relatively diminutive on the court. His scruffy goatee adds some years to his appearance, but he still comes off as a boy among men. But look at some old pictures of Curry, from his college days or his younger years in the NBA. And look at him now. He appears to have taken a sip of the same serum Steve Rogers used to become Captain America.

Curry is surprisingly chiseled, the result of meticulous sculpting. He doesn't bulge out of his uniform with guns that beg for muscle shirts. His physique is less eye test and more advanced analytics. He leans on science and technology and nutrition, pairing it with a motor that wows his professional athlete colleagues, squeezing every ounce of ability from his frame. It requires a special diligence for Curry to maintain his physical sweet spot. He can't get too big or be too light. He can't wear himself down but must push his limits.

His stiffest competitors all boast the staples of basketball excellence, some jaw-dropping combination of size, hops, speed, and strength. Curry counters by maximizing his particular blend of athleticism and skill.

Understanding Curry's gifts requires rethinking traditional notions of athleticism. Because the intangibles that scouts missed with Curry, as they were too focused on speed and leaping ability, are what make him a surreal talent. They are a key and understated part of how he has pulled this off. How Curry manipulates his athletic strengths is a window into where athletics have been trending—emphasizing efficiency, technology, and skill.

"He's a phenomenal athlete," Hall of Fame–bound point guard Steve Nash said. "He's off the charts in so many ways as an athlete. We sometimes get so enamored by explosion. Athleticism is what you can do within the parameters of the game: the ball, opponent, space, time, execution. There are so many things. We lose track of what a phenomenal athlete he is."

After every practice, Nick U'Ren can be found under the same basket. He and assistant coach Bruce Fraser work with Curry through his regular routine. Fraser comes up with the drills for Curry to sharpen his game, work on techniques. U'Ren helps, including grabbing the ball out of the net. He and Fraser have probably assisted on more Curry 3-pointers than anyone else in the Warriors organization.

U'Ren marvels at Curry's "touch." He talks about it with the wonder an archaeologist might have for a dinosaur fossil.

"He must have extra senses in his fingertips," U'Ren said. "His ability to, in a split second, manipulate the ball is incredible. It's just a miniscule fraction of an adjustment—to loft it a little higher, or change the angle with a defender coming at him. But he can feel it and make the change instantly."

Basketball is full of utility words, these generic descriptions that sum up intangibles too difficult to describe. *Feel* is one of them, as in "he has a great feel for the game." It is a way of describing players' instincts, their understanding of how to navigate the nuances of the game, the fluidity of their reading and reacting.

Another one of those terms is *touch*. It is most often used in discussing shooting but can also apply to passing. It is an attempt to encapsulate a specific intangible ability. Shooting a basketball has a list of mechanics: point hips toward the basket, spread feet shoulder-width apart, generate power from the legs, keep shooting elbow close to the body, leave space between the palm of the guide hand and the ball, focus on the rim, snap the wrist for a firm follow-through. Any basketball technique video can teach a player the proper shooting form and he or she would probably improve at shooting. But touch is unteachable. Touch is taking the unspoken calculations in measuring a shot—how hard to shoot it, how much arc to give it, how much rotation to use, the angle of the release—and having the ability to execute them.

This ability that has been crammed into oversimplified vernacular is an athletic skill. It's called dexterity—the skillful manipulation of the hands.

Hands is another one of those terms, used to encompass catching and throwing, to describe the speed and strength in a player's mitts. Curry has phenomenal hands. His dexterity is off the charts.

It's how he can finger roll from the free throw line, in an NBA game, and it is not luck. It is how he can shoot from thirty feet with the same efficiency as a seven-footer from five feet. It is how he can cut back door and catch a pass in traffic—you will rarely see Curry not catch a pass he gets his hands on. It is why if the ball is exposed before him, he's likely going to swipe it. It's why he can drive to the basket and, with either hand, spin the ball perfectly off the glass or loft it at the perfect height to get the right bounce.

U'Ren gets to see it every day. It blows him away. And he formerly worked with Nash. He also worked with Phoenix Mercury star Diana Taurasi, one of the greatest players in women's basketball history.

"He must feel things in his fingertips that most people don't feel," U'Ren said, looking at his own digits as he rubbed them together. "It's like he has more nerve endings. He makes these adjustments on the fly, in tenths or hundreds of a second. It's incredible."

If there was a genetic marker Curry received from his sharpshooting father, it was probably dexterity. It's an inherent, unteachable benefit that big men across America wish they had.

Whenever a player is poor at shooting free throws, fans take it as an indictment of his work ethic, as if free throw shooting is purely a matter of repetitions. No doubt, since the distance is constant, enough practice can create muscle memory. But it is a skill to be able to adjust to other varying factors. Players with great dexterity can have their mechanics be imperfect on a particular free throw—such as fatigue preventing the full use of the legs—but make up for it, instantly, in their release. If the free throw is too hard, dexterity is the skill that allows a player to take a little bit off the shot to get it perfectly in the middle on the next one. Curry can do this from deep, accounting for the variables of defense, position on the court, movement before the shot, and fatigue.

A great example came against the Clippers at Oracle in March 2015. Another night he brought all his weapons to bear on Chris Paul, his favorite rival. He split the double-team of Chris Paul and Matt Barnes with a couple of low, quick dribbles. He then evaded on-charging big man DeAndre Jordan with a through-the-legs-and-behind-the-back dribble, a move that again slipped him past Paul, who continued his pursuit from behind. Curry took one more dribble, away from the basket toward the top of the key, before suddenly turning and shooting in a blink. Nailed it dead center. Four Clippers in his wake.

Kerr, who had thrown his hands in the air wondering what Curry was doing, shook his head and walked back to his seat after the shot went in. He had no words. That all happened in four seconds.

What might have happened if this skill had been attributed to him early, and manipulated? While most guards come out of college needing to learn how to shoot, Curry came out with an incredible skill that opened up a world of shots. Not just spot-on 3-pointers. But mid-range jumpers, runners, off-the-dribble pull-ups, and more. Maybe if that skill had been recognized it would have been clearer that he had the tools to be a master at the pick-and-roll, which might have gotten him to a major college, or higher in the draft, or a coach that was patient with his development. Getting passed over worked out perfectly for Curry, but how will the next undersized guard with supercharged skills be received?

Another area Curry is an athletic freak: hand-eye coordination.

There was an underrated play in November of 2016 that illustrated Curry's gift. It was Kevin Durant's first game against the Oklahoma City Thunder, which he had left to join the Warriors. Everybody on the team knew Durant wanted to play well and beat his former team. They were feeding him from the outset. One sequence began with Durant's missed pull-up jumper being deflected right back to him and him draining a 3. On the ensuing defensive possession, the Warriors forced a turnover and Curry scooped up the loose ball on the run. He took two dribbles with his left hand, then curled the ball around his back to the right side. But it wasn't a dribble, it was a pass. And one bounce later, Durant stepped right into it for the pull-up 3-pointer.

The crowd at Oracle Arena was going crazy because Durant had hit back-to-back 3s. The overlooked spectacle in that sequence was Curry's pass. With his off hand, he'd dropped in a perfect pass. In a split second he had to calculate Durant's positioning and speed, then figure where he wanted to place the ball—safely away from defense but in Durant's already set path. It takes incredible hand-eye coordination to analyze the parameters he needed to hit, then hit them. He added a degree of difficulty by making it an around-the-back pass, still getting the right amount of height on his bounce and the perfect trajectory so Durant could catch it in stride.

Hand-eye coordination is why Curry is so good at golf. He could go pro if he picked up the sport full-time.

Curry's ability to see, measure, decide, then do is on an elite level. Even among exceptional athletes, he is exceptional in this area. In 2015–16, Curry made fifty shots from at least twenty-eight feet, which is well behind the 3-point line. The second most was Portland guard Damian Lillard at sixteen. Curry made 48.1 percent of his attempts from that distance, which is a higher percentage than what Phoenix's seven-foot-one center Alex Len shot from ten feet or closer.

Deep shooting isn't just about showing off. It's about spreading the floor. The farther Curry proves he can make shots from with regularity, the farther out the defense has to come to defend him. That stretches the floor, giving the whole offense more space to work with.

Jerry Rice was known for speeding up Bay Area mountainsides. Kobe Bryant is reputed to log hours and hours at the gym. Tiger Woods worked himself into the most sculpted golfer ever.

Curry has that kind of drive. It is quiet, unassuming, and self-sustaining. But the uniqueness of Curry's work is in its aim. He doesn't work for the sake of working, to simply be in peak condition and avoid fatigue. He does the strength- and endurance-training stuff. Payne even made him throw up a couple times. But Curry's pursuit is to enhance skill, to build up the physical elements that help him master his style of play.

Eric Housen, the Warriors do-it-all equipment manager and travel secretary, has seen his share of tireless workers. He got his start as a ball boy and became invaluable to the franchise by rebounding for Chris Mullin into the wee hours of the night. He's seen guys like Jason Richardson and Harrison Barnes, who live at the facility, putting in the sweat equity.

Yet Housen can't help but sometimes watch Curry work. He'll sit on the balcony that overlooks the Warriors' practice facility and just watch Curry. It's not the time he puts in, or how grueling the load. Housen is amazed at the technical difficulty. Curry practices the difficult until it becomes normal. He sets the bar so high in practice that his dazzling is monotonous in the games.

His pregame warm-up, which is a spectacle, is but a glimpse into Curry's behind-the-scenes workout. He doesn't work on 3-pointers, he works on 3-pointers from deep after three-pronged dribble moves. He doesn't practice free throws. He practices left-handed floaters from the free throw line.

And once the insane has become normalized, he turns up the

heat. He'll wear a mask to simulate altitude, tiring himself out faster—and saving the wear and tear on his body—so he can get comfortable shooting 3s while fatigued. After the step-back became normal, as did the step-to-the-side 3, he worked incessantly until he got down the side-stepping, around-the-back 3-pointer.

"There will never be another person who spends more time in the gym than Mully," Housen said of Mullin, who is widely known as a workout maniac. "If Mully wasn't sharp, if he wasn't more fit than anybody else . . . he needed that to be who he was. I don't think Steph has to do what Chris has to do. It's not that Steph doesn't work like that, but his work is just, man, it's just unbelievable. The things he works on and how hard they are. And he'll work on it until he can do it five times in a row, no matter how many times it takes. It's crazy, all the things he does before he gets to his shot."

Lanny Smith sat in Legends gym in Houston in the summer of 2016 watching young players warm up. It was John Lucas's big-time AAU tournament, assuredly featuring some future NBA ballers.

Smith is well known by the kids. Not because he played a couple years in the NBA Development League, spent a summer league with the Rockets and a preseason with the Sacramento Kings. They know him as a friend of Curry. He is owner of the faith-based apparel line Active Faith. He met Curry through Anthony Tolliver, who was with him on the Kings training camp roster. Curry believed in the product and became a shareholder early on, and the two are now friends.

Smith was amazed at how this gym full of high schoolers were all emulating Curry. He couldn't help himself. He had to go talk to them. He wanted to know if they were practicing the shots they were taking. He had to ask if they had mastered those moves through repetition during the extra work they got in on their own time.

He felt it was his duty to make sure they knew Curry wasn't hitting those shots on the fly, that he worked on them. He wanted to emphasize that the player they imitated was as diligent as they came.

"I had to pull a couple of kids to the side and ask," Smith said. "How many of those are you taking at practice? There is a reason Steph is able to do it at a high level. He gets in the repetitions. All that crazy stuff you see him doing, he's able to do it because he's worked on it."

Count Smith among the many floored by Curry's inner drive. Smith was a point guard all his life before injury forced him to give up his hoop dreams. He always prided himself on being able to handle the rock. Yet what Curry can do leaves him shaking his head.

This is part of Brandon Payne's work with Curry at his Accelerate Basketball program, making the crazy normal. The way they highlight Curry's skills is by making those skills operational under nearly any circumstance. The way to do that is to get Curry comfortable executing in such adverse circumstances that in-game situations are easy. It's akin to learning to get your work done with a headache by inducing a migraine on your off day and practicing that work.

Payne calls it overloading. He overwhelms Curry's senses so he can be conditioned under duress. Some of Curry's drills are ridiculous. The quarters drill is just one of them.

Many of his drills are to be done with one hand while dribbling a ball in the other. Making layups and close-range shots. Whipping a heavy rope. Catching tennis balls.

Payne uses technology to ramp it up. Curry might have to catch a tennis ball while dribbling and wearing sensory goggles. There is a light machine that flashes colors, and each color represents a dribble move Curry is to execute before touching it. He might have to do it while bouncing a tennis ball off the wall. And one of Payne's team members will hold up a sign that gives Curry another task.

So when he is dribbling up the court, and a defender reaches while Curry is trying to get the play call from the bench, he can handle all three tasks and make the right decision, even if he is tired.

Payne calls it "neuromuscular efficiency." To get this level of mastery pushes Curry to the brink of physical and mental exhaustion—and he soaks it up.

"I love every day I get to say I work with Stephen Curry," Payne said. "It's a joy and a challenge at the same time. It's a joy because he comes to work. There is no yelling or screaming. When we're on the floor, it just kind of flows. It's a challenge because I have to help this guy who seems to master everything in the first ten minutes I give it to him. I can show the guy something brand-new, and he will look like Bambi right out of the womb on the first three runs. And on the fourth or fifth run, he will look like he has been doing it all his life. And once he gets it, it's locked in."

Before the 2016 playoffs, Payne gave Curry an assignment: give him a list of things he wanted to work on over the summer. Payne wanted them before the playoffs started so he could prepare a regimen.

Curry was winding down the best season of his career, one of the most productive campaigns in NBA history. He was a virtual lock for a second straight MVP and awaiting him was another run for the title. Yet when he and Payne met up, both bringing their off-season to-do list, Curry had the longer list. And Payne said Curry's list was better, even though Payne prides himself on being a straight shooter who tells Curry the truth.

Curry's list included improving his footwork, dealing with circumnavigating big men with long arms, new ways for Curry to create space and score against the schemes defenses used against him. From the input of both of them, they crafted a set of goals that was the most extensive they'd had in their years working together.

This, as much as anything, illustrates Curry's work ethic. The most comprehensive regimen of his career is coming at a time when his schedule is as packed as ever. For Curry, it's not about how backbreaking the work is, but about the discipline it takes to get it all done. He works in the mornings and late at night, making sure he can take his daughters to school and tuck them in for bed. He carves out the time to work toward a black belt in basketball technique while still keeping a gazillion obligations to his endorsements and the Warriors.

He made sure to support his wife's booming career as a celebrity chef and still made sure to work on finishing through contact.

"If people only knew how crazy his schedule is," Housen said, "yet there is always basketball in it. And you don't even understand the man's passion for golf. He seems like the most balanced, hardest working guy in the world."

Balance is a specialty of Curry's, part of another stellar athletic skill of his: agility.

As part of his ankle rehabilitation, and building up his body to prevent further injury, Curry enhanced an overlooked part of the body: the hip. This actually improved his balance—i.e., his agility.

Keke Lyles, who spent three seasons as the Warriors' director of performance, taught Curry how to use his hips as the foundation of his shifty game. Curry, to compensate for not having broadband speed, leans heavily on changing directions and sudden bursts. That put a lot of pressure on his ankles. But retraining to use his hips gave him the same results without the ankle stress.

In the process, Lyles came to marvel at Curry's capacity. He had the Warriors star learning yoga techniques and developing his core strength. Curry's proficiency at hip hinges was the foundation for him being able to deadlift four hundred pounds. He trained until he himself became an expert. He could handle anything Lyles threw at him.

Watch Curry curve around screens, contort his way through traffic with sudden lunges, take shots from awkward angles, shift on a dime without breaking stride. It is all part of his astonishing agility.

"A normal person couldn't even move the way Steph does," Warriors assistant GM Kirk Lacob said. "They would fall over or hurt themselves just trying. His balance, his coordination, his core strength, they are second to none."

Curry is a master of his body. He can tell you how much he weighs to within a pound or two. He likes to play at about 192 pounds because he knows that's his best balance of size and quickness. He doesn't live in the gym; he just works smart to get the same quality of work done within two hours.

He doesn't get quicker by shaving seconds off his forty time, but by refining his footwork to get to the spot with fewer steps. He doesn't add strength so he can bully guards in the post, but to give him more explosion on his first step.

What Curry has done is sculpt himself into a machine. As Payne put it, Curry has taken his genetic makeup and pushed it to its ceiling. And not so he can wow with athleticism, but so the skills that make him great can flourish.

This is how Curry takes down Goliath, by sharpening his rocks and becoming a wizard with the slingshot.

The way Lanny Smith explains it, Curry's work ethic is connected to his faith. The drive within him is fueled by his strong belief system. He points to Curry's favorite scripture, Philippians 4:13, which inspired the tagline for his Under Armour brand: "I can do all things."

The widely accepted understanding is that Curry points to the verse because God allows him to accomplish success, that his faith is so strong that he can achieve the greatest heights. Smith says that misses the mark.

He believes the real point of the verse Curry chose, and the teaching behind it, is that through faith he can handle anything thrown his way.

That includes success, but it also includes failure. It includes fighting back from a career-threatening ankle injury *and* remaining humble despite the spoils of global fame. It includes diligently doing his best despite playing for a terrible franchise *and* maintaining that diligence when the franchise becomes elite.

That would explain why Curry works just as hard as a two-time MVP as he did when he was perceived as overrated and making it on his daddy's name. That would explain why he is willing to push himself to the limit and try whatever Payne throws his way without ever griping, because he is certain he can endure.

Curry's answer to his naysayers, his response to criticism, his rebuttal to injury, is to work. In the process, because of his natural talent and sheer determination, he molded himself into an MVP.

"He wasn't a guy who was built like he was going to be the man," said champion boxer Andre Ward, an Oakland native who has become good friends with Curry. "He was always kind of overlooked and not paid attention to. That's either going to discourage you and you're going to start to believe what they're saying. Or you're going to turn into a monster. And you're going to get in that gym and you're going to work and become what you know you can become. You're seeing the fruits of all his labor . . . I see work ethic. I see unwavering belief."

Underdog

o   o   o

"He didn't pass the eye test. He was so small. He jumps much better now than he did then. Wasn't the fastest. His jersey swallowed him."

—Shonn Brown

CHAPTER 10

Curry watched as LeBron James buckled to the Oracle Arena hardwood, his teammates piling on top of him. Many of Curry's teammates retreated to the locker room so their hearts could crumble in private. But Curry soaked it up. He stayed on the court and watched the Cavaliers celebrate. He swallowed the embarrassment of being unable to save the Warriors.

It was the biggest game of his life. Game 7 of the NBA Finals. A showdown with one of the greatest to ever play the game. On the same court where he had often been so magical, brazen in his domination. And Curry had looked flat-out subpar. He had turned in one of the worst performances of his career, certainly the worst since he'd become MVP.

He wasn't good for the majority of the NBA Finals. Or for the majority of the playoffs. He had a few moments, stretches where he looked like the once-in-a-generation superstar. But most of the Warriors' march for a championship revealed a suspect Curry. He had a chance to salvage it all, to negate his postseason struggles by doing merely what he'd pulled off regularly—being the closer. One more ounce of Curry magic and these playoffs would have been more gutsy than gut-wrenching.

Game 7 had ground to a halt down the stretch. The Warriors, who led by as much as 8 points and trailed by as much as 7 in the third quarter, found themselves with a 4-point lead with 5:37 left for a second consecutive championship. It felt like so many other games at Oracle, where the opponent would hang close only for an inevitable Warriors surge to reassert their superiority and set the world as it should be.

But head coach Steve Kerr injected some life into the Cavaliers by subbing in Festus Ezeli, who started as Andrew Bogut missed the game with a knee injury. And Ezeli never looked as if he was ready for the moment. He hadn't been the same since knee surgery in February. And he looked to be the perfect foil to Cleveland's struggles scoring.

James immediately attacked Ezeli, who was playing Game 7 with a jitteriness that made Warriors fans nervous. He had played just over 8 minutes of the game so far, and they hadn't inspired much confidence as Kerr kept him glued to the bench. But it was winning time, and Kerr was nervous about not having a shot blocker in the game to protect the rim. So he went back to Ezeli. It proved to be the opening James needed.

He immediately put Ezeli in the pick-and-roll, forcing the Warriors' center to defend the future Hall of Famer out on the perimeter. Less than a minute after he checked into the game, Ezeli found himself trying to defend James out past the 3-point line. No trap came from the Warriors to take the ball out of James's hands. He gave a hard pump fake, baiting Ezeli to jump. While the Warriors center was coming back down, James pulled up for a 3-pointer, making sure he drew contact with Ezeli and drew a foul. And since fouling a player shooting a 3-pointer gets three free throws, James's duping of Ezeli was extra costly. He made all three free throws.

Then the worst of Curry resurfaced. The knock that's followed him throughout his career flared up at the most inopportune of times.

Desperately needing a basket to keep the Cavaliers at bay, Curry dribbled the ball on the right side, well beyond the 3-point line, Kyrie Irving on his back. He bought time by banging into Irving while Thompson used an Ezeli screen to evade J. R. Smith. With his back to Thompson, and Irving applying pressure, Curry didn't pick up his dribble and pivot to make a clean pass to the cutting Thompson. Instead, Curry did what he often does, as Thompson curled from the top of the key toward the right sideline of the court—he zipped an around-the-back pass to the moving target. He missed wide. Turnover.

A viral video clip perfectly captured the moment: a baseline replay of Curry's behind-the-back pass sailing away from Thompson and out of bounds. But the championship trophy was superimposed over the ball. The Warriors title bounced errantly out of bounds.

The next time down, James went at Ezeli again. Draymond Green bailed Ezeli out with a sudden and timely switch onto James. But James was determined to get Ezeli to defend him, so he backed up, started over, and called for another screen to get Ezeli to switch onto him. Having fouled James the last time, Ezeli was hesitant to press up. That gave James the space to rise up with ease, draining a 3 over Ezeli. Just like that, the Warriors were trailing.

A Klay Thompson layup tied the game at 89 with 4:39 left. The weight of the stakes dragged the game into a grueling display; the defenses tightened and the pressure mounted. A missed 3 by Curry followed a missed jumper by James. Then James and Thompson traded bricked fadeaways. Then Andre Iguodala blocked a layup by James.

Three minutes left.

Iguodala missed a 3, and Kevin Love missed a hook shot, and Green a 3, and Kyrie Irving a runner. With each brick, the tension in Oracle thickened like cement. A moment was forming that would be carved in basketball history. This was Curry's chance to save the day, like he normally did, and erase the memories of his playoff struggles. His chance to make his rash of injuries the subplot for his heroism. His chance to transform his turnovers and 3-point binging from a flaw in his game to a testament of his perseverance.

One minute, fifty-five seconds left.

No doubt, James was taking his best shot at the superstar finish. He was bent on covering his own struggles with timely greatness. An Irving miss led to a fast-break attempt for Iguodala. He gave it up to Curry, who bounce-passed it right back to Iguodala for an open layup. But James soared from behind the play, blocking Iguodala's layup off the glass and keeping the game tied. It was one of the most clutch defensive stops in NBA history.

James followed by missing a running hook, setting the stage for Curry. But like he had done for most of the Finals, he went hunting for a 3-pointer. His quick attempt coming off a screen at the top missed wide right, banking off the glass. At this point, it was clear that Curry didn't have it. One of the game's best closers, the Warriors' reliable superstar, was out of gas in the most gargantuan of times.

Irving upped the stakes by breaking the three-minute, forty-six-second drought. He became a legend by drilling a step-back 3-pointer over Curry's outstretched arms, giving the Cavaliers a 92–89 lead with fifty-three seconds left. It was probably the first time all series non-Cavaliers fans thought the Warriors were actually going to lose the Finals.

Curry had one last chance to save the Warriors, to end the spiral of his most trying postseason. He came off a screen and had Kevin Love in front of him, the most ideal of circumstances. Love is probably the Cavaliers' worst defender due to his poor lateral movement and worse instincts. Curry feasts on players like Love.

But after a couple of crossover moves, he couldn't find a comfortable look. He passed the ball to Green, who gave it back, and Curry tried again. A couple more moves and Love was still there. Eventually, Curry hoisted an off-balance 3-pointer as if time were running out. Desperation had kicked in. It rimmed out. The title was lost.

The last play was the most telling moment of how not-Curry

he actually was. The same guy who had averaged 30 points while shooting greater than 50 percent couldn't score. The same guy who habitually left defenders confused and at his mercy couldn't get the best of Love, who often couldn't be on the court at the end of games because his defense was so poor.

Curry wouldn't reveal the details about his ailing knee despite numerous attempts from the media to pry. But he was on a strenuous regimen to protect his knee while playing on it, around-the-clock treatment to get his knee ready for game action. Rest, ice, stimulation would get his knee feeling good, then another intense playoff game would take it away. More treatment would get it feeling good, then he would play again and inflame the sprained ligament. With each game, the treatment became less effective because it included less rest. The games were churning too fast. But Curry kept playing.

Game 7 of the NBA Finals was the sixteenth time he'd gone through that cycle of strengthening and stressing his sprained ligament.

The biggest tell that his knee injury was worse than he was letting on: Curry pulled out of the 2016 Olympics. This was a huge deal for Curry, a high-priority bucket list item. He had set his sights on 2016, reestablished himself as a key part of Team USA in the 2014 FIBA World Championships, winning another gold medal, and was a lock to make the team bound for Rio.

It killed him to have to pull out. Many thought it was the Zika virus that kept Curry from the Olympics, as he was the first basketball player to publicly say he wasn't going to Brazil. But one of his main causes is the fight against malaria, and he went to Tanzania to personally deliver nets. He wasn't afraid of Zika.

It was his knee keeping him from his Olympic dreams. That was the trade-off he was making—not resting and healing his sprained ligament in May and June, instead of not doing so in July and August. If Curry agreed to that, it meant his knee must have been a legitimate problem. And by the final moments of

Game 7, it was clear it was. In the biggest quarter of the year, he was 1-for-6 with 3 points and a turnover for the ages.

But it wasn't just his knee working against him. Curry wasn't good. Players of his status have been known to play well despite their injury. They summon a level of greatness that defies logic. Curry's injury, though, made him more normal than ever. It seemed to bring out the worst in him.

He shot 43.8 percent from the field, way down from his regular season average of 50.4 percent. He averaged 5.2 assists and 4.2 turnovers, the worst assist-to-turnover ratio he had ever posted in the playoffs. During the regular season, his efficiency was off the charts. In the playoffs, he peppered a few spectacular games in a postseason that was an utmost struggle.

"I take it on the chin because I know I didn't play my best," Curry said a day after the series ended. "That's something that I will have to deal with. That's my own expectation and my own kind of self-assessment. I don't need anybody else to tell me that. I don't need analysts all summer breaking down why I didn't do this, why I didn't do that. My team didn't win. I didn't play my best. That's not going to be the end of the story. That's just a down chapter in the book . . . If I'm in that position again, I know I will be better equipped to handle it."

Eight times during the playoffs, in which Curry played eighteen games, the Warriors were outscored in the minutes he was on the court. That only happened six times in his seventy-nine regular season games.

Hobbled by injury throughout the playoffs, Curry didn't become a smarter player. He didn't compensate for his physical limitations by upping his cerebral game. Instead, he seemed to lose focus more. He didn't hunker down and become more efficient, leaning on his experience and high basketball IQ. Instead, Curry leaned on his ability to pull off the magical.

It worked a few times. And when it did, it produced incredible moments.

Game 4 in the NBA Finals was one of those moments. It wasn't a marvel of a performance, but he was the best player on the court in Cleveland. Curry controlled the game as he maneuvered the Cavaliers' double-teams and traps. He was the unstoppable force on the court, outdueling Kyrie Irving while LeBron James struggled. Curry scored 24 of his 38 points in the second half. He made seven of his thirteen 3-pointers, three in the third quarter as the Warriors took control of the game and the series. Curry asserted his dominance and LeBron James was left scrambling. The Warriors were up 3–1 in the series and headed home on the brink of a second consecutive title.

But things began to unravel for the team. In the fourth quarter, Draymond Green got into it with James. With the game and the series slipping away, James started getting testy. Green set a screen on James, who bullied through the screen and threw Green to the hardwood. Getting back into the play, James stepped over Green. That is a no-no in the unwritten rules of basketball, famously broken by Allen Iverson in the 2001 NBA Finals, who stepped over Lakers guard Tyronn Lue—now the Cavaliers' head coach.

What happened next depends on who you believe. Many Warriors fans believe Green's explanation: he was pushing James from overtop him and his hand accidentally hit James in the groin. Most everyone else believes Green was throwing a cheap shot at James's groin. And since this was the third such incident in the playoffs, all over an eleven-game span, that narrative became much more plausible.

The NBA ruled with the latter crowd, deeming Green's swing a flagrant foul, exceeding his limit for the postseason and triggering a one-game suspension. In Game 5, which Green missed, Andrew Bogut suffered his own knee injury that knocked him out for the rest of the series.

The Warriors needed one more big game from Curry. The problem, though, was that pursuit of the postseason flurry was getting Curry out of his game. The result was a drastic decline in his 3-point percentage and an uptick in his turnovers. His big games had produced expectations for more heroics, exacerbating his inability to pull them off.

Over the last four games of the Finals, Curry had attempted fifty-five 3-pointers. It was the third most he'd attempted over a four-game span all season. The previous times, he shot 49 and 56.9 percent. This time, just 40 percent.

Curry couldn't stop the disappointing end to the Warriors' dream season. The largest audience of the NBA season was on the Warriors, and they didn't get to see the same Curry who had looked otherworldly all season.

His struggles shined especially in comparison to James, who went legacy hunting. Pitted against the Cleveland star in a battle for basketball's best, LeBron was the one who looked sensational, the one who looked ready to take down history. Curry at times didn't look ready for the moment.

He was pretty good. But beating Cleveland required greatness. The bar set by back-to-back MVPs demanded that he be extraordinary on such a platform. Pretty good wasn't enough.

In blue Hawaii-themed board shorts and a gray T-shirt, both from his SC30 collection with Under Armour, a cream-and-blue Warriors cap turned backwards on his head, Curry sluggishly walked away from his last interview of the season. He had done his exit interview with general manager Bob Myers and Steve Kerr, and he'd spent nearly fourteen minutes addressing the Warriors' epic collapse. Finally, he was retreating to the off-season. His attire, the drag in his stroll, his play to end the season—it was clear he was ready for a break.

But halfway across the practice court, Curry stopped to talk some more. He was asked about the favor he'd lost, about how rapidly he went from beloved to derided. The last game of the regular season, he scored 46 points and eclipsed four hundred made 3-pointers in a season, leading the Warriors to an NBA-record seventy-third win. His favorables were at peak levels. Just over two months later, he was walking off as the goat, carrying the weight of the Warriors' epic collapse.

Curry flashed his half-a-smile as he scratched his left arm and looked toward the hardwood while digesting one more question. He started walking away as he began to answer.

"I'm fine with it," Curry said. "It's not like I haven't been here before."

The land of the doubted isn't foreign territory to Curry. He is familiar with the not-good-enough label. Losing in the NBA Finals the way the Warriors did brought him back to well-known territory.

No moment signified that decline in stature like in the fourth quarter of Game 6 of the 2016 NBA Finals. The Cavaliers had all the momentum, and Curry, down 13 with just over four minutes left, was trying to stem the tide and silence the crowd. Facing down LeBron James at the top of the key, Curry drove down an open lane against Cleveland's star. He tried to dupe James with a fake to the right side of the rim, extending the ball with his right hand as he shuffled to a stop. But since James was behind him, Curry couldn't see that James didn't bite on the fake and was still waiting on Curry to shoot. And when the Warriors star tried to sneak a left-handed layup off the glass, James emphatically swatted it out of bounds.

It was more than a block. It was a message. A moment. LeBron made Curry look inferior, unworthy. LeBron was announcing that this newcomer to the all-time-great discussion didn't belong.

Is this the player who was mentioned in the same breath as Jordan? Is this the revolutionary who was reconstructing the game itself?

The question isn't whether Curry is a star. The doubt surrounding him now is whether he was as good as he had appeared. Whether he ever really deserved the relentless hype and historical comparisons. Whether the novelty of his dominance led to an exaggeration of that dominance. Whether he really is in the ilk of LeBron and Kobe Bryant, the once-in-a-generation types who carried the league to new heights.

Now, it's fair game to question his postseason record, which is littered with magical performances but overall doesn't match his regular season gaudiness. It's common to explain away his high-volume production as the result of something other than his worthiness.

He thrives because he has the ultimate green light.

His production is high because his teammates are good.

He is only doing this because the league is watered down.

The stakes are different, the level is higher, but the position is all too familiar. Curry is now shrouded in doubt. He is back in the position where he needs to prove himself. Undoubtedly, there are many who believe in his greatness. His NBA Finals performance didn't hijack all his support. Players, coaches, media analysts, and past legends—Curry can find credible support in every circle. But as has always been the case with Curry, he hears the haters clearest. The people who believe in his talent are appreciated; the people who doubt his talent keep him motivated.

If past is preface, a swollen negative rating is a good thing for Curry, and his team. He has two MVPs in his trophy case, a championship ring on his finger, a name that resonates globally, wealth greater than he's probably ever prayed for—and a chip on his shoulder. And nothing has been as great a motivator for Curry than having to disprove his critics and avenge his name. This is how it has been all his life. And just when it looked as if he had answered all questions, vanquished all skepticism, he is right back in this space. In his head, whispering, "I'll show you."

It was like that in high school. Though his skills screamed prodigy, few could get over the slightness of his build. He couldn't make enough 3-pointers to cover for how feeble he looked with his baggy jersey draped on his frail frame. He couldn't drop enough dimes to convince people he wasn't a one-trick pony, the basketball version of a carnival gimmick. He couldn't make enough smart plays to ensure recruiters they wouldn't look dumb for taking a chance on him.

It was a tall order to begin with. Charlotte Christian is smaller than a small school. And it plays in a private school league. Some of those private schools are big, with reputed sports programs, but Curry's school was a small school in that circle. And Curry didn't play AAU ball, the other popular way of getting your name out there.

When Curry was a junior, which is when the good players start narrowing down their list, he wasn't even an afterthought on the college scene. It took his senior year of high school—and growing to six-foot-two, 160 pounds with ankle weights on—for him to start showing up on recruitment radars as a viable option. He didn't make the rankings of the best players in the nation, per Rivals.com, a respected prep sports site. He didn't make the rankings at his position. He wasn't even among the best players in his state.

Another site, 24Sports, gave Curry a composite score that ranked him 281st in the nation. He ranked No. 51 among point guards and No. 16 in North Carolina.

Curry didn't get a sniff from Duke or North Carolina, the dream of nearly every Carolina boy who dribbled a basketball. Neither did Wake Forest or North Carolina State think he was on the level of the second- and third-tier recruits they get after the Tobacco Road schools get the cream of the crop. Adding insult to injury, all of the big-named Carolina schools gave scholarships to small point guards.

North Carolina landed Ty Lawson, who Rivals ranked as the No. 3 guard in the country. Wake Forest nabbed Ish Smith out of Concord, North Carolina.

"Scouts had their way of evaluating," said Shonn Brown, Curry's high school coach. "We'd hear stuff like 'My guard right now will eat him up.' We would tell them he could shoot better than any player they have right now. You could see his skill. The question was his size. Would he grow into his feet—he wore a size 13 then—and get there physically?"

The perfect fit figured to be Virginia Tech, where Curry had a personal connection to the school: both his parents went there. Both were stars, too. Dell had led the school to the NCAA tournament and was one of the few Hokies to get drafted into the NBA. Sonya was a stud on the volleyball team, helping to establish the young program.

Virginia was in Curry's blood. His mother grew up twenty minutes from the Virginia Tech campus in Blacksburg, and his dad's origins were just a two-hour drive away. Curry being a Hokie made perfect sense.

And Virginia Tech lived on sleeper recruits while trying to make noise in the highly regarded Atlantic Coast Conference. They offered Curry a chance to get revenge on the Carolina schools that wouldn't give him the time of day.

But even that was a long shot. Seth Greenberg, the men's basketball coach at the time, wanted Curry. But his offer came with conditions: he wanted Curry to redshirt his first season as a walk-on, then he'd get a four-year scholarship. He didn't have a scholarship to offer Curry at the time. Presumably, Curry's parents could afford to pay his way to Virginia Tech for a year. But for Curry it was all part of a grand slight to his game. In his mind, he was worthy of a Division I scholarship. To be a walk-on was akin to accepting the analysis of the analysts. *Walk-on* is a label that carries with it a connotation of unworthiness. It would have been a confession that Curry wasn't good enough.

Greenberg already had his starting back court set with two senior guards, Zabian Dowdell and Jamon Gordon. And a year earlier, he had landed Nigel Munson, a six-foot guard who committed to Virginia Tech after his junior season. Munson was a star at DeMatha High School, a known hotbed of basketball talent, and finished his high school career ranked No. 109 on Rivals.

Curry was a project, a flyer Greenberg was interested in taking.

But it didn't make sense for Greenberg to burn a scholarship on a guy who wasn't going to play. So the hope was Curry would walk on and wait.

Davidson coach Bob McKillop had been on Curry the whole time. Other small schools showed serious interest in Curry: Virginia Commonwealth, High Point, William & Mary. But Davidson won him over. His mother edged him that way because of the school's strong academic reputation. And McKillop was offering Curry a chance to play right away. So Curry swallowed his ACC hopes and settled on the mid-major school that was much more like his high school than the intense, high-level college hoop he'd watched as a teenager.

It's a slight Curry carries with him to this day, though he considers attending Davidson a genius move. At a time when he was supposed to be weighing options and visiting campuses and being wooed by coaches he saw on TV, Curry was being told he wasn't quite ready for that level.

And even after he proved they had all made a mistake, even Duke and North Carolina, the slights didn't stop. He led the nation in scoring and carried his small school to the Elite Eight of the NCAA tournament. Yet when the draft came, he was back in this same place.

The dissenters didn't own the consensus. Three NBA teams for sure coveted Curry.

Warriors general manager Larry Riley fell in love with Curry during Davidson's 2008 NCAA run. As fruit from the tree of Don Nelson, who'd groomed Steve Nash into an MVP, Riley was all over a point guard who could shoot.

In Curry's following season, Riley went to see Davidson play at Purdue. It was one of Curry's worst games that season and it sold Riley on him.

"The talk was that he wasn't tough enough," Riley said. "I went to Indianapolis to see him play against Purdue. A Big Ten school that's usually tough. I wanted to see how he would do.

Now, Purdue beat them pretty bad. Steph didn't shoot the ball well. I wasn't worried about his shooting. I know he can shoot. I wanted to see how he would handle the physicality. They beat the crap out of him. They fouled him all game. They were determined to not let him score. And he took it. He made the right plays. He passed the ball. He didn't get rattled. I was impressed. That was all I needed to see."

The Knicks also wanted Curry badly. They were desperate for a player to be the face of their franchise, and Curry had growing name recognition and unique game to make him an instant draw in New York. And Curry wanted the Knicks, too. Playing in Madison Square Garden, headlining one of the NBA's premier franchises, would have been the kind of validation Curry had sought but never received. It was the stage on which he had always been sure he belonged.

The Phoenix Suns were hot on his trail, too. With Nash exiting his prime, the Suns saw Curry as the heir apparent.

The Suns' general manager? Steve Kerr.

But the fact that all three teams would have a remote shot at getting Curry turned out to be evidence of his persistent underdog status. The Warriors had the highest of the picks in the 2009 draft at No. 7. The Knicks were at No. 8. The Suns had the No. 14 pick.

The Warriors never thought Curry would make it to them in the draft. They had him as the second-best player behind Blake Griffin. His being available at No. 7 was a fantasy. They were resigned to get big man Jordan Hill out of Arizona State. The Knicks prayed for a miracle while Phoenix worked to trade up for Curry.

Oddly enough, the Suns found a trade partner in the Warriors. Riley agreed to trade the No. 7 pick to Phoenix for Amar'e Stoudemire, with other pieces making the deal work.

In a strange turn of events, though, point guards kept coming off the board and none of them was named Stephen Curry.

Griffin went No. 1 overall to the Clippers, as everyone expected.

Hasheem Thabeet, a seven-footer from UConn, went No. 2 to Memphis, and James Harden to Oklahoma City. The first point guard taken was Tyreke Evans, a freshman from Memphis who was really more of a combo guard, by Sacramento at No. 4. Minnesota had picks Nos. 5 and 6. In a history-altering blunder, what will surely be remembered as one of the worst moves in sports history, the Timberwolves selected two point guards not named Stephen Curry: Jonny Flynn and Ricky Rubio.

The three point guards taken first in the draft were each an indictment on Curry. Their strengths contrasted with the weaknesses in Curry's scouting report. They typified how many basketball executives thought, possessed what general managers usually valued. And Curry didn't.

Tyreke Evans was six-foot-five with the bulk of an NBA veteran, though he had played just one season at Memphis. Size is always seducing in the NBA. Height has a way of hypnotizing decision makers into imagining what could be. Muscles automatically translate to readiness.

Evans had both. He wasn't a traditional point guard. But he could handle the ball and get to the basket. And he was big—which meant if he was groomed to be a solid point guard he could turn out to be a nightmare for other teams.

Curry was six-foot-three if he let his hair grow out. He didn't have the height or the bulk to create many possibilities. Instead, his size inspired a perceived inevitability: that he would be battered into futility in a merciless league.

Flynn was five-eleven on a stack of Bibles. But he was strong and blazing fast. He had the athleticism of a shooting guard just compacted like a crushed can. His dunks were a sight to see, his first step a weapon. Explosive athleticism is also seducing to basketball brains.

Curry didn't have that kind of athleticism. He couldn't jump out of the gym. His speed wasn't on a par with other point guards. His biceps didn't inspire.

Making matters worse, Derrick Rose, another one-and-done from Memphis, was tearing up the league. A freakish athlete, Rose made immediate impact for the Bulls. That only made other teams want a Rose of their own. Curry wasn't close.

Ricky Rubio was a teen prodigy from Spain who'd dazzled in the Olympics. He had the kind of game that suggested he was born to be a point guard. His game dripped with instinct and intelligence, was laced with an entertaining flair.

While scouts didn't know for sure what position Curry would be, there was no doubt what position Rubio played. Curry's game was flagged for poor shot selection and an inability to penetrate and finish inside. Meanwhile, Rubio was a bona fide floor general.

Because of the doubts about Curry, he landed in a place that thought the world of him. The Warriors were so elated Curry fell to them at No. 7, they backed out of the deal with the Suns—whose draft room erupted in celebration when Minnesota selected Rubio and thought they were getting Curry.

Riley drafted Curry. Even though Curry declined to work out for the Warriors. Even though Curry's agent practically begged the Warriors to not draft the Davidson star, so New York could take him. Even though Riley and Nelson had recently flown out to Memphis to smooth things over with disgruntled star Monta Ellis, assuring him they wouldn't draft a point guard.

The Warriors happily selected Curry. Nelson was giddy as he publicly declared the deal with the Suns dead.

This window of rampant love was short-lived.

"You can't put two small guys out there and try to play the one and the two when you've got two big guards in the league," Ellis, who like Curry was six-foot-three and light in the pants, declared during Curry's first media day. "You just can't do it. OK, yes, we're going to move up and down fast, but eventually the game is going to slow down. You can't do it."

The way Curry's career started supported Ellis's belief that he and Curry couldn't win together. Curry closed 2009 trying to find his rhythm. He averaged 11.8 points on 44.3 percent shooting in his first thirty-one games. He made just forty 3-pointers during that opening stretch to his career, at a 39.6 percent clip. And the Warriors were 9–22.

The talk about Curry not being ready had some credence. Analysts wondered if he was qualified for point guard at this level. Critics suggested he was destined to be a shooter off the bench, at best a change-of-pace Sixth Man. On top of that, rookie point guard Brandon Jennings, taken three spots after Curry, was tearing it up along with Tyreke Evans.

Eventually, Nelson turned the team over to Curry. He took the ball out of Ellis's hands and let Curry run the show. The rookie took off. By the end of the season, Curry had vindicated himself.

The team was sold over the summer, and Nelson was fired shortly before Curry's second season. Assistant coach Keith Smart was tapped to be the interim head coach, a form of audition for the new owners who didn't get the time to do an exhaustive coaching search.

With Nelson gone, the team was back in Ellis's control. Smart, hoping to prove he deserved a long-term gig, rode Ellis's talents to every win he could squeeze out. In pursuit of the best record he could muster, the interim head coach didn't have the patience for Curry's turnovers.

And Curry's assist-to-turnover ratio for his second season dipped below two-to-one, raising questions again about his ability to play point guard.

Late in close games, Smart made a habit of benching Curry after a bad turnover. He turned to backup point guard Acie Law, a steadier hand that Smart trusted. Curry went from a team-high 700 fourth-quarter minutes as a rookie to 523 his second year, fifth highest. Swingman Reggie Williams, in his second season with the Warriors after being called up from the NBA Development League, totaled 617 fourth-quarter minutes.

Curry's turnover issues were clearly a problem. The crowd

would let out a here-we-go-again sigh when he'd cough it up in a crucial moment. An angry Smart would yell for Law, and Curry would walk somberly to the bench, even put a towel over his head on occasion.

"You could see that he wanted to be out there," recalled Law, who played seven NBA seasons before going overseas, where he won two European titles. "He was a young player, turning the ball over. Just growing pains, you know. It was just a challenge for him. It was probably good for him to go through that, to have to earn his minutes."

His frustration was twofold. For starters, it was embarrassing, getting yanked like that. Here he was, the No. 7 pick who as a rookie was pulling off feats accomplished only by Oscar Robertson, spending close games watching like a role player.

On the other hand, there was frustration over his development. How could he learn without getting comfortable under the weight of the moment? Curry was a franchise centerpiece and Law was a backup. In a doomed season, it seemed to make more sense to give those minutes to Curry for his growth.

Or had Smart simply come to grips with the reality that Curry, Warriors fans, and management didn't want to admit: that Curry wasn't an NBA-caliber point guard? The doubt followed Curry like Pig-Pen's dust cloud. And it drove him to reach another level.

"That kid worked. He busted his butt," Law said. "I always considered myself a hard worker. I always put in an extra thirty minutes or so after practice. He would be on the other end for two hours. I would be done getting my shots, done getting iced, got a message, and getting ready to go. And he would be just finishing."

The Warriors did not retain Smart after his one-season interim stint. Instead, Mark Jackson was hired, and he immediately declared Curry his starting point guard. But before Curry could validate that choice by redeeming himself from the rough sophomore season, ankle injuries derailed his season.

The 2012–13 season was a breakout year for Curry. He set the NBA record for 3-pointers made. His career-high averages in points (22.9), assists (6.9), and minutes (38.2) trivialized the importance of his turnovers, which hovered around three a game again. Jackson's coaching and the overhaul of the roster around him, giving him talent to complement his own, brought out a new level to Curry's game. He led the Warriors to its first play-off appearance in six seasons. Playing through another sprained ankle, Curry averaged 23.4 points and 8.1 assists in twelve play-off games, upsetting Denver and putting a scare in San Antonio.

His postseason debut produced some moments that silenced his critics and reaffirmed why he had been coveted by some in the NBA draft. His doubters were muzzled by the blatancy of his potential and the magnetism of his game.

He had gone from fragile to the future. He exited the 2011–12 season, his career threatened by injury, then exited the 2012–13 season as a threat to the NBA elite. Once again, Curry had overcome.

Then Nike brought him right back to that place.

With his deal up, and having become the talk of the NBA after his postseason performance, Curry was expecting that success would impact his pending shoe deal. A Nike athlete his whole career, his contract was expiring right when Curry was blowing up.

But Nike wasn't all in on Curry. They didn't woo him with talks of a signature shoe, didn't excitedly share their plan for his brand moving forward and how they would capitalize off his buzz. It was clear to Curry that they never saw him as more. In an exposé on the breakup of Curry and Nike, written by ESPN's Ethan Strauss, Nike's PowerPoint in a meeting with Curry featured Kevin Durant's name. It came across like they had just thrown together a quick, thoughtless presentation centered on one they had already done for Durant and were so indifferent about Curry they didn't proof it.

Curry hadn't been made an all-star yet. Nike had giants on its roster in Durant, LeBron James, and Kobe Bryant. And Nike already had a point guard on the roster, 2011 No. 1 overall pick Kyrie Irving, so they couldn't go all in on another point guard.

It had to be like déjà vu for Curry.

Under Armour, known for its football apparel but looking to increase its share of the basketball market, came hard after Curry. They recruited in much the way Davidson's Bob McKillop had. They told him how special he would be with them. They made up for lack in stature by showing they cared about him, investing in getting to know him. They had a vision for what things could be.

When Curry went to Nike for a counteroffer, they conveyed to him that leaving would be his loss, a mistake he'd regret. He would be severing ties with the company permanently. And that was it for Curry. He was out.

Curry signed with Under Armour and started another cycle of proving himself. He was ridiculed for the move. Nike is a powerhouse with urban credibility and a legacy of design excellence. Why would he leave them? Under Armour wasn't highly regarded in sneaker culture or the basketball community. Curry was affixing himself to mediocrity, dooming his brand for more money. In the minds of many, even though he was clearly on deck for NBA elite, this move was evidence for why he would never be on the highest level. He was a cute underdog story with a shoe endorsement to match.

Once again it was proved that this is Curry's zone, the space where the soil is most fertilized and produces his best crop. He took the doubt and the mocking, the ceiling placed above him by outside forces, and produced another career season.

He averaged 24 points and 8.5 assists, became an all-star and led the Warriors to its highest win total (fifty-one) in twenty-two seasons.

This is the pattern of Curry's basketball life: having to earn respect, he does so, and then something prompts him to need to earn it all again. And every time he is put in a position to prove his worth, it propels him to a new level.

What can be proved after back-to-back MVPs? What is the level after putting together one of the most efficient seasons ever, bested only by Wilt Chamberlain? All that's left is NBA Finals dominance. It's the one card his critics can play.

His thirteen NBA Finals appearances have produced only two signature Curry games. He's had a few solid performances, by his standards. But on the biggest stage, with the most viewers tuned in, his explosions haven't come as frequently. There are several legitimate explanations, but they don't explain away the end result most will focus on: in the Finals, he's had more of the uncharacteristically poor Curry games than he has had the sensational, this-dude-is-ridiculous showings.

The guy who has been driven by doubters, fueled by analysts and critics telling him what he can't do and what he isn't, has more fuel. He is back in the space of having to prove himself again. Curry got to this level because this is a comfort zone for him. The international stardom and grocery list of accolades are evidence of, and validation for, his belief in himself. But his best work is usually done staring down narratives that anticipate his demise.

Which means we'll probably want to see what's next.

EPILOGUE

Christmas Day 2016, and Stephen Curry was looking like he didn't get his Red Rider BB gun. His slumped shoulders and drooping head, his patchy beard, the way he randomly shook his head "no" while staring off into nowhere.

Postgame dejection isn't rare for Curry, who is one of the more outwardly emotional professional athletes. What was rare was his inability to shake it. Normally, by the time the media gets access, he's cooling down. By the time he speaks, he's found the proper bow to put on the situation. But this time, the frustration wasn't dissipating. He was still fighting to keep it below the surface when he was first asked about the Christmas disappointment.

The Cavaliers had just won their fourth straight over the Warriors—the first three coming in the 2016 NBA Finals. Cleveland pulled off a nail-biter over the Warriors on Christmas Day, which for the first time in this rivalry featured Kevin Durant. Cavaliers guard Kyrie Irving nailed the game-winner in dramatic fashion. Again.

Curry, meanwhile, had 15 points, making just four of his eleven shots. He was a non-factor when the game was on the line, and this time he wasn't playing with a sprained knee. On the key possession, when Irving did his one-on-one magic, Curry was on the bench, the towel on his head failing to hide his anger. Kerr sat him for defensive purposes, putting in a taller defender, so Curry had to sit and watch Irving stick a turnaround jumper over Klay Thompson.

Curry bore the burden of the loss, though Durant, who was the

Warriors' best player all game, had just 2 points and missed all five of his shots after the Warriors built a 14-point lead with nine minutes left. Draymond Green had three turnovers in five minutes to help feed Cleveland's comeback. And Coach Steve Kerr waited until it was a 3-point game to put his best players on the court together.

But the postgame narrative was dominated by Curry's ineffectiveness, his latest failure to measure up to LeBron James's lofty standard. Or even Irving's. But while the focus was on another riveting installation in the Warriors-Cavaliers matchup, the bigger issue wasn't Cleveland. It was Durant. Specifically, the impact of his presence on Curry.

For weeks, in the opening leg of the 2016–17 season, Curry sacrificed the potency of his game to promote chemistry on offense. He was diligent about getting his teammates going and facilitating the kind of ball movement that fuels the Warriors' offense. The aggressiveness that made him MVP, the type of shots that captivated basketball fans, were shelved in pursuit of better shots for his talented teammates. Per Curry's basketball IQ, that was the smart move considering how defenses were constantly pressuring him.

This adjustment by Curry came at a price, and Cleveland served as the expense report in the biggest game of the regular season.

"I can't take eleven shots," Curry said after the Warriors' loss at Quicken Loans Arena, stopping in his tracks, stiffening his posture, and sharpening his stare. "I don't care what is happening or who is on the floor. I can't take eleven shots."

The word *meek* finds its origins in a Greek word that is transliterated *praus*. It is used to describe strength that has been subdued, power suppressed into something gentle.

It was a military term used to describe a war horse. The Greek army would get wild horses from the mountains and train them. An exclusive group emerged fit for battle. They were called meek, for they were powerful, strong, fierce, and courageous. But they were disciplined enough to control their nature, able to contain their power well enough to respond to even the slightest instructions.

But nuance gets lost in translation and *meek* becomes synonymous with *weak*. It is a term commonly connected to that which is submissive and feeble. The power and strength components have been stripped from the connotation. As a result, what was an admirable trait has become an indictment. Being meek, an incredibly hard thing to do, is instead deemed soft.

And now you understand Curry's burden. Now you have some insight into why his historic merger with his MVP predecessor was a struggle.

It was not because Durant insisted he be the primary scorer. He has shown nothing but willingness to fit into the Warriors' style of play. He's been a model superstar whom his teammates have to prod to take over. He's been outwardly and obviously about his support of his teammates and the occasions they dominate.

But Curry's amenability comes from within. The hospitality he extended to Durant, the focus on being the glue of this new super-team, was of his own volition. He volunteered to suppress his status and basketball might.

What Curry may not have fully understood was the difficulty of actually changing his existence on this team. It was an adjustment he was willing to endure, but still a definite adjustment. He probably thought he would just be sacrificing prestige, which he would take pride in doing. He likely presumed it would shave his scoring down, cut back on his OMG moments. That's a tithe he's happy to pay.

But it seems he didn't know it would cost him his rhythm, the life blood of his unique game. What he probably didn't foresee was how focusing on team flow would cost him his own, a reverb that would affect his shooting and comfort.

Starting games passively and then trying to turn it on in a snap wasn't a reliable game plan. He went nine straight games taking fewer than twenty shots, which hadn't happened since the first half of 2014. It sounds crazy, a point guard not getting twenty shots being a sign of passivity. But in the Warriors' context, the franchise changed when the offense centered on Curry's playmaking. They won a championship on his shooting and the world of options that opened because he aggressively looked for his shot.

Going spells without shooting and getting shots randomly, based on the playmaking of his teammates, disrupted the music to his game and made him a less efficient player. Curry dropped back to normal standards, missing a ton of open looks, which was a jarring sight after making more than four hundred 3-pointers on 45.4 percent shooting.

"I think Steph has probably had the biggest adjustment of all of our players from Kevin's arrival," Coach Steve Kerr said. "I think if you look at it from a practical standpoint, he's doing great. His numbers are still fantastic. Forty percent from three, twenty-four points per game. But he also happens to be coming off the greatest shooting season in the history of mankind last year. He has set the bar so high for himself that it's going to be a point of discussion."

However unexpected those ramifications may have been, they weren't the hardest part. That wasn't what made Curry rethink his approach. It was the insult that came with the injury. His sacrifice was being taken for weakness. His noble choice, coupled with his rare execution, to take a back seat was being heralded as an example of his inability.

He is a two-time MVP, the first unanimous selection. He is the face of a franchise, one that has become a perennial championship contender. He is a household name whose adoration has global reach. And yet he scooted over to make room on his throne for Durant. He invited a Hall of Famer to join his team. He welcomed a presence potent enough to carve into his territory.

There is a long list of former All-Stars who wouldn't dare approve such an alliance. Durant was chided by the fraternity of NBA stars for wanting to play with the Warriors. Curry, especially after failing to take down LeBron, doesn't come across as tough by all but begging Durant to join him.

In a series of text messages to Durant, Curry practically renounced his throne like Eddie Murphy on the subway near the end of *Coming to America.* Curry told Durant he didn't care who dominated the spotlight, or who sold the most sneakers, or who scored the most points. If Durant wound up heralded as the better player, that was an acceptable outcome for Curry in exchange for winning championships.

Such was the work of his reputed humility, a rare and emphatic display of unselfishness. It was the kind of sacrifice that illustrated why people close to him rave about Curry, an example of why parents and corporations embrace him. Stars typically leverage their influence for personal gain—playing de facto general managers, making coaches miserable, cashing in breaks, and getting a different set of rules. Curry treated his clout like injera, breaking off a piece and sharing it with Durant.

Curry was ten during the 1998–99 NBA lockout. The players and their exorbitant contracts were cast as spoiled and greedy, a national narrative aided by visuals such as Anthony Mason showing up at an exhibition game in a white fur coat. Curry was starting his junior season of high school when the Malice in the Palace happened. The fight between the Pacers players—most infamously the former Ron Artest, Stephen Jackson, and Jermaine O'Neal—and the Detroit Pistons fans at the Palace of Auburn Hills gave NBA players a black eye. They were portrayed as unruly and ruthless. Curry had just finished his rookie season in the NBA when LeBron James rendered "The Decision," ditching Cleveland to create a super-team in Miami. James was the poster boy for the selfish and ungrateful stigma on NBA players.

His entire career, Curry has been cognizant of giving NBA players a good name and not justifying the stereotypes. He wants to play the right way. Be unselfish. Avoid scandals and illegalities. Be happy and personable. Doing so has made him a likeable celebrity. It is intentional yet genuine as his public persona closely matches his private disposition. Still, Curry has capitalized off contradicting these generalizations. He has cashed in on being an atypical star.

But now his greatest sacrifice was putting him in a tough spot. The crown jewel in his legacy of selflessness was working against him.

Some in Curry's camp did not want the Warriors to get Durant. Some, obviously, saw the business ramifications of pairing with such a big star. Recruiting Durant was inviting competition for his off-the-court ventures. But a few didn't want Curry to lose what he had built. His DNA was infused into the Warriors' success. Adding Durant would change the composition, and those results couldn't be guaranteed. The same logic had many Warriors fans wanting to keep Harrison Barnes instead of going after Durant, wary of how the loss of chemistry would change the formula that led to 140 regular season wins and a championship in two seasons.

Getting Durant did change the chemistry, and Curry felt it the most.

He became an overlooked part of the offense. Kerr, in tinkering with how best to use all these all-stars, wound up taking his star for granted. The offense focused on infiltrating Durant (along with new starting center Zaza Pachulia and several new bench pieces) and assumed Curry would just find his way. In close games, Kerr would take the ball out of Curry's hands, seemingly not considering the psychological impact of Curry being reduced to a decoy underneath the weight of unanimous MVP expectations.

It wasn't until the fallout from the Christmas Day game that getting Curry going became a focus. Kerr stopped waiting for Curry to find his way and got more active in helping him. Five games after the Christmas Day showdown, it was clear why

Curry needs Kerr's help: he has a hard time deciphering when to override his better judgment.

The Warriors had all but squandered a 24-point, third-quarter lead to Memphis. They found themselves in a tight ball game in Oakland.

The Warriors were up 111–109 inside a minute remaining. Curry missed a 3-pointer but Klay Thompson grabbed the offensive rebound. With just under 40 seconds left, the Warriors had the chance to milk the clock and ice the game with one more basket.

Thompson passed the ball to Green, who gave it to Curry out near half-court. The play they were going to run was the pick-and-roll, the Warriors' bread and butter in crunch time. It used to be with Curry and Green. But after the Christmas Day debacle, Kerr had been using the Curry and Durant pick-and-roll more. That was the call for this final possession.

Memphis big man Zach Randolph, in his mid-thirties and with some 35,000 NBA minutes on his legs, was defending Durant. Grizzlies point guard Mike Conley Jr., an avid defender, was locked on Curry. Durant was supposed to set a screen for Curry and coax the Grizzlies defenders into switching. The goal was to get the much-slower Randolph onto Curry and the much-shorter Conley onto Durant. The Warriors love making it so a big man is defending Curry, giving him a speed and quickness advantage. But Durant with a point guard trying to cover him is equally as daunting. The Warriors had their pick of options to exploit.

But Durant saw he had the much slower Randolph on him. He knew he could take Randolph, so he clapped for Curry to pass him the ball. Curry rebutted Durant initially, gesturing for him to set the screen and run the play. Green joined Curry in telling Durant to run the play. Durant insisted by gesturing for Curry to pass him the ball. Curry sighed and passed the ball. Green was angry enough to throw his hands in the air and scream at Durant.

It got worse. Curry tried to set the screen for Durant. That way they could still run the play even if the ball-handler was different. Durant waved that off, too. He wanted to take Randolph one-on-one. So Curry got out of the way and joined his three other teammates standing near the sidelines. Durant missed the 3-pointer he took over Randolph. The Grizzlies wound up tying the game and winning in overtime.

Curry had a game-high 40 points at the time, but he gave up the ball. Green was livid, walking to the sidelines shaking his head and yelling in the huddle during the timeout. After the game, Green was vocal with the media about his frustrations, criticizing the Warriors' crunch-time offense. With his uninhibited passion and unflinching audacity, Green chided his teammates and himself publicly.

And it all happened, one could argue, because Curry gave up the ball. If he had Green's disposition, he would have demanded Durant run the play. He would have exercised his right to be authoritative, a right he earned by previously carrying the Warriors to a championship in 2015 and toppling Durant's Oklahoma City Thunder in the 2016 playoffs. Green, instead, emerged as the valiant leader, the one willing to say the hard thing and be demanding of his teammates.

What looked like dysfunction, though, was actually a moment of growth. What came off as poor leadership was really a window into the benefits of Curry's leadership style and how it helps make this all work.

Curry's meekness can be frustrating even for his staunchest supporters. Some occasions call for the best player to speak up. His unselfishness can be a detriment as it can skew his understanding of right and wrong on the court. He doesn't always see how his forcing a shot can be better than an open shot by his teammate. The trickle-down effect he brings to an offense sometimes requires a greed that has always warred with his conscience.

It took nearly half a season, but it became clear that Curry is the team's best playmaker and the axis on which the Warriors spin—even with Durant. The Warriors have four all-NBA talents, and Curry is the one that most needs to be activated. Him being aggressive, attacking within the Warriors' system of movement, playing his game, is the special sauce that makes this team so good.

"It's important that this team remains Steph Curry's team," Baron Davis said. "KD is a phenomenal scorer, a phenomenal player, another MVP candidate. But I just think for Steph, his personality and who he is has to remain the face of this team and the personality of this team. Because that's when they play their best. . . . I think their showmanship is the X factor, and Steph has to have that swagger and that showmanship every night."

Curry's struggles to open the season with Durant underscores the freshness of this Warriors era and how Curry is still a toddler at this NBA superstar level. It wasn't until February 2013, when he scored 54 at Madison Square Garden, that he popped up on the radar of the elite. After the two ensuing postseasons, he still hadn't arrived, humbled by the San Antonio Spurs in the 2013 playoffs and Chris Paul in the 2014 playoffs.

So Curry is in his third season as a marquee player, a tier that has a unique set of issues and challenges. He is still learning how to wield his power, still trying to craft a voice, still getting settled in the thin atmosphere of MVP expectations. It's possible he never finds it.

Curry is not one for confrontation, which in the arena of high-level pro sports, governed by ego and machismo, isn't a revered quality. He won't get points for leadership until he is seen as being in control. That requires being domineering, holding his teammates accountable, even breaking away from script. Any of that, or all of it, as modus operandi would be Curry altering who he is. It's not in his makeup to argue with a teammate in public, or blatantly disregard the coach's wishes.

He could get away with it if he did. His name comes with some rope. He's built up years of good favor. What's more, he entered the 2016–17 season a pending free agent—a star player's free pass to be high maintenance since teams don't want to do anything to force him away. Curry could plant an article about his willingness to leave, take matters into his own hands on the court (since he has the ball the most), or do the time-honored pouting tradition of distancing himself while saying nothing is wrong.

Instead, his typical response is to look inward and figure out how he can win over his critics and teammates. What Curry is learning, though, is that some people are only won over by force; some moments require him to be domineering. He has mastered the ability to subdue his stature; the next step is him learning how to exercise it constructively.

But Curry's meekness isn't all bad. His leadership style, the tone he sets, the way he carries himself, has been the Warriors' biggest bait.

Kerr turned down the New York Knicks job Phil Jackson had offered him, in part, so he could coach Curry. Not just for his talent but for his coachability.

Andre Iguodala turned down more money in Sacramento and Denver because, in part, he wanted to play with Curry. After the 2013 first-round series between the Warriors and Denver, Iguodala weaved around the crowd of players on the Oracle court in pursuit of Curry. The two embraced as Iguodala shared how much he respected how Curry carried himself. Three months later, Iguodala was a Warrior. Just over two years later, Iguodala was NBA Finals MVP.

Draymond Green passed on the free agent market in part because of Curry. The second round draft pick rose to be an invaluable piece in the Warriors' championship puzzle. And after making less than a million in each of his first three seasons, Green was in line for a huge payday. But before he hit the market, he agreed to a lucrative deal with the Warriors that turned out to be below market value. He and Curry had built a bond. Green made himself a force next to Curry. He couldn't envision leaving at the time.

Before Green, Klay Thompson did the same thing—accepted below the maximum salary he could have gotten to stay with the Warriors and next to Curry.

And now Durant was lured by the Warriors' chemistry.

"To see them together, they all walked in and it looked like they were holding hands," Durant said. "It was just a family. I could tell they enjoyed being around each other. When I met these guys, I felt as comfortable as I've ever felt. It was organic, it was authentic, it was real, and it was a feeling I couldn't ignore."

That aura is built on Curry. He was the one who started changing the air of bitterness and discontent previous stars left behind for him. At one point, Curry was the fifth highest paid player on the team and never uttered so much as a peep of discontent, which prevented any other player from complaining about being underpaid.

His playfulness and joy keeps a certain spirit around the team. His comfort with others being vocal has allowed Green to flourish as a leader. His perpetual availability, especially his willingness to address the media and answer questions even after the toughest of losses, takes some of the pressure off his teammates.

It is an unusual style of leadership. But it fits, as Curry is an unusual type of star. He just needs to trust that he's as a good a player as the rest of us know he is.

INDEX

INDEX

INDEX

ABOUT THE AUTHOR

Marcus Thompson II is a sports columnist for the *Mercury News* and the *East Bay Times*, the flagship publications of Bay Area News Group. Before expanding to reporting on the NFL, MLB, and other Bay Area sports, he covered the Golden State Warriors exclusively as beat writer for ten seasons. Thompson is a graduate of Clark Atlanta University. He lives with his wife, Dawn, and daughter, Sharon, in their hometown of Oakland, California.